EMPLOYMENT AND WORK RELATIONS IN CONTEXT SERIES

Series Editors

Tony Elger and Peter Fairbrother

Centre for Comparative Labour Studies,

Department of Sociology,

University of Warwick

The aim of the Employment and Work Relations in Context series is to address questions relating to the evolving patterns of work, employment and industrial relations in specific workplaces, localities and regions. This focus arises primarily from a concern to trace out the ways in which wider policy making, especially by national governments and transnational corporations, impinges upon specific workplaces, labour markets and localities in distinctive ways. A particular feature of the series is the consideration of forms of worker and citizen organization and mobilization in these circumstances. Thus the studies will address major analytical and policy issues through case-study and comparative research.

THE STATE, YOUNG PEOPLE AND YOUTH TRAINING

In and Against the Training State

Phil Mizen

MANSELL

First published 1995 by
Mansell Publishing Limited, *A Cassell Imprint*
Villiers House, 41/47 Strand, London WC2N 5JE, England
387 Park Avenue South, New York, NY 10016-8810, USA

British Library Cataloguing-in-Publication Data
A catalogue record for this book is available from the British Library.

ISBN 0-7201-2169-8 (Hardback)
ISBN 0-7201-2247-3 (Paperback)

Library of Congress Cataloging-in-Publication Data
Mizen, Phil.
    The state, young people and youth training : In and against the
training state / Phil Mizen.
        p.   cm.—(Employment and work relations in context series)
    Includes bibliographical references and index.
    ISBN 0-7201-2169-8 : $80.00
    1. Occupational training—Great Britain—Coventry.
    2. Occupational training—Government policy—Great Britain.
    3. Youth—Employment—Great Britain—Coventry.   I. Title.
    II. Series: Employment and work relations in context.
    HD5715.5.G72C685   1994
    331.3'42592'0942498—dc20   94-13545
                                                          CIP

Typeset by Colset Ltd, Singapore
Printed and bound in Great Britain by Biddles Ltd,
Guildford and King's Lynn

CONTENTS

TABLES

PREFACE AND ACKNOWLEDGEMENTS

This book has grown out of a desire to examine the ways in which the young working class have responded to the restructuring of work and employment over the past 15 years. In particular, the intention has been to provide an empirically based account of the ways in which the young working class have sought to confront changes in the organization of the social relations of production, through the development of the *training state* and, more specifically, through their everyday struggles *in and against* youth training. For more than a decade now, the Youth Training Scheme[1] has been a central feature in the restructuring of work and employment and to this end is held up as a shining example of the drive to 'modernize' an ailing British economy. It has claimed to provide working class school leavers with the opportunity to acquire the skills they are told employers need, to give them the 'right' attitudes to work demanded by an internationally successful economy, the chance to undertake quality foundation training for jobs and also to learn the necessity of 'pricing themselves back into jobs' if they ever want to work again. The result, we are told, has been a 'revolution' in the provision of skills training for school leavers and the radical transformation of attitudes to work and training among school leavers.

This book takes these claims seriously. Over three million school leavers have been through the scheme in the past decade, over two million of whom have already gone through the two-year youth training programme. What is more, many of these trainees have known nothing other than large-scale unemployment among both their communities and the population at large, and most are acutely aware that even fewer jobs exist for school leavers. Each of the subsequent chapters of this book therefore examines a central aspect of this youth training provision and relates it to the experiences of the young people concerned. This is important because although research focused on the social world of young people and the impact of the restructuring of work, unemployment and training has grown extensively in recent years, very few of these studies have examined the experiences of those for whom youth training is an everyday reality.

This book therefore not only seeks to add to our overall knowledge of young people's behaviour in relation to work, unemployment and training; its intention is to do so by letting the young people concerned speak for themselves. Through a case study of two different groups of young people in Coventry, one group of school pupils approaching the final year of their compulsory education and another group near the end of their first year's youth training, the claims which have accompanied the development of youth training are put to the test.

But the book also has a second intention and one that goes well beyond its place as just another contribution to the extensive body of literature that the topic has already generated. It has been a distinctive feature of the intense research interest in young people, work, unemployment and training over the past 15 to 20 years that there have been few sustained attempts to make sense of all this research activity and to speculate upon what all these 'facts' really mean. We therefore currently find ourselves in the situation of knowing quite a lot about the ways in which working class school leavers behave but very little about why they actually do so. Recently one or two attempts have been made to undertake such a task and this book must be judged alongside these contributions. But it is from a committed belief that it is only through an empirically based *analysis*, one in which theory is generated and informed by developments in the 'real world', that we can further our understanding of the current trends and processes in which working class young people are currently embroiled. This is not to argue that the attempt to do so here is complete or that the ideas contained in the initial sections are fully worked out. Yet it is hoped that it will be viewed as the beginning of an attempt to engage with the issues identified by other research and to develop its own distinctive contribution.

To this end, Chapter 1[2] attempts to outline an approach which argues that we should view working class young people's behaviour in relation to youth training as being constituted in and against its form. It does so by arguing that attempts to resurrect the previously influential culturalist perspectives on 'youth' are of only limited value, and can therefore offer no sustained logical or historical analysis. They cannot explain the complexity of young people's behaviour in relation to youth training and, because of their preoccupation with culture and ideology, they remain firmly rooted at the level of appearances. This means that many of the pronouncements that accompany the development of the training state have been taken at face value by the culturalists, with the result that their conclusions seek consensus and incorporation where none exists. In contrast, by seeking to understand young people's social relationships as materially constituted in and against the social relations of production, the chapter argues that we can begin to explore the behaviour of the young working class, propelled into training schemes out of necessity, while simultaneously realizing that such schemes involve new disciplines and constraints which remain unresponsive to their wider needs and aspirations.

It must also be pointed out that being in and against youth training necessitates constant struggles to resist its tendency to reduce all social relationships to those of exploitation and domination. Many of the struggles, the ways in which working class young people attempt to confront youth training's disciplines, are not the spectacular displays which other sociological accounts in the past have pointed to as acts of resistance. The struggles pointed to here are the struggles of everyday life but they are struggles nonetheless and should be recognized as such. Not only do these struggles show youth training's normal condition to be one of disruption, dissatisfaction and instability, but they are also important because the struggles forged through youth training are defined by their opposition to the scheme's dominant values and therefore to its essential objectives and aims.

As the analysis presented here is an empirically based one, the following chapters each present accounts of different aspects of social life which define being a youth trainee, and the contradictions and struggles these involve. Chapter 2 begins by outlining what it is like to be young in Coventry and how the intense restructuring of work and employment in the city has had particularly acute implications for school leavers. The chapter also gives a brief account of how the research was undertaken, the methodology involved and the other significant sources of information on which it draws.[3]

Chapter 3 begins the wider analysis by examining the 'deficiency model' on which the training state has developed. Using as its justification the idea that young workers in particular are deficient of those qualities that they are told they need to secure a job today, the state has put in place an extensive institutional network of training schemes which seek to apply a training remedy to these deficiencies. However, as the chapter demonstrates, the young working class are not deficient in the ways that youth training seeks to portray. Most immediately, the chapter argues that through child working the majority of working class young people gain a wide and extensive knowledge of the social relations of production before they have even finished their compulsory education.

Chapter 4 seeks to relate the evolution of young people as distinctive forms of labour power to the movement onto training schemes. It identifies the ways in which final-year school pupils assess the prospect of youth training through a consideration of its freedoms and constraints, rooted in their knowledge of work, training and local labour markets. It is this contradictory assessment of youth training which defines young people's reactions to the prospect of youth training and which permeates all aspects of a trainee's life. And it is with these factors in mind that they set out to negotiate a perilous labour market in the search for *real jobs*.

Chapter 5 takes up the issue of youth training for skills and examines these claims in relation to case studies of trainees' experiences of training across a range of schemes. It seeks to challenge claims that youth training has delivered its promise of quality foundation training for life and seeks to establish that what has been put in place essentially represents a period of work experience dominated by the demands of semi-skilled and unskilled work. It further argues that it is precisely because trainees recognize the generality of youth training that it has set up new tensions and contradictions, the most important of which is examined in Chapter 6, which considers the successes of the scheme in training school leavers for jobs. Against the formidable claims made for the scheme, the chapter uses wider data to question the scheme's actual ability to lead trainees into jobs and it outlines trainees' evaluation of the scheme as a springboard into work. Seen in the context of the scheme's failure to lead trainees into jobs, the chapter also examines the significance of the persistent tendency of trainees to leave their schemes early.

Chapter 7 completes the analysis of the empirical data by looking at struggles in and against youth training's attempts to 'price young workers back into jobs'. It argues that the low level of allowance remains the most resented aspect of youth training's imposition and that the hardships and material deprivations it entails continue to constitute a major factor in young people's opposition to training. It also examines opposition to the low level of the allowance in the context of young people's reluctance to succumb to the inevitability of youth training's economic logic.

Notes

1. In 1990 the YTS changed to Youth Training. Although the 'new scheme' heralded some important changes in the structure of YTS, most noticeably in its flexibility and funding arrangements, there remained strong underlying continuities. Therefore, throughout the book youth training will be used as a generic term to cover both phases in its development.

2. Chapter 1 is based on an article which appeared in the Summer 1994 issue of *Capital and Class* (Mizen, 1994). My thanks to the editorial committee and two anonymous referees for their comments.

3. Some of the material contained in Chapter 2 was published in an article in the *British Journal of Education and Work* (Mizen, 1992).

Acknowledgements

As with every study of this kind it is impossible to thank individually all those who contributed to its success or made it possible. However, this work stems primarily from an Economic and Social Research Council grant for a PhD, in the Department of Sociology at the University of Warwick, and although the version here has been substantially revised it would have been impossible without such funding. Thanks must also go to Mikey and all the other teachers and pupils who gave their cooperation and without whose assistance the survey phase of the research would never have been completed. A similar acknowledgement must also be made to the managing agents, trainers and especially the trainees, all of whom who were so generous with their time and willingness to discuss a whole range of aspects relating to their rapidly changing lives. Without their help this project would never have gone beyond the planning stage.

Special thanks must also go to a number of people who have been crucial to the development of the ideas contained within this book. Helen Rainbird, Dan Finn and Teresa Rees all, at some stage or another, provided invaluable advice, assistance and constructive criticism. Ian Procter contributed tireless enthusiasm and encouragement, and was an unending source of support without which this project would never have been concluded so effectively. Peter Burnham and Ray Kiely took time to read parts of this work and provide incisive and thoughtful comment, and thanks must also go to Peter Fairbrother and Tony Elger. As well as being understanding and conscientious editors, over the years I have known them they have also displayed a long-standing interest in and enthusiasm for my work. Finally, I must acknowledge the patience and support of Jane McAllister, not least because of the sacrifices she had to make to see this project come to a conclusion. If this work has any merit, much of the credit lies with them. Needless to say, its shortcomings are entirely my own responsibility.

List of Abbreviations

CSE   Certificate of Secondary Education
CPVE   Certificate of Pre-Vocational Education
DHSS   Department of Social Security
EITB   Engineering Industry Training Board
ET   Employment Training
GCSE   General Certificate of Education
ITB   Industrial Training Board
LEA   Local education authority
LECs   Local Enterprise Councils
MaC   Maintenance and construction
MSC   Manpower Services Commission
MVM   Motor vehicle maintenance
NNEB   Nursery Nursing Education Board
NTI   New Training Initiative
RSA   Royal Society of Arts
PSV   Public service vehicle
SCPR   Social and Community Planning Research
TA   Training Agency
TECs   Training and Enterprise Councils
TOC   Training Occupational Classification
TUC   Trades Union Congress
YOP   Youth Opportunities Programme
YT   Youth Training
YTS   Youth Training Scheme

1 IN AND AGAINST THE TRAINING STATE

The postwar period has witnessed far-reaching changes in the ways in which working class young people have left school and entered employment. As little as a generation ago, most working class young people found few difficulties in finding work on leaving school, taking advantage of the relatively abundant opportunities for apprentice training or the large-scale need for young workers to fill the numerous semi-skilled and unskilled positions available (Keil *et al.*, 1966). It seems almost incredible now but demand for young workers was such that, throughout the initial decades after World War II, unemployment rates for the under-25s lagged behind those for the population as a whole (Deacon, 1981). Indeed, much of the academic and policy-related literature of the time reflects the feeling that young people's movement into work was a relatively unproblematic stage in their lives. In summing up the period one important review concluded that 'for most young people there is a basic continuity in their experience at home, at school and at work' (Ashton and Field, 1976, p. 12). Another seminal study of the time also argued that

> for many children the values of school had always appeared irrelevant to life as it was actually lived, but the values of work fitted in with those of home and in the neighbourhood. (Carter, 1962, p. 210)

Work, it was felt, 'gave a dignity and a sense of freedom which had not been felt at school' (Carter, 1962, p. 210).

As we are now all too well aware, such a period of relative prosperity did not last for long and the limited 'dignity' once offered by work has rapidly given way to the despair of unemployment. This is not to overlook the real continuities which exist between the experiences of young people in the labour market during the 1950s and 1960s, and those of their children during the 1980s and 1990s. Then, as now, working class young people's opportunities were constrained by their gender and, as increasingly recognized, by their ethnicity; the work they were required to do was often unpleasant, physically demanding, intrinsically unrewarding and relatively low paid; and young workers sought to avoid such work if it was at all possible. However, much has also changed over the ensuing years as repeated crises have consistently exposed the vulnerability of young workers to the vicious restructuring of work and employment. Today, in the 1990s, far from being easy, finding a job directly on leaving school has become the exception rather than the rule and many young workers are now forced to confront the realities of a hostile labour market in ways unimaginable even 20 years ago.

What has emerged as a central feature in this whole sorrowful episode has been the real changes in the way in which the state has sought actively to intervene in restructuring young people's initial years in the adult labour market. It is not the intention of this book to outline in any detail the development of the training state, driven by its relentless need to tackle the problem of unemployed young workers by forcing them to train. Others have already done this (e.g. Ainley and Corney, 1990; Finn, 1987; Keep, 1986) and more must surely follow. Yet for over 15 years, hundreds of thousands of young people each year have begun their adult working lives steeped in the institutional and ideological context of an emergent new vocationalism, with its whole new vocabulary of preparatory training and vocational skills (Rees and Atkinson, 1982).

In particular, the most systematic of these forms of state intervention, youth training, has recently entered its tenth year. Although any celebrations have been conspicuous by their absence, what is evident for all to see is that during this decade of training a new and extensive set of institutions have been put in place which purport to offer unemployed school leavers the opportunity to acquire the skills and qualities they are told they need to succeed in the contemporary labour market. The 'jewel' in the first Thatcher government's crown (Finn, 1986), youth training, has developed into a massive exercise in state intervention costing billions of pounds of public money, employing thousands of trainers and administrators, covering millions of school leavers and creating a whole new form of state activity centered around the idea of training and vocational preparation. With the re-election of a fourth consecutive Conservative government in 1992, committed to further entrenching this 'training revolution' (Conservative Party, 1992, p. 19), and with the spectre of mass unemployment once again a reality, the training state looks set to remain a distinctive feature in the lives of large numbers of working class young people.

Making Sense of It All

Today, as before, young people remain an object of intense sociological enquiry, but as the training state has grown bigger and its activities ever more expansive, there has been a growth in the number of studies intent on finding out what this training revolution actually means for those on the receiving end. The scale of the youth training initiative has, in part, been matched by a whole host of academic and policy-related studies examining the impact of unemployment and training on the lives of the young working class (e.g. Banks *et al.*, 1992; Wallace and Cross, 1990; Raffe, 1988; Brown and Ashton, 1987). Self-consciously empirical, these studies have generated a wealth of information on all aspects of working class life, as young people have been forced to negotiate their way through an increasingly treacherous labour market.

However, apart from the often innovative and sympathetic research that has emerged, what also stands out from all this frenetic activity is a clear feeling that the sociological imagination has failed to match this thirst for hard facts. The recent emphasis on empirical research has often overshadowed any equal concern for what all this enterprising research activity means. As the grand theoreticism of the 1970s (e.g. Brake, 1980; Hall and Jefferson, 1976) has failed to meet the challenge of these new conditions, quickly giving way under the weight of mass unemployment, a new 'abstract empiricism' (Wright Mills, 1959) has emerged which enables us to know a lot about the ways in which young people behave during their first years in the adult labour market, but pitifully little about why they behave as they do. Consequently, we currently face a situation in which empirically informed analysis of youth unemployment and training is the exception rather than the rule and, simply stated, speculation on the wider meaning of these facts has been sadly lacking from wider debates.

To the credit of some, these absences have been noted and a sense of unease about what all these data actually mean often pervades its pages. However, the consistent failure to deal in any detail with the meaning and significance of the forms of youthful behaviour identified by this research has meant that even sympathetic accounts have been forced into shallow and unsupported hypothesizing. To suggest that what we are currently witnessing is 'a redefinition of youth in capitalist societies . . . possibly associated with the perceived need to extend education in line with technology' (Wallace and Cross, 1990, p. 8) is clearly inadequate. Apart from such technicist explanations echoing the right's efforts to discipline the young working class by exhorting them to play their part 'in creating the highly skilled and innovative workforce required to meet the employment needs of new technologies' (Department of Employment, 1985), a closer examination reveals that youth training has never been about training for new technology. They also ignore at their peril powerful arguments which suggest that the state has actively sought to restructure social relations as a precondition for the introduction of new technology (Pollert, 1988; Holloway, 1987). What is more, they largely exclude the actions of young people themselves, who have steadfastly resisted their subjugation to the new forms of discipline associated with the training state.

One result of this reluctance to speculate on the meaning of these changing forms of working class life has been the re-emergence of a form of narrow empiricism which, as Cohen (1990) has pointed out, has actively conspired in perpetuating accounts which identify young people as a social problem only when there are too many. A declining youthful population, it was argued, together with an upturn in the economy would relegate the 'youth problem' once more to the margins of both political and academic concerns. However, the continuing inability of British capitalism to resolve its tendency towards recurrent crisis has once again exposed the superficiality of claims that the 'youth problem' would disappear in the predicted new golden age for young labour during the late 1980s. Wittingly or unwittingly, many sociologists have therefore become entwined in a form of sociology concerned with 'a numbers game . . . devoted to the surveillance and control of youthful populations' (Cohen 1990). Such conclusions may come as little surprise given the weak and long-discredited social democratic framework that many of these approaches are now endeavouring to resurrect (e.g. Jones and Wallace, 1992). Yet a second trend, more worrying to those convinced that the real problems currently faced by working class young people are not about numbers but go to the very heart of the organization of social life, is constituted by more recent attempts to provide a 'radical' socialist account of working class responses to the training state by resurrecting a culturalist understanding of 'youth'.

These attempts draw primarily on a long tradition of studies of working class 'youth', most closely associated with the work of the Centre for Contemporary Cultural Studies at the University of Birmingham (McGuigan, 1992, chapter 3). While distancing itself from the more obvious limitations of those now 'classic' accounts which have emerged from the centre, the work of Hollands (1990, 1991) in particular has set about reformulating a culturalist understanding of youthful forms of behaviour commensurate with the impact of Thatcherism.[1] Located broadly within Hall's (1983) wider analysis of the Thatcher years, and their successes in generating and sustaining some form of hegemonic leadership during the 1980s, Hollands wants to identify the ways in which the new vocationalism has proved central in generating new forms of behaviour which were essential if Thatcherism was to succeed. More specifically, using 'the YTS as a key focus for exploring and evaluating a much broader historical shift in working class transitions, identities and lifestyles' (Hollands, 1990, p. 2), Hollands sets himself the task of explaining why the new vocationalism has been so successful in winning the hearts and minds of the young working class; and why it has had such a considerable impact in transforming common sense assumptions about welfare and full employment into those more attuned to the discipline of training programmes and the politics of the market-place.

Hollands's concern, therefore, is not with the emergent institutional context of the new vocationalism but the ways in which the working class has been incorporated and persuaded to accept as legitimate these new institutions and their associated values. To this end, he begins by identifying the importance of political and ideological struggle for this process of transformation through his assertion that

> the preparation of youth labour has never been simply about matching supply with demand but has always involved a much deeper state concern with respect to the cultural remoulding of the working class. (Hollands, 1991, p. 8)

Under Thatcherism, Hollands wants to argue, the political and ideological levels have taken on a new, sharper and modern dimension whereby working class young people have become the specific object of far-reaching and sustained attempts to redefine the relationship between the working class and the labour market, to profoundly 'influence the population's experiences and indeed expectations of work' (Hollands, 1990, p. 1). It is precisely through an appreciation of Thatcherism as a political and ideological project that its 'success in mobilising a kind of consensus around the youth training issue' (Hollands, 1990, p. 201), not least among the trainees themselves, can best be understood.

The extent to which this individualism has been normalized is illustrated through the findings of an extensive ethnographic study. Reflecting this emphasis on the cultural level in the changing 'transition from school to work', Hollands uses his empirical evidence to illustrate the extent to which traditional forms of working class behaviour have been displaced by new and more fragmented ones 'bear[ing] the logo of the Conservative Party's long reign in office' (Hollands, 1991, p. 40). Through the new vocationalism's emphasis on individual opportunity and career progression, Hollands wants to demonstrate that older, more collectivist forms of working class activity are being superseded by new ones working 'to prepare particular kinds of youth labour required in the political economy of Thatcherism' (Hollands, 1991, p. 38). Among young women this has taken the form of an enthusiasm for 'transitions, lifestyles and identities' which echo youth training's claims to offer training in jobs in 'glam' (glamorous) work, mainly in offices, hairdressers', beauty salons and with fashion designers (Hollands, 1990, p. 105); new 'paraprofessional/ domestic' work with children and the elderly; and factory jobs, mainly in clothing manufacture and warehouse distribution. For young men, the enthusiasm for white-collar work as a source of possible upward mobility 'and a growing conservative and corporate view of business' (Hollands, 1990, p. 199) is seen as responsible for eroding the traditional collectivist appeal of manual labour; and an enthusiasm for self-employment and entrepreneurialism is seen to cut right across the entire range of these new 'transitions'.

Not surprisingly, a new generation of school leavers bearing the ideological and political imprint of Conservative Central Office has profound implications for any possibilities of socialist renewal since 'it is clear that the transitions thrown up by the new vocationalism have influenced the identities and politics of a whole new generation of young people' (Hollands, 1990, p. 13). Echoing Hall's (1988) exhortations to the Labour Party to learn from the politics of Thatcherism, Hollands asserts that it is precisely the labour movement's

> absolute failure to contest the ideological grounds of the new
> vocationalism and provide an overall alternative form of youth politics

[which] has meant they have . . . been forced to accept the economic and political necessity of current government schemes. (Hollands, 1990, p. 2)

Taken at face value, such an approach therefore appears to offer a powerful explanatory account of youth training's success in both defusing any sustained opposition to mass unemployment, and recomposing existing forms of working class behaviour in ways conducive to Thatcherism and its successors.

Working Class Transitions 'Old' and 'New'

However, to begin with, the most striking aspect of these 'transitions' is that they do not seem so new after all. Critics of *The Coming of the Post-Industrial Society* (Bell, 1973) have long argued that the emergence of a new social order, premised on the general growth of a service economy and characterized by large-scale white-collar employment, has been part of a longer process of capitalist development stretching back into the nineteenth century (Williams, 1985; Kumar, 1978). More recently, attempts to construct a theory of post-Fordism (see Hall and Jacques, 1989; Lash and Urry, 1987), signifying the end of an era of Fordist mass production and consumption and its replacement by a new regime of disorganized capitalist production and fragmented culture, have also neglected the historically diverse forms taken by working class life (Callinicos, 1989; Costello *et al.*, 1989). Transitions into service sector and white-collar work have been a fact of life for the majority of postwar British school leavers. Manufacturing industry has traditionally employed relatively few young people, with school leavers considerably more likely to begin their working lives in the service sector (Jackson, 1985). Both young men and young women have tended to enter the distribution and miscellaneous services sectors, while young women have also tended to enter the clothing and footwear sectors in relatively large numbers (Makeham, 1980). More generally, 'since the Second World War agriculture, clothing, construction, distribution and miscellaneous services have been Britain's main youth industries' (Roberts *et al.*, 1986a, p. 34), the last sector consisting primarily of hairdressing, hotel trade and catering work.

As well as echoing claims that youth training has been accepted as a new and innovative way into training and work, Hollands's suggestion that

working class young people perceive youth training as a viable and progressive alternative to traditional patterns of work entry is also highly
problematic. At one level his own data do not always readily support such
an assertion; for example, the young women's discussions of paraprofes-
sionalism seems more amenable to an interpretation which stresses conflict
between youth training's ideology of careerism and personal success, and
the harsh constraints of everyday life on a training scheme. More disturb-
ing, however, is that although both Hollands and Cohen are correct to
highlight the dangerous complicity of numbers game sociology, this is
taken as a pretext for ignoring the opportunity to interrogate a whole host
of studies examining the new vocationalism's impact on young people's
lives. Any such consideration would immediately illustrate the fundamental contradictions which underpin youth training's attempts to
discipline further the young working class and expose the tenuous foundations on which any claims to an emergent consensus rest.

Without pre-empting the more detailed discussion of these issues contained in subsequent chapters, it is necessary to point out here that a closer
inspection of the wider material would quickly illustrate that the young
working class experience youth training in complex and distinctly contradictory ways which are not too dissimilar from wider working class
experiences of institutional forms of state activity which appear to provide
real benefits, but only in forms that simultaneously impose distinct limits
on freedom and which erect further barriers to the control working class
people feel they have over their lives (London Edinburgh Weekend
Return Group, 1980). This is most vividly illustrated by the instrumental
ways in which the young working class have continued to resist incorporation into youth training. Research among Scottish young people has
consistently illustrated an appreciation of youth training's limited opportunities for work experience and training, alongside a sustained and
deeply felt cynicism concerning both employers' and government's
ulterior motives (Raffe, 1989; Raffe and Smith, 1987). The experience of
young people in England and Wales reflects these findings, suggesting that
they too appreciate youth training's limited opportunities for work
experience, where no alternative jobs exist, while criticisms of its exploitation and low pay remain severe (Lee *et al.*, 1990; Courtenay, 1988). More
recent research in England and Scotland also found a pervasive instrumentalism towards youth training's perceived freedoms and constraints,
leading even these numbers game sociologists to conclude that 'despite
all the Thatcher government's efforts to establish a universal "training

culture" on Continental lines, there were few signs . . . that most school leavers had taken it on' (Banks *et al.*, 1992, p. 44).

Despite their notoriously selective presentation, the state's own data also fail to conceal a further important manifestation of this contradiction: young people's persistent tendency to leave their training schemes before the duration of their planned training. During youth training's first three years early leavers accounted for about half of all entrants, with over one-third leaving before six months had been completed and with trainees spending an average of only 40 weeks on the 12-month programme (Gray and King, 1986). Recent data from the Training and Enterprise Councils (TECs) show that even with unemployment hovering close to the three million mark, around half of all trainees are still leaving their schemes early (Unemployment Unit/Youthaid, 1993a). Reasons for leaving are dominated by criticisms of the scheme's performance, the quality of training and the lack of money, and even though the single biggest group said they had left for a job, the extent to which 17- and 18-year-olds work in 'blind alley' employment (Courtenay, 1988) in mainly unskilled work, devoid of any security, hardly represents an endorsement of youth training as a viable and progressive route into work.

The idea of a young working class of would-be entrepreneurs also fails to withstand a rigorous examination. It has been pointed out at length that the concept of enterprise is itself a diffuse and highly contradictory concept (Coffield, 1991; Rees, 1986), and that this ambiguity has been reflected in the deep-seated pessimism characterizing young people's response to this broad enterprise movement. A detailed study of young entrepreneurs in the north-east of England found that self-employment was more likely to be a reaction to restricted employment opportunities than indicative of active support for the enterprise initiative (MacDonald and Coffield, 1991). This initial cynicism was largely confirmed by the actual experience of self-employment which, more accurately, was defined by a 'phlegmatic realism . . . a determined and hopeful, but also stoical attitude to the practice of enterprise' (MacDonald and Coffield, 1991, p. 145) rather than the kindling spirit of wealth creation fostered by the Department of Trade and Industry. Further evidence from Liverpool found that less than 10 per cent of a sample of young people thought it likely that they would become self-employed (Roberts and Parsell, 1989), and research among sixth form pupils concluded that there has 'not been a major increase in levels of enterprise-mindedness among young people' (Curran and Blackburn, 1990, p. 42). Indeed, it has been argued that trainees on schemes appear even less likely to embrace the values of enterprise than either their employed or unemployed peers, so that 'the evidence points away from the idea that young people have absorbed much of the enterprise ethic which has been so enthusiastically advanced in the last decade' (Ashford and Bynner, 1991, p. 60).

Young people do go on youth training, considerably more than three million since its inception, but this in no way represents a consensus or even an endorsement. Culturalist accounts like Hollands's completely neglect any discussion of the state's coercive power in getting young people on to schemes, whether through direct benefit sanctions aimed at further penalizing unemployed school leavers or through the ways in which it has allowed working class young people to bear the brunt of the restructuring of British industry. Furthermore, the wider evidence suggests that even where they have gone on to schemes, working class young people have continued to resist youth training's claims to offer new opportunities for individual career progression and development, and that they have met the call to enterprise with a momentous blast of indifference. Every stage of the scheme's development has been met with new forms of resistance and struggle, not least represented by young people's sustained instrumentalism, high rates of early leaving and the maintenance of something approaching a 'moral economy . . . a dissociation between economic values on the one hand and social and moral obligations on the other' (Thompson, 1978a, p. 292) over the paucity of the training allowance. Despite the repeated attempts by the training state to subjugate further the young working class to the discipline of training, this is the continuing reality of everyday struggle on youth training, something evacuated and sterilized by culturalists, and it is here that the significance of trainee forms of behaviour can be found.

The Appearance of Youth

What is at issue then is not just a matter of exchanging examples of data in claim and counter-claim, although a wider review of the literature does point compellingly away from accounts of ideological incorporation and political consensus. Nor is it simply a matter of political differences, although contrasting strategic positions do necessarily follow. More fundamentally, it is also a methodological and conceptual issue of whether culturalist accounts like Hollands's, which present working class youthful forms of behaviour as the outcome of ideological and political processes, can explain the complexity of the attitudes and behaviour displayed by working class young people, let alone provide us with some insight into the determining pressures which give shape to and modify these forms. It is precisely because Hollands treats forms of working class youthful behaviour as constituted ideologically and politically that his account remains only partial. The consequent inability to relate aspects of this behaviour to the specific conditions and organization of social life means that analysis never gets beyond the level of appearances and that the conclusions offered tend to mirror the grander ideological facade which has accompanied the development of the institutional forms which characterize the training state.

This tendency to separate ideological and political forms from the ways in which social life is materially organized can be traced to the two major accounts on which Hollands's analysis rests. To begin with, he follows Clarke (1979) in locating the development and recomposition of the post-war working class within its cultural forms. Here tensions between the demands of the economy and the need to secure the social conditions through which production is maintained and reproduced, tensions between the 'sphere of production and the sphere of reproduction' (Clarke, 1979, p. 247) are seen as generating new 'cultural solutions' in which to live the experience of being working class. Changes in the sphere of production, associated with the concentration and centralization of capital, the introduction of new technology and the decline of heavy industry, are seen as giving rise to changes in the sphere of reproduction, manifest in the changing appearance and differing character of working class culture as new forms appear and old forms are replaced. Although no simple causal relation is alleged, nor a plain process of substitution, changing production relations are seen as demanding new forms of cultural articulation if working class people are to make sense of living with capitalism.

Clarke's account therefore establishes a functional separation between the sphere of production and the sphere of reproduction in which the demands of the economy are reflected in the cultural activities of the working class. For Clarke capitalism is structured by a variety of different and relatively autonomous levels, each of which is defined according to the function it fulfils in relation to the needs of the social formation as a whole. Material production, or the sphere of production, is given primacy because of the assumed need to guarantee the physical survival of the whole, with the political and ideological levels, the sphere of reproduction, seen as distributive relations functioning to ensure that individuals are both allocated to the means of production and able to fulfil their roles as good citizens. As Simon Clarke neatly puts it, such theorists argue that 'the economic level is thus the technical realm of material production, the political and ideological levels are the social realms which establish the social conditions of material production' (S. Clarke, 1991, p. 83).

The necessary consequence of such a functional distinction is that the significance attributed to forms of working class culture lay in their ideological role of representing 'the subject's imaginary relation to its conditions of existence' (McGuigan, 1992, p. 30). Any changes or restructuring in these conditions of existence are seen to 'require the elaboration of new cultural practices and repertoires which are capable of producing . . . new cultural frameworks in which to live the experiences of being working class' (Clarke, 1979, p. 247). By obscuring the real contradictions which characterize social life, these writers treat culture's importance, like ideology, as arising from its role in ensuring that working class forms of life are conducive to the maintenance and reproduction of capitalist relations of production. Working class culture is therefore inherently passive, a reified form of activity which is sucked dry of any real-life contradictory activity, before being assimilated uneasily into the function of ideology through its role in articulating new forms of imaginary relations conducive to the reorganization of production. Instead of recognizing working class culture as both the product and process of struggle, riven by conflict and the transforming possibilities of everyday life (Thompson, 1978b), culture becomes little more than a static and alien structure responding to the imperatives of production by defining the limits within which even the most visible cultural forms, 'the area of youth' (Clarke, 1979, p. 241), are simply boxed in and contained. The significance of forms of working class behaviour is therefore lost because these forms represent, at best, no more than defensive routines of everyday survival in response to capital's need to reproduce itself and, at worst, the actions of individuals fully incorporated by the dominant ideology.

The importance that Hollands attributes to the ideological level is both taken a stage further and given a specifically youthful dimension through the elevation of politics and ideology to a pre-eminent role in shaping social life. As Meiksins Wood points out, what initially appears a paradox in such accounts between a latent economic determinism and voluntaristic accounts of politics and ideology 'is nothing more than a flip of the structuralist coin' (Meiksins Wood, 1985, p. 79). It is precisely because such accounts tend to assume that the social formation is characterized by distinct and separate spheres that analysis can move between these levels with impunity and without regard for their logical or historical connections. In order to escape accusations of reductionism, politics and ideology are usually given some form of autonomy from the economic with the consequence that social relations become constituted politically and ideologically, rather than by reference to any specific historical forces grounded in the organization of social life. Taken to their post-structuralist extremes, politics and ideology increasingly become alienated from the social and historical relations which give them their form, eventually giving way to ideas or discourse as both the sole determinants of individual subjectivities and the formative factors in establishing the conditions in which social and political forces are actually constituted.

Within Hollands's account, this tendency can be traced to his heavy reliance on Cohen's (1986) attempt to 'rethink the youth question'. In a long and often only partially developed working paper, Cohen wants to replace orthodox accounts of youth grounded in biological or psychological definitions with one which can locate the specific appearances of youth within their historical context. For Cohen, youth does not correspond to a timeless biological or psychological process even if it is construed as such for the purposes of political or moral regulation, but is better understood as an imaginary category with a life of its own. This imaginary category stems from the structural organization of capitalism into relatively autonomous economic, political and ideological levels:

> it is the discontinuities between these structures which pose the youth question as a specific instance of their articulation; this takes the paradoxical form of creating the conditions of an imaginary unity out of the real social relations which distribute young people to different social locations. (Cohen, 1986, p. 53)

Although it is by no means clear how these relatively autonomous structures logically and historically evolve, or in which ways they actually combine to produce an imaginary category labelled youth, what Cohen offers is an essentially pluralist framework. This is a framework which proceeds from the assertion that society has no fundamental determinants, that each level of society has equal weight in any analysis and that all levels have real autonomy of action from others (Burnham, 1991). However, a necessary corollary of this pluralism is that analysis remains dogged by its inability to relate the forms taken by social life to the material organization of society which actually gives them their distinctiveness. Despite the supposed equal emphasis given to each factor, analysis rarely proceeds beyond the level of politics and ideology because it is through ideology, and ultimately even 'discourse' (Cohen, 1986, p. 54), that individuals are constituted as social beings and through which political and social forces are actually defined. Cohen thus rightly dismisses one approach, because it eternalizes in the form of (bio)ideology what are historically specific social relations, only to replace it with another which also cannot go beyond considerations of youthful behaviour as constituted by ideology and discourse, by relating them to the specific organization of social life.

The consequence is that analysis necessarily remains at the level of surface appearances and, as we have demonstrated, its conclusions tend to illustrate a remarkable complicity with the ideological assertions of the state (Williamson, 1989). This is most graphically illustrated by what Cohen treats as just one instance of youth, the young working class, and it is here that the limitations of Hollands's culturalism firmly rest. For Cohen, class relations under capitalism are no longer experienced in straightforward ways, as direct economic relations, but increasingly take the form of imaginary relations which appear in non-class forms:

> In other words, class positions are rarely registered in a simple and immediate form (e.g. in the conflict between Capital and Labour) they are lived through a series of non-class positions which they invisibly connect and inflect *at the level of cultural reproduction*. (Cohen, 1986, p. 56, original emphasis)

More specifically these 'non-class' positions take the form of 'reproduction codes' or 'cultural forms' (Hollands, 1990, p. 15) which, taken in their totality, provide the cultural framework within which individual subjectivities are constituted as working class young people mature. It is through these cultural markers that the meanings associated with working class childhood, adolescence and adulthood are defined; struggles over their definition, something uniquely appreciated by the politics of Thatcherism (Cohen, 1983), are important in constituting the specific forms taken by working class life.

To see class as reproduced in indirect and alien ways is to follow Cohen in seeing class as a technical or an economic relation. It is a relation whereby factors such as labour and machinery are combined within the technical process of material production, the economy, to make commodities, and which takes place *within* ideologically and politically constituted parameters (S. Clarke, 1991). Class, however, is neither a technical nor an economic relation, and its development is not more or less synonymous with the technical ways in which commodities are produced or one whose history can be read off against essentially neutral laws of technological progress (Meiksins Wood, 1990). Under capitalism class is a social relation, a relation rooted in the social organization of production in which the production of commodities necessarily entails a relationship between a class who own and control the means of production, and a class of wage labourers who are forced to return to the labour market each day just in order to survive. It is therefore a social relation of exploitation and domination in which the production of commodities necessarily involves the production and reproduction of social, and thus class, relations. In this way class cannot be seen as something separate from other social relations: ideology, politics and culture. Rather, 'the relations of production in their totality constitute what are called the social relations, society, and specifically, society at a definite stage of historical development' (Marx, 1977, p. 256).

It is precisely this that defines the historical significance of capital as a social relation which imposes itself throughout society and which finds expression in all that society's activities and forms. Class cannot be defined purely economically, in terms of the immediate labour process or at the level of the enterprise, but is a social relation of exploitation and domination which expresses itself in economic, political and ideological forms (S. Clarke, 1991). As E. P. Thompson so eloquently puts it:

> take up the essential defining productive relationship (private ownership of the means of production, and production for profit) and turn it round, and it reveals itself now in one aspect (wage labour), now in another (an acquisitive ethos), and now in another (the alienation of such intellectual faculties as are not required by the worker in his productive role).
> (Thompson, 1978b, p. 294)

It is here that we must search for the real substance of patterns of working class youthful behaviour because it is in the generality of the capital relation, and the necessary struggles against its tendency to reduce all social relationships to those of exploitation and domination, that the significance of these activities ultimately lies.

The Working Class and the Training State

This is not to deny that there is something specific about working class young people, that they face particular predicaments and that their forms of behaviour continue to pose serious problems for capital. The difficulty for analysis, however, is to explain these forms of behaviour without resort to accounts of ideology and discourse whose relationship to the organization of social life remains, at best, ambiguous and which say nothing about the concrete struggles with which the young are constantly involved. As McGuigan (1992) has pointed out, Cohen's (1972) earlier work was seminal in defining an analytical approach to youthful forms of behaviour whose class insights were overshadowed by its assertion that there was 'something specifically privileged about the *generational experience* of the young (Clarke *et al.*, 1976, p. 49, original emphasis). What actually constituted this privilege remained unclear beyond abstract concerns with distinctive subcultures as ideological forms of resistance and an inherent analytical exclusivity, stemming from its preoccupation with the most visible forms of behaviour, which ultimately offered few insights into the lives of the wider working class young (G. Clarke, 1991).

More recently, Cohen has restated this belief in the privilege of youth through his claim that 'there is a relation between generations and the views they hold' (Cohen, 1985, p. 33). Yet beyond the obvious truisms of such a statement a more fundamental problem remains, since for Cohen the specificity of generation can only be defined ideologically, through the idea of 'reproduction codes' as 'landmarks for historical generations' (Cohen, 1986, p. 57). Not only are we forced back into the superficiality and incoherence of culturalist accounts, youth constituted ideologically and politically, but by emphasizing generation a false separation between the experiences of young people and those of their parents is necessarily invoked; between the formative experiences of trainees today and those of their parents as products of the affluent 1950s and 1960s. However, 'even if they [working class young people] are involved with different institutions from their parents (schools etc.) all the evidence is that their response to them is based on similar values' (Corrigan and Frith, 1976), ones forged in and against the continuity of the capital relation.

To take a pertinent example, despite the lack of systematic research and analysis into the impact of adult training schemes, it is also instructive to remember that the young have not been the only section of the working class subjected to the onslaught of the training state, and what information there is suggests real continuities between their experiences and those of youth trainees. Evidence points strongly towards the failure of these new training opportunities for the adult unemployed to attract and retain trainees in ways not too dissimilar to those which characterized the development of the Youth Opportunities Programme (YOP) and the so-called 'new deal' offered by YTS (Finn, 1987). Unemployed adults, like their younger brothers and sisters, and indeed their own children, have remained deeply ambivalent towards this promise of training, despite the creation of a whole new network of training and benefit regimes aimed at coercing them into taking up places (Finn, 1988).

The most recent scheme, in particular, Employment Training[2] (ET), has continually suffered from low rates of participation analogous to youth training. Although it was originally expected to cater for 600 000 trainees per year on programmes lasting six months, with 300 000 trainees on the programme at any one time (Department of Employment, 1988b), numbers were quickly revised downwards to 450 000 per year and ET currently has around 250 000 participants (Unemployment Unit/Youthaid, 1992b). Because of the initial poor response, participation was extended from six months to a maximum of one year, but of those who joined during its first 18 months, just over half who were actually referred to a scheme completed their initial assessment period and, among those who stayed, more than two-thirds left early (Training Agency Employment Department, 1990). The latest evidence shows that this ambivalence has persisted, and by March 1992 only 41 per cent of trainees were completing their agreed training programme (Unemployment Unit/Youthaid, 1992a). In the context of this sustained opposition it is therefore unsurprising that the adult unemployed are now facing the prospect of further discipline through 'workfare' schemes in ways now long familiar to the young unemployed.

In and Against the Training State

The significance of forms of trainee behaviour must therefore be located within an analysis of class in general. Young people display many of the same values and responses as those of the wider working class and so it is to an appreciation of class as a social relation that we must look in order to further our understanding:

> working class young people are, in sociological terms, an actual and potential labour force and it is this (and not their youth) which determines their social relationships and structures their institutional relationships. (Corrigan and Frith, 1976, p. 236)

Youth is a class concept and what is specific about the behaviour of working class young people is not best understood by some ambiguous reference to ideology and politics, but to the ways in which youthful forms of labour have historically been constituted through struggles in and against the capital relation.

As Simon Frith pointed out some time ago, the 'concern of training programmes is young collective labour' (Frith, 1980, p. 38) and the problems of control it poses. These problems historically arise from the constant failure of young workers to display the same longer-term commitment to work, generally more characteristic of older workers with family responsibilities and mortgages to pay. The young working class's knowledge that work, more often than not, entails a harsh, negative and alienating experience has proved a constant source of tension in the development of capitalist social relations. Research has consistently illustrated that young people have a 'wide range of knowledge about their work situations . . . often acquired *before work begins*' (Keil, 1976, pp. 134–5, original emphasis). Young people, at least those entering manual labour, do not expect to find neat jobs and a comfortable working environment but dirty, noisy and smelly types of work (Simon, 1977; Ashton and Field, 1976). It was this familiarity with work which accounted for 'young workers' restlessness, their readiness to chop and change jobs for "trivial reasons", their immunity from the constraints of long-term instrumentality' (Frith, 1980, p. 38). While the postwar boom continued, employers' recruitment strategies anticipated the consequent disruptions and high levels of turnover this entailed (Ainley, 1988). However, as the boom gave way to crises, it was young workers' willingness and ability to act on the knowledge that work was often unpleasant, repetitive and intrinsically unrewarding which could no longer be allowed to persist.

It is therefore significant that the state has increasingly attempted to regulate these forms of behaviour through the evolution of forms of activity centred around the discipline of training. Nevertheless, following the culturalists in seeing this as the realm of some relatively autonomous ideological and political action is clearly inadequate. Such an approach ultimately echoes the state's claim of consensus where none exists; it cannot account for the complexity of trainee behaviour and it ultimately offers few clues as to how these forms relate to the organization of social life. What is needed, instead, is an analysis which begins from the centrality of the capital relation and the necessary struggle which takes place in and against its forms. Such an approach recognizes that the apparent separation of the political and the economic is intrinsic to the rise of capitalism (Clarke, 1988; Holloway and Picciotto, 1977, 1978) and seeks to demonstrate that the state and its activities are, both logically and historically, a specific form taken by capitalist social relations of production. Not only does such an approach therefore force us to confront the state's role in maintaining class rule through its differing forms of discipline and control, but it also compels us to understand how the state actually undertakes this task through the ways in which it projects certain forms of organization on to our lives. These are forms of social organization which continually seek to deny the transforming possibilities of class by attempting to individualize the ways in which we relate to each other in the everyday experience of our lives, whether as individual voters, consumers, tax-payers, social security recipients or trainees.

As a social relation of production, the state and its institutional forms are therefore subject to the same contradictions, antagonisms and constant struggles characteristic of the ways in which labour is established in and against the capital relation. Put simply, labour is historically constituted *in* the capital relation as a workforce necessary if capital is to continue to exist. Yet, simultaneously, because labour is subject to capital's tendency to reduce all social relationships to one of exploitation and domination, it is also necessarily *against* the capital relation. The implication of such a position is that struggles to resist the imposition of the capital relation, including the forms of the state, permeate all levels of capitalist life and that capitalism as a system of organizing social relations is inherently unstable. Moreover, because the forms which the capital relation takes are not simply established at the dawn of the capitalist epoch, they must constantly be fought out and re-established through determinant forms of concrete, historical struggles. Translated into everyday life:

> we can see all around us that the 'normal' condition of things is one of
> *instability*: factories, families, schools — are all riven by conflict,
> disruptions and impermanence . . . The veneer of equality and harmony
> scarcely conceal the daily eruptions of state violence and discrimination
> on the one hand, and on the other the sabotage, truancy, absenteeism,

> vandalism and the million other acts of rebellion which capital is
> constantly seeking to control or suppress. (Holloway, 1991a, p. 237,
> original emphasis)

Such a position therefore urges an approach to understanding young people's social world which emphasizes the unity of theory and practical research. While theory opens up the issues and lays bare the interpretations of social reality, theory itself can only progress by incorporating substantive research into its wider development. In this way, theory must remain open and sensitive to the demands and insights established by empirical research, but its categories and assumptions must reciprocate this openness by remaining sensitive to the complexities, contradictions and movement of social existence which ultimately underpin them. It is only in this way that a self-critical understanding of the social world can develop.[3]

To this end, we must therefore begin our analysis from the centrality of the capital relation, by identifying its differing historical forms and by recognizing the necessary struggles in and against these forms. It is in the practical struggles to resist capital's disciplines that the significance of working class behaviour lies and it is these struggles which represent the reality of being young and on a government training scheme. It may be 'grinding, everyday, unspectacular' (Holloway, 1991b, p. 171) class struggle but it must be understood as class struggle all the same. Without such an appreciation the significance of 'youthful' forms of working class behaviour will be lost and so it is to a consideration of these practical realities that we are now compelled to turn.

Notes

1. Hollands is not alone in this – see also Bates (n.d.) – but at the time of writing his account represents the most sophisticated attempt to develop such a position.

2. The 'guarantee group' for ET covers all 18–24-year-olds who have been out of work for six months or more; and the 'aim group' covers all those between 18 and 50 who have been out of work for two years or more.

3. For a considerably more detailed account of the necessity of an 'open' analysis, see the two volumes edited by Bonefeld et al. (1992).

2 YOUTH TRAINING IN COVENTRY

Coventry, the ninth largest city in Britain, with a population just under 300 000 (Office of Population Censuses and Surveys, 1992), lies about 20 miles to the south-east of Birmingham in what was once referred to as the 'manufacturing Midlands' of Britain. It is a city once famed for its prosperity and relative affluence, and was a symbol of all that was held precious by those who celebrated the postwar consensus. However, by the close of the 1980s the boom years had long since vanished; to talk of the 'good times' in Coventry's recent past may bring a flicker of recognition from some who shared in this brief moment of relative prosperity, but for more recent generations of young Coventarians The Specials' haunting 'Ghost Town' (a Coventry band's number one hit about the city) provides a much more pertinent backdrop. When people talk of Coventry, the epithet 'from boom town to doom town' tends to enter the conversation at some point or other as the experience of prosperity, war and recession have all left their indelible mark.[1]

One important mark of this prosperity was Coventry's position as the fastest-growing city in Britain during the first half of the twentieth century. Between 1900 and 1950 the population increased by around three times, so that by the end of World War II, swollen with the migrant labour which had been directed to work in the city's munitions factories, Coventry could boast a population of around a quarter of a million inhabitants. Such a rapid expansion was largely driven by Coventry's historical associations with the engineering industry (Thomas and Donnelly, 1986). A city once renowned for its textiles, especially its silk and ribbon weaving, by the late nineteenth century Coventry had already become established as a major centre of watch and bicycle production. It was this which laid the foundations for the city's later reputation as the home of the British motor cycle and motor vehicle industries, and for the subsequent development of a significant aircraft and aerospace industry. Textiles may have retained a substantial place in the local economy, undergoing something of a revival during the 1920s, but it was engineering, and particularly motors, that fuelled the city's expansion, and when engineering was thriving the rest of the city prospered too.

Even the ravages of war seemed a short-lived impediment. As a centre of engineering the city was an obvious target, and the suffering its people were subjected to during the early years of World War II was experienced by few others in Britain. At the height of the bombing campaign against the city between 1940 and 1943, over 1100 people were killed or injured; 55 000 houses were either damaged or destroyed; around 160 workshops, factories or warehouses were flattened; and most of the city's medieval centre was laid to waste (Mason, 1986). It is testament to the resilience of the local population that the war years were quickly overcome after such devastation, and prosperity was once again forthcoming. Indeed, Coventry's rebirth became one of the major symbols of Britain's wider post-war reconstruction, promising its citizens a not previously experienced affluence and a new planned way of life. A massive new shopping precinct was built, a city centre ring road was built to match the surge in car owner-ship, a huge new hospital was constructed on the edge of the city, a college of further education was put in place, a polytechnic followed and later came a new university (Beechey and Perkins, 1987).

For a while the boom times also meant relatively high wages in the newly rebuilt factories, and the city's labour-hungry industries attracted large numbers of migrant workers from all over the UK and beyond. The city had long been a central focus for inward migration, and as the tradi-tional industries declined in the early decades of the century, miners from South Wales and the north-east of England, displaced textile workers from Lancashire and metal workers from London all made their way to the city in significant numbers (Lancaster, 1986). Later, many itinerant Irish workers were to come to the city and settle as the postwar rebuilding pro-gramme provided abundant construction work, and the initial community established by a small number of Indian workers, brought over to work in the munitions factories, was to develop into a distinctive feature of the city's contemporary make-up. To say that Coventry is now a melting pot may be stretching the metaphor to its limits, but its once insatiable appetite for labour has ensured that the city now plays host to a richly contrasting and diverse series of ethnic groupings and cultures.

Nonetheless, Coventry has remained essentially a working class city which temporarily offered the prize of 'high earnings, rising consumption and new aspirations' (Tolliday, 1986, p. 205) for those willing and able to endure its monotonous and intense factory routines. For a while, workers in Coventry's expansive motor industry earned themselves a reputation as a 'blue-collar bourgeoisie' and enjoyed a standard of living mostly unavailable to the working class elsewhere. Yet it was a relative affluence which was not to last, and as early as the mid-1950s alarm bells were already beginning to sound. Engineering had been the postwar salvation of the city but the cost had been an ever-narrowing economic base, as the motor, aircraft and metal working industries increasingly dominated the local economy (Thomas and Donnelly, 1986). For the greater part of the postwar period, almost one-third of Coventry's total employment was accounted for by the motor industry alone, although few of the major British component manufacturers actually relocated there. The dominance of manufacturing was also underlined by the fact that, in 1978, the top five employers still provided 58 per cent of the city's manufacturing jobs and 32 per cent of its total jobs (Confederation of British Industry Special Programmes Unit, 1983). However, as with the motor industry, of the multinationals which dominated the local economy none chose to locate their head offices in the city. As a result, Coventry could boast few of the administrative jobs which normally accompany large-scale manufacturing and, as late as 1981, 40 per cent of the city's workforce was still employed in the engineering sector against a national average of 13 per cent (Dutton, 1987). There was significant expansion in public sector employment, particularly associated with local government, education, health and welfare, but in the provision of jobs in the wider service sector Coventry continues to fall well below the national average.

Even through the still prosperous 1960s many of Coventry's engineering workers were already familiar with fluctuations in their earnings, short-time working, frequent interruptions to production and even the occasional lay-off (Tolliday, 1986). Throughout the 1960s the motor industry had undergone widespread restructuring, and 11 000 aviation jobs were lost to the city between 1962 and 1967 (Blissett, 1989). These insecurities became further apparent during the early 1970s as the impact of recession began to expose the vulnerability of the local economy. Most significantly, the large-scale redundancies announced by Rolls-Royce's liquidation and its subsequent government take-over in 1972 signalled what was to come, a message reinforced shortly afterwards by British

Leyland's near bankruptcy and the threat from Chrysler to close its two Coventry plants. Nevertheless, it still came as a shock when, between 1975 and 1982, redundancy plans were introduced in all the city's top 15 firms as their workforces were halved, so that at the height of the early 1980s recession the city was shedding jobs at the terrifying rate of 520 a month; 1520 went in December 1982 alone (Thomas and Donnelly, 1986). The result was an estimated 2.5 million square feet of empty factory space and, as the temporary respite provided by relatively high redundancy payments and income-related social security benefits dried up, the city's high street shops also responded by laying off staff.

What had once been seen as the city's great strength now became a major weakness as the collapse in manufacturing overwhelmed any modest expansion of the service sector. Between 1971 and 1982 the service sector could add only 9000 extra jobs to the local economy (Blissett, 1989) and, as a consequence, between 1973 and 1981 the number of people in employment in the city fell by almost a quarter. As a result, unemployment, which had still been running at only 3 per cent in 1975, topped 20 per cent in 1982 as the city's downward slide turned into something approaching a full-scale slump (Coventry City Council, 1989).

The young were hit particularly hard as new generations of young people entered the labour market only to find that the previous opportunities for school leavers in Coventry's factories no longer existed. As manufacturing contracted, so too did the openings in low-skilled but relatively well-paid jobs traditionally taken by the city's school leavers. The young were therefore forced to take their chances and battle for those vacancies that remained with an ever-growing pool of available adult workers, themselves desperately trying to stave off unemployment. The availability of apprenticeships, the only types of work for which the young face no competition from older workers, also underwent a vicious contraction, declining from 456 in 1980 to only 248 the following year (Confederation of British Industry Special Programmes Unit 1983).

It was a fight for jobs that the young could never really win, and in 1983, when unemployment in the city among the 16–18-year age group peaked, some 7506 16- to 18-year-olds were registered with the careers service as either unemployed or on a government programme (Coventry City Council, 1989). Although many continued to view the situation as a temporary phenomenon, including many young people themselves, others were not so sanguine. Writing towards the end of the 1970s, Frith (n.d.) was already arguing that the extent of unemployment among school leavers in Coventry reflected a far-reaching restructuring of the city's economic and social relationships. For him, the plight of the young unemployed 'had become a permanent feature of the Coventry economy' (Frith, n.d., p. 21).

Frith's conclusions have, unfortunately, proved well-founded and now, around fifteen years later, widespread unemployment remains a major problem for the city's school leavers. By late 1989, when this research was being concluded, the situation had changed very little and few inroads had been made into the real problems facing many of Coventry's school leavers. The expansion of the city's financial sector had continued throughout the 1980s and, more importantly, manufacturing industry had undergone something of a limited renaissance, so that by 1989 it had 'once again [become] the dominant employer in the Coventry economy' (Blissett, 1989, p. 6). Nevertheless, a major study of the local workforce estimated that growth in employment had primarily come through increases in part-time working and self-employment, and that the level of full-time working had remained more or less constant (Elias and Owen, 1989).

With few full-time jobs available, unemployment in the city remained a major problem. At the height of the late 1980s boom, the city council estimated that there were still 12 274 officially unemployed people in the city and that this represented around 8 per cent of the working population (Coventry City Council, 1989). Over two in five of these were long-term unemployed and in some areas the general rate was closer to 20 per cent. For Asian and Afro-Caribbean people living in Coventry, unemployment levels have remained about twice as high as the figure for the city as a whole (Elias and Owen, 1989). School leavers were faring only marginally better, with some 4230 16- to 18-year-olds either looking for work or on government schemes. Indeed, a measure of the problem facing these young people was that the proportion of school leavers on training schemes or special programmes had increased from 31 per cent in 1980 to 62 per cent in 1989 (Coventry City Council, 1989).

It is for these reasons that Coventry represents an ideal city in which to undertake a detailed consideration of the ways in which the young working class have confronted the development of youth training. The collapse of the manufacturing base and the squeezing of the service sector had deprived many of the current generation of school leaver of the work that they were previously anticipating. By the end of the 1980s, youth training had grown to become a formidable feature of the city's post-school landscape, with over one third of 16-year-olds leaving school only to enter a scheme.

Like elsewhere (e.g. Lee *et al.*, 1990), the expansion of work experience and training programmes for unemployed school leavers in the city had been far from simple. Suspicion from both potential trainees and placement providers dogged its early stages (Frith, n.d.) and, in particular, for a number of individuals and institutions involved in the crucial process of guiding trainees into places, youth training remained a sensitive issue. Here my initial attempts to talk to school pupils about their perceptions and experience of youth training met with an uncompromising rebuttal, as careers advisers argued that to do so would have been 'inappropriate for the school' and would therefore have provoked 'a storm of protests from the parents'. However, although such concerns may have been manifest at a surface level, it later became apparent that they reflected more deeply the ways in which the careers service and the schools structured the movement into training schemes.[2]

At the time, Coventry operated a decentralized system of careers guidance and counselling for pupils which gave the service a direct presence in each of the city's comprehensive schools. This system of directing careers advice within the city had developed alongside national changes in the careers service, which had seen it take on an increasingly direct role in managing high levels of youth unemployment and administering to the needs of the burgeoning youth training programme (Bates, 1984). Traditionally, the national careers service had been set up as a quasi-autonomous organization which had prided itself in providing school leavers with specialist advice from professionally trained counsellors. Regardless of the demands of employers and the state, the careers service saw its primary role as one of offering independent advice, guidance and information best suited to the needs of individual pupils.

However, as the opportunities for direct entry into jobs declined, the limitations of this autonomy became increasingly apparent as the service became progressively associated with placing school leavers into schemes. Thus, for example, in 1987 the careers service nationally undertook over a million individual careers guidance interviews and placed 92 000 young people in jobs. However, over the same period it placed 244 000 young people in youth training schemes (Cross *et al.*, 1990). In the same year, 74 per cent of the schemes' total recruitment came via the careers service, and its success in placing young people in jobs declined from 59 per cent of all placements in 1978 to only 26 per cent eight years later.

As we will see in the following chapters, for many school leavers the careers service has become little more than a functionary of youth training and, as a result, hostility, suspicion and frustration towards it remain widespread. It is in this context that the decisions of the careers advisers to block my attempts to talk with the pupils appears less surprising, together with the fact that the careers service actually had the power to prevent me from doing so. Revealingly, one of the advisers even commented that 'because most young people have a negative image of YTS' his school did not treat youth training as a separate component of careers education, preferring instead to lump it in with a number of other post-school issues under a catch-all session on 'opportunities for young people in jobs and training'. Youth training's significance was therefore consciously underplayed by this school's careers curriculum despite the probability that around one-third of its leavers would be destined to start on the scheme. More alarmingly, it was also revealed that some of these young people actually entered schemes believing them to be jobs, initially unaware of their impending status as youth trainees.

Apart from the questionable moral and political implications of placing young people into training schemes without their full knowledge, or possibly even consent, the underhand and almost clandestine treatment of youth training points towards a mutual awareness among both staff and pupils that the scheme remained distinctly unpopular. It has been noted elsewhere that it is precisely during this later phase of education that the fragility of the education/job 'exchange' becomes more fully exposed (Corrigan, 1979; Willis, 1977). 'Teachers exchange knowledge and qualifications for respect and good behaviour from pupils' (Stafford, 1981, p. 61) and as pupils become more aware that this 'fair exchange' may not be rewarded with jobs, maintaining control and discipline becomes more problematic. This is implicitly acknowledged here by the failure of the schools to treat youth training in any systematic and direct way, and by the careers advisers' reluctance to countenance research which would bring to the surface many of the subterranean issues they sought to suppress. At a time when many fifth-form pupils are actively contemplating how best to make their way in a hostile labour market, any undue attention to aspects of post-school life which could have further undermined an already fragile 'exchange' would be a far from welcome intrusion. This is despite the fact that the lack of free and open debate in school can only eventually serve to further underline the feelings of irrelevance that many working class young people already have towards their formal education.

Furthermore, as will be seen in Chapter 4, despite the school's surreptitious approach to youth training, pupils do have a considerable knowledge and appreciation of youth training's opportunities and constraints. Failing to acknowledge the significance of training does not make it any less of a reality for a large number of working class school leavers.

The Schools and Their Pupils

The first school to agree to cooperate with the research, Crompton School and Community College,[3] was one of the city's most recent secondary schools and was housed in modern, purpose-built accommodation. Standing on the outskirts of the city, it drew its mainly white pupils primarily from a large surrounding council estate which had grown progressively larger throughout the 1960s and 1970s. As one of the city's smaller comprehensive schools, with a capacity of well under 1000 pupils, its role for the previous academic year stood at considerably less than the maximum, including a small sixth form attended by around 40 pupils. The school's relatively modern origins were also reflected in its overall design and appearance. From the outside the two-storey buildings looked smart and in a generally good state of repair, as did the well-kept surrounding lawns and flower beds. To the back of the school there were expansive playing fields marked out for rugby, football, hockey and cricket, and at the front was a floodlit area used for tennis, netball, hockey and five-a-side football. The school also boasted an annexe which was used for its community and youth club activities. Crompton's overall newness was reflected in the spacious and light classrooms, which were both well decorated and relatively well equipped, and by its centre-piece large sports and assembly hall from which the remainder of the school buildings radiated off. The pupils were also provided with a purpose-built tuck shop and the teachers enjoyed a relatively expansive staffroom, with a small but impressive open-plan office space shared by the deputy heads and senior teachers.

In contrast, Harwood School had a much more familiar feel to anyone who has been through the comprehensive system. Originally established as a single-sex grammar school at the turn of the century, the school had become a mixed comprehensive during the 1970s and a designated community college shortly afterwards. Its longer and more varied history was immediately evident from the newer 1960s-type developments grafted on to the original brick school buildings and from the provision of temporary classroom facilities, which grew as education cuts took their toll. In spite of attempts to liven up the school with the pupils' often colourful art and design work, the school had a more subdued feel than Crompton, with its dark corridors and murky and smaller classrooms adding to the overall gloomy feel. It too had its own surrounding playing fields adjacent to the main complex, but immediately around the school buildings grass had now given way to bare earth under the constant pounding of the pupils' feet.

Harwood School stood just outside the inner city, drawing its pupils from a large, long-established working class area. The mainly terraced housing of the surrounding streets was punctuated by workshop and factory units, and patches of derelict ground now stood where factories had once supplied the locals with work. Coventry's deindustrialization had taken a particularly aggressive form in and around the local community and the school's then catchment area was dominated by one of the city's poorer districts. It had recently been identified by the local education authority (LEA) as 'having particular problems' with 'high or above average' ratings for a group of socio-economic indicators used as measures of local social deprivation. The catchment area was also racially diverse, with a lively and long-established Asian[4] community nearby. According to the school's prospectus, approximately one-third of its pupils had their 'origins outside the UK', with the consequence that the school was actively committed to a multi-cultural education and 'an anti-racist policy which it pursues with vigour'. Harwood had also recently been threatened with closure due to contracting pupil numbers across the city but 'after a fierce campaign by teachers, parents and pupils' the LEA had finally backed down. By 1989, its roll stood at just under 1000 pupils, of whom about 70 attended the small sixth form.

The combined final-year groups of pupils from both schools represented about an eight per cent sample of Coventry's then fifth-form population. Both groups of final-year pupils were requested to fill out an eight-page questionnaire as part of either their careers teaching programme or as the basis for a social studies lesson. The questionnaires were administered on a form group by form group basis and, as Table 2.1 shows, the final coverage included a cross-section of both girls and boys, and pupils of European and non-European descent.

In all, 152 questionnaires were completed and returned, 81 from Harwood (57 per cent) and 71 from Crompton (43 per cent), which taken together covered 51 per cent of the total number of pupils in both final

Table 2.1 *Breakdown of School Pupil Survey*

	Male	Female	Total	European	Non-European
Harwood	43	38	81	45	36
Crompton	44	27	71	71	0
Total	87	65	152	116	36

years. This represented a disappointing response rate, although not out of line with those found in similar types of survey work, given the 'captive' audience anticipated. In one school, although it was never explicitly acknowledged, an administrative error meant that at least one form group had not been given the questionnaire to complete, and at the other school, including the unused questionnaires which were also returned, there were 27 less than the original number delivered. Despite repeated enquiries and the promise of another 'twenty odd' in a couple of weeks, these too were unforthcoming.

The timing of the survey also undoubtedly contributed to the low response rate, as the original intention had been to carry out this phase of the research shortly before the Christmas break. However, delays in obtaining access meant that it was not undertaken until near the end of the spring term when, according to staff at both schools, large numbers of pupils had made up their minds about leaving and were already voting with their feet. For many of these, attendance at school in these final few months was sporadic and this undoubtedly contributed to the overall low returns. The loss of this group also had implications for the quality of the data generated by the survey, as the idea had been to carry out a census of each school's fifth year to capture the entire range of pupil experience. Failure to capture the feelings of those pupils who had already left meant that an important component of the schools' cohort of final-year pupils was only partially represented. This is particularly important for assessing the significance and extent of child labour discussed in Chapter 3, because having already rejected school these were the pupils most likely to have been involved. Furthermore, it was precisely this group of pupils who were more likely to leave school with few or no qualifications, and therefore they represented the most obvious group for whom youth training was destined to become a reality (Banks *et al.*, 1992).

It is also probable that a number of pupils simply refused to complete the questionnaire, or at least were not interested enough to bother, because of the research's associations with school. The school's staff took responsibility for administering the questionnaire and, in this respect, it may have been perceived as just another mundane aspect of the school's activities. Certainly, Corrigan (1979) warns of the dangers of researchers in schools becoming too associated with the institution they are researching. Despite my being given the opportunity to talk to pupils about the research and to urge on them both its independence from the school and the genuine desire to gain some sense of their feelings and experience regarding youth training, it is doubtful whether the survey could ever have freed itself totally from any institutional associations. Taking all these caveats into consideration, the survey did, however, ascertain the experiences and feeling of a cross-section of both school's final-year populations. To this extent, the views expressed in the following discussions are a representative selection of pupil experiences.

The Schemes and Their Trainees

The second phase of the research focused on a small number of youth training schemes considered broadly representative of both the concentration and distribution of trainees in the city. According to the Training Agency's *Two Year YTS 100 Per Cent Follow Up Survey* (Training Agency, 1990), discussed in more detail below, youth training in Britain is dominated by a small number of Training Occupational Classifications (TOCs).[5] Between April 1988 and March 1990 70 per cent of all leavers nationally came from just six TOCs: 20 per cent from 'Office Work', 14 per cent from 'Selling/Warehouse Work', 14 per cent from 'Building/Construction Work', 11 per cent from 'Engineering Work', 8 per cent from 'Community/Health Service Work' and 7 per cent from 'Repairing Motor Vehicles', with the remaining 11 TOCs accounting for the rest. Notwithstanding small local variations, these national figures were closely mirrored by the pattern for Coventry, with the same six TOCs accounting for 73 per cent of all leavers. Together with a scheme which trained young people in the 'Cooking/Service/Food' TOC, as Table 2.2 shows, it was from these training areas that the schemes to be researched were eventually drawn.

Discussions with the Assistant Principal Careers Officer for Coventry

Table 2.2 *Managing Agents, Schemes and Trainees (n = 42)*

	Male	Female	Total
Chamber of commerce			
Retail scheme	2	2	4
Clerical scheme	0	4	4
Engineering scheme	4	0	4
City council			
Carpentry scheme	3	0	3
Plumbing scheme	2	0	2
Clerical scheme	1	4	5
The college			
Public service vehicle (PSV) scheme	4	0	4
Horticulture scheme	2	2	4
Community care scheme	2	2	4
The centre			
Catering scheme	0	4	4
Motor vehicle maintenance (MVM) scheme	2	0	2
Maintenance and construction (MaC) scheme	2	0	2
Total	**24**	**18**	**42**

identified a number of managing agents who offered schemes in the selected TOCs and who, it was felt, would provide something approaching a representative selection. These are also outlined in Table 2.2. Each scheme was visited regularly during the fieldwork period, where most of the time was spent with the trainees during their off-the-job provision. At the time, training providers were still required to provide a minimum of 20 weeks' off-the-job training, although this has subsequently been relaxed to allow greater 'flexibility'. As most of the off-the-job training was provided in-house by the managing agents themselves, spending time with the trainees in this way offered the advantage of ensuring virtually unlimited access and overcame some of the more problematic issues raised when interviewing young people (see Roberts *et al.*, 1986a). This was also greatly facilitated by the extensive cooperation from the managing agents and individual staff from the schemes, all of whom gave their time freely and generously provided the opportunity and facilities to open up more detailed discussions with trainees. Moreover, it was even mentioned on a number of occasions that my presence was a welcome distraction from the usual routines, a further way to occupy the trainee's time and, for the staff, it was even mentioned that 'it's nice to get them out of my hair for a while'.

At each scheme I was therefore permitted to come and go virtually unhindered, and while one or two schemes asked for short notice before visiting, no requests to visit were ever refused. This allowed me to spend a considerable amount of time with the trainees, sitting in on training sessions, observing individual lessons and socializing with the trainees at lunch times and during tea breaks. The first intention was to get to know the trainees better and then to develop some sense of what was involved in being a trainee, and then to establish some opportunities to follow up these issues through more detailed discussions and interviews. Across the period of the research, most of the trainees I met and spoke to were more than willing to discuss their views on a whole range of subjects but, as Table 2.2 also shows, only 42 were singled out for a more detailed interview. The interviews lasted between 40 minutes and two hours, and included 18 young women and 24 young men, of whom three of the total were of Asian descent.

It is from these 42 interviews that the material used in the subsequent chapters is taken and, much to their credit, none of the trainees approached for a more detailed discussion actually refused to be interviewed. At all times, individual trainees were selected to ensure the research retained its commitment to some sort of representative cohort and this was achieved through my own observations of the trainees and in discussion with training scheme staff. Because of the crucial gender dynamic to youth training (Cockburn, 1987), approximately equal numbers of young men and women were interviewed, although the surprising finding of two young men on the community care scheme slightly skewed the final numbers. Interestingly, the availability of individual trainees was often determined by whether the young person in question had bothered to turn up on a particular day. The problem with sporadic attendance became increasingly clear as the research progressed and the training staff often expressed the view that 'we don't know who's coming from one week to the next'.

For the managing agents and training scheme staff, attendance problems were a manifestation of wider problems of discipline and control. For the researcher it meant four return trips across a three-week period, until the interview with one young person could eventually be secured. The trainees interviewed also displayed varying levels of academic ability but again they were representative of the general trainee population. Two interviewed were said to have 'learning difficulties', one 'behavioural problems' and, at the other end of the spectrum, one trainee, much to my surprise, had nine O levels. Like countless other working class young people, most had sat some exams while they were still at school, only to either fail or not bother to find out how they had got on or, for the more successful, scrape one or two passes.

One final point needs to be made on the selection of trainees because it again has important wider implications for the organization of youth training. Considering the significance of ethnicity in youth training (Cross and Smith, 1987), one of the explicit intentions of the research was to explore the experiences of being a young black trainee. Three Asian young people were eventually interviewed, two young men and a young woman, but it was obvious that black trainees were remarkably under-represented on the schemes identified for research. This is unfortunate because, as we shall see in some detail in Chapter 4, black trainees face particular obstacles when training.

It is worth noting here, however, that the failure of the research to identify significant numbers of Asian trainees, especially given the fact that Asian people now constitute around 9 per cent of Coventry's overall population (Office of Population Censuses and Surveys, 1992), is indicative of the wider ways in which youth training has become embedded in a pre-existing racial division of labour. There is now a growing literature on the particular problems faced by black trainees (see Chapter 4) but little discussion of the more subtle processes influencing young black people's entrance into training. The discriminatory practices of employers, managing agents and the careers service have been well documented, especially the now stock response that these types of young people do not apply for places in the first place. Yet what this fails to recognize is that many young black people's acute desires to avoid unemployment or youth training further locks them into a vicious circle of low-status jobs. For example, other research in Coventry has illustrated the particular importance of 'friends, acquaintances and relatives' (Hoel, 1982, p. 82) for young Asian women's ability to avoid unemployment. Family and kinship networks often provide Asian young people with alternative routes into work but at the cost of accepting 'sweated' work in Coventry's extensive clothing factories, where wages are low, hours long and job security almost non-existent. For some Asian school leavers this may provide an alternative to unemployment or training schemes, and a route into much prized jobs. However, in doing so, it further illustrates the ways in which the scheme has initiated new forms of resistance among certain sections of the young working class through its failure to address some of the fundamental discriminatory processes which reproduce racialized forms of training. Through Asian young people's desires to avoid training schemes and in their continued preferences for jobs outside the scheme, or 'real jobs' as many of the young people referred to them, they effectively become locked into a series of networks which lead into low-paid, arduous work that offers few possibilities for any real training or further career development. In this way, the position of young black people in the lower levels of the job market is indirectly reproduced by the failure of youth training to engage in any meaningful way with its overt commitment to equal opportunities and quality training for all.

The Two-Year YTS 100 Per Cent Follow Up Survey

One last comment needs to be made about the final source of data on which the arguments presented here often draw. The official record of youth training's development and performance comes from data previously supplied by the *Two Year YTS 100 Per Cent Follow Up Survey* of leavers and now by the *YT National Follow Up Survey*.

The former consists of empirical data generated by the Manpower Services Commission (MSC) and more latterly by the Department of Employment, up until the delivery of the scheme was taken over by TECs in England and Wales, and Local Enterprise Companies (LECs) in Scotland, at the beginning of the 1990s (see Peck, 1993). The *Follow Up Survey* represents an impressive piece of research and was undertaken for the Department of Employment by the Social and Community Planning Research (SCPR) market research organization. Its scale is such that for the last full survey, between April 1988 and March 1990 (covering the period of research here), 706 006 questionnaires were issued of which

384 594 were completed and returned; a response rate of 54 per cent (Training Agency, 1990). A copy of the questionnaire was sent to every trainee three months after leaving the scheme, together with a pre-paid envelope for its return. The survey results were updated every three months, with copies placed in the House of Commons library, broken down on a national, regional and local level. It was from the survey's findings that government ministers made their claims for the scheme's performance, that the Department of Employment answered questions tabled in Parliament, and that various claims were made in the pages of such publications as *Youth Training News*. Close scrutiny of the leavers survey, as it appeared in the House of Commons library, illustrates the ways in which successive governments have been 'economical' with its findings. Apart from getting regular and detailed coverage in the Unemployment Unit/Youthaid's excellent *Working Brief*, the results of the survey rarely achieved any detailed public scrutiny or dissemination, allowing the official claims for the scheme to be put to the test. Attempts to do so are made in the following chapters.

Since the TEC initiative, however, the survey has undergone substantial reorganization as individual TECs have become responsible for monitoring their own schemes' performances. One consequence of decentralizing the monitoring process has been that, post-1990, the collection and presentation of data on the progress of leavers have taken place largely on an *ad hoc* and unsystematic basis. Results from the new system were extremely slow to emerge and many TECs have failed to submit returns or release any figures.[6] Close and careful monitoring of youth training, never easy to begin with, has therefore become an increasingly difficult task to perform. Apart from its implications for local democracy and the accountability of institutions which are responsible for receiving extremely large sums of public money, as with so many other government statistics we are now faced with partial and often superficial data in a period in which unemployment for 16- to 24-year-olds has once again risen to around the one million mark.

Notes

1. The analysis presented here is, in large part, developed from an empirically based research project which examined working class young

people's responses to youth training in Coventry at the end of the 1980s (see Mizen, 1990b).

2. The research addressed the question of young people's relationships to youth training in two phases. The first phase examined how young people approaching the end of their compulsory schooling, and contemplating an immediate entry into the labour market, faced the prospect of beginning their working lives proper as trainees. The second phase sought to go further by undertaking a detailed examination of what it was actually like to be a trainee on a Coventry scheme.

With this two-stage approach, the first requirement was undertaken through a one-off survey of a representative sample of school pupils in the last year of their compulsory schooling. At the time, the number of young people in their final year of compulsory schooling stood at just under 4000, in 19 different comprehensive schools. The intention was therefore to generate a 10 per cent sample. The second phase, as described in more detail later in this chapter, drew in a number of trainees from a cross-section of the city's training schemes.

3. For reasons of confidentiality the names of both schools have been changed.

4. Asian is used throughout the book to denote those young people of Indian, Pakistani, Bangladeshi and Sri Lankan descent.

5. For a more detailed discussion of Training Occupational Classifications, see Chapter 5.

6. For a full list of TECs that, at the time of writing, have failed to make their youth training returns available, see Unemployment Unit/ Youthaid (1993a).

3 HAVING TO LEARN THE HARD WAY: THE SIGNIFICANCE OF CHILD LABOUR

It has been pointed out that at the heart of the training state lies a 'deficiency model' (Davies, 1986) of young workers. This is a model which equates young people's inability to secure paid employment less with the ways in which capitalist social relations structure and organize work, and more with the presumed inability of individual young workers to display those basic attributes that they are told employers need. Today young workers are consistently portrayed as individually wanting in the basic abilities needed to secure and hold down a job in a dynamic economy. Institutionalized in successive government initiatives from the YOP to YT and from Restart through to ET, an ever-widening training network has been put in place shaped largely by the demands of capitalist restructuring and articulated through the 'needs' of employers (Ainley and Corney, 1990; Finn, 1982).

What these needs actually are, however, has remained far from clear beyond continual and generalized references to the need for a better trained, more productive and increasingly flexible workforce. Employers' concerns over the quality of young labour are nothing new and recur throughout the postwar period, but what was specific to the late 1970s was the increasing urgency of these worries as one after another leading politicians, industrialists and employers became ever more vocal in their criticisms of new recruits coming into the labour market (Davies, 1986). On the one hand, the education system came in for a sustained and aggressive critique as comprehensives, inappropriate curricula, left-wing teachers and progressive teaching methods were all blamed for falling educational standards. On the other hand, a sustained offensive took place against successive generations of working class school leavers who were singled out as being unprepared for the demands of working life, oblivious to the imperatives of a successful and vibrant economy, and unable to demonstrate to employers that they were up to the tasks they were required to do. As the object of much derision, it was claimed that 'after one of the longest periods of compulsory education in Europe, young people seemed ill-equipped for almost any kind of employment and woefully ignorant about the basic economic facts' (Sir John Methven, Director General of the Confederation of British Industry, quoted in Brown, 1987, p. 108).

Despite the emphasis on declining standards, what employers wanted could never be expressed solely in terms of their technical requirements. Not only did different employers require different capacities and skills from their workforces, but these technical qualities were subject to pressures from constant variation, innovation and change. Significantly, employers were 'more concerned with the general, social dispositions and characteristics of their workers than with their particular abilities to carry out specific tasks' (Finn, 1982, p. 44). Closely wrapped up in their technical worries was therefore a more pressing preoccupation with the forms of behaviour that the young working class continued to show. Employers saw young workers as a 'headache' with 'a reputation for moving in and out of jobs in a casual, undisciplined and aimless way; [and] of performing poorly in jobs they do hold down however temporarily' (Industrial Training Research unit, 1979, p. 2). Institutionalized in the Holland Report, it was working class school leavers' lack of 'attitude/personality, appearance/manners and inadequate knowledge of the "three Rs"' (Manpower Services Commission, 1977, p. 17) which was the real issue at stake. Declining academic and technical standards may have been the pretext for such interventions, but increasingly apparent in all this was the belligerence of employers' complaints concerning the character of the young labour on which they were having to draw (Frith, 1980).

Yet paradoxically, it was not their new recruits' woeful ignorance of the basic economic facts which lay at the heart of these accusations. On the contrary, it was an awareness among young workers that employers' needs meant undertaking gruelling, unpleasant and alienating forms of work which fuelled these forms of behaviour and the problems of discipline they posed. It was this that made young workers such an unattractive source of labour for employers and, in the words of Sir Richard O'Brien, then chairperson of the MSC, what they needed was 'knowledge of what it means to have a job . . . its opportunities, disciplines and rights' (quoted in Finn, 1984, p. 17). Expressed most thoroughly through the New Training Initiative (NTI) and its plans for a comprehensive youth training scheme, these deficiencies were to be remedied by the imposition of new forms of discipline on the young working class: the discipline of training. The young unemployed were first and foremost to be subjected to a period of vocational preparation which would equip them to

> adapt successfully to the demands of employment; to have a fuller appreciation of the world of industry, business and technology in which they will be working; and to develop basic and recognised skills which employers will require in the future. (Department of Employment, 1981, p. 7)

Thus the deficiency model represents nothing more than an attempt to subject the young working class to new forms of discipline in the guise of training. However, what it fails to appreciate is that the importance of work does not just begin when a young person leaves school. What the deficiency model is continually seeking to suppress is that working class young people do have a substantial knowledge of the world of work, and that this is a knowledge of work as a profoundly harsh and alienating experience. Working class young people grow up in working communities (despite the often savage levels of unemployment many of these communities are forced to endure), are themselves brought up to work and gain intimate knowledge and information about working life from family, relatives and friends (Moore, 1984). Most importantly of all, young people gain immediate and direct knowledge of work through their experiences of child labour.

It is through exploring the significance of child labour that this chapter seeks to question the validity of the deficiency model. By looking at the importance of work in its most immediate form for school pupils, I establish the extent to which the young working class are directly constituted as wage labourers before they finish their compulsory education. More specifically, I assess the extent to which school leavers are already involved in paid employment before they leave school and the significance this has for their movement into training schemes. Through an examination of the extent of child working and the jobs child workers actually do, I explore what it means to be a child worker and assess the wider implications of this experience for the relationship between school, work and training.

The Significance of Child Labour

There have been a number of attempts to provide a more rigorous and detailed understanding of the contemporary extent and significance of child working but many of these have been limited by their narrow focus. On the whole they have tended to concentrate on specific issues concerning the mechanics of child labour, like the efficacy of existing legislation, its implications for young people's schooling and examination performance, and its wider significance for issues of moral and social regulation (e.g. Fyfe, 1989). While these issues obviously demand serious critical attention, concentrating on such specifics has meant that the wider significance of child working has until recently gone largely unexplored. In particular, research is only just beginning to consider the content and meaning of child working for those for whom it is an everyday reality, the child workers themselves, and as such the importance of child labour for growing up working class is only just emerging.

One of the few attempts to evaluate systematically its significance has sought to highlight the significance of child labour in defining the movement from school into work. For Dan Finn, young people are directly constituted as a distinct form of labour power from an early age and it is through working while still below the minimum compulsory school leaving age that young people gain their first direct taste of waged labour. This gradual accumulation of a wide-ranging knowledge of the immediate social relations of production is essentially a 'learning experience' (Finn, 1984, p. 44), whereby child workers begin to directly appreciate the relative freedoms and coercions endemic in earning a wage. Child labour is therefore the beginning of a process through which young people start to consciously fashion many of the qualities needed for later working life. They begin to learn the skills necessary to find, secure and hold down paid employment; they suffer at first hand the demands and coercions imposed by the discipline of work; they learn how to successfully negotiate and manage employment relationships with employers; and they begin to experience the relative freedoms associated with the command of an independent wage. This experience is all the more significant because it often involves experience of work at its most mundane, where 'contact with the "dull compulsion" of capitalist economic relations is with capital at its dullest' (Finn, 1984 p. 18). It is through directly experiencing hard work devoid of any intrinsic value that the young working class are forced to confront the realities of wage labour the hard way.

It is this constitution of pre-school leavers as a distinct source of labour power that, according to Finn, proves one of the central features in defining the continuity between the social relations of adolescence and schooling, and those of the adult world of work. For him, the state's attempt to portray the young working class as ignorant of, and ill-prepared for, working life obscures the realities of social life by denying that the struggle to find and maintain a living wage is one of its defining features (Finn, 1982). While not insensitive to a whole series of tensions and uncertainties contained within the movement from school to work, and the ways in which waged labour is given a distinctive form through its interrelationship with patriarchal forms of social relations, Finn's emphasis is on child labour's role in providing young people with a prefigurative framework for later adult working life. Through child working young people accumulate a considerable reservoir of knowledge and experience on which they can constantly draw, so that far from being ill-prepared for adult working life or unaware of what it entails, the majority of working class young people leave school 'ready culturally and socially to make the transition to work' (Finn, 1984, p. 59).

The significance that Finn attaches to pre-school working as a source of work experience is not an uncontested one. For Roberts *et al.*, Finn overemphasizes the role of child working in preparing the young working class for adult life and they question the extent to which 'spare-time' working can be generalized into a youthful experience. They also doubt the role of child labour in allowing young people to 'become streetwise, learn how to hold jobs, to earn and spend their own money and to handle relationships with employers' (Roberts *et al.*, 1986a, p. 91). Where they do see some significance for spare-time working, however, is for young people who remain in full-time education beyond their final compulsory year at school. They suggest that an Americanization of attitudes is taking place whereby parents are increasingly encouraging their children to supplement any pocket money through working while remaining in full-time education (see also Hutson and Cheung, 1992). It is precisely these 'bright sixth formers and college students' that employers prefer to fill their part-time and temporary vacancies, thus squeezing opportunities for 'less able pupils' (Roberts *et al.*, 1986a, p. 92). Thus a movement away from associations of spare-time working with working class origins and educational failure is taking place, and Finn's emphasis on viewing child labour in relation to working class rejection of school is, increasingly, a misplaced notion.

The Extent of Child Labour

As there are no nationally recognized figures and no centrally administered source of statistics, precise estimates of the extent of child working in Britain are difficult to gauge and longer-term trends and patterns almost impossible to assess. What research is available would suggest that child working is extensive and includes, at any one time, between one-third and two-thirds of all school pupils. The Emrys Davis Report, commissioned for the then Department of Health and Social Security (DHSS) in 1972, covered 40 schools in 10 different regions and found that three-quarters of 13- to 15-year-olds were involved in some form of work, around half of them holding a paid job (quoted in TUC/UNICEF, 1985). Three years later a DHSS estimate of the effects of legislating for the compulsory registration of child workers put the initial figure at 33 per cent of the child population for the first year of registration. Its figures for yearly additions implied that one in four children were involved in part-time working other than baby-sitting and running errands (quoted in MacLennan et al., 1985).

These estimates have been complemented by the findings of other large-scale survey research. In Scotland, evidence from the Scottish Young People's Survey found that 45 per cent of pupils held a term-time job and, had holiday jobs been included, the proportion would have been substantially higher (Howieson, 1990). The annual survey of 33 000 school pupils by Exeter University's Health Education Unit has consistently found that, at 15, around half of their sample held a paid job during term-time (*Guardian*, 29 November 1989). A series of studies by the Low Pay Unit have also consistently reinforced this picture of extensive child working. In their survey of Child Labour in London (Low Pay Unit, 1982) in the early 1980s they found that 35 per cent of their sample from six comprehensive schools were currently working and, in a larger-scale follow-up, 40 per cent of pupils were found to be in paid employment during term-time (MacLennan et al., 1985). From their most recent survey of child workers, it was calculated that nationally around half of Britain's four million children of secondary school age were currently involved in some form of waged labour (Low Pay Unit, 1991).

Although the extent of part-time working is undoubtedly influenced by the structure and opportunities of local labour markets, more specific and localized studies tend to reinforce these general findings. The strength of the conclusions of Roberts et al. (1986a) is surprising given that

42 per cent of their sample had worked before leaving school, a far from insignificant minority. An early 1980s study of a South Wales comprehensive school found that around half the fifth-form pupils held a part-time job (Brown, 1987), and a study of young people on the Isle of Sheppey found that every one of the respondents 'already had extensive work experience before they left school' (Wallace, 1987a, p. 64), usually in the form of part-time or casual working.

Finn's (1984) own conclusions were drawn from research in Rugby and Coventry, where 75 per cent of his sample of fifth formers had at one time held a part-time job, and many of these had started working during their early teens. A senior teacher at a Scarborough comprehensive school, prompted by falling attendances for out-of-school activities, carried out an informal survey among his pupils and found that around 75 per cent of the second-year pupils reported having a job. Although many jobs involved dog walking or digging the garden, he found a 'worrying' number working as baby-sitters, delivering newspapers and working in the hotel and catering sector of Scarborough's tourist industry. Furthermore he felt it was an increasing trend:

> the clash between school commitments and a part-time job is not something new, but it used to be a Saturday morning problem confined to the 15 plus age group. Now many youngsters aged from 12 upwards have jobs before and after school. (Combes, 1987, p. 22)

This pattern of extensive child labour was also confirmed among the Coventry young people who took part in my research. Of the 152 school pupils who had been surveyed, 104 (69 per cent) had held a part-time job at one time or another and, as Table 3.1 illustrates, a clear distinction in rates of activity emerged between those who intended to leave school at the earliest possible moment and those who had decided to stay on. The division of pupils into stayers and leavers loosely reflects a long-standing distinction between groups of working class pupils who see education as offering opportunities for advance and the majority of 'ordinary' girls and boys who reject school in favour of work (Ainley, 1988). Clearly, finding and securing paid work while still at school was considerably more important for the leavers than it was for the stayers, and this was again reflected by the rates of child working recalled by the youth trainees. Among the 42 trainees, 32 (76 per cent) had worked in a variety of jobs before reaching the minimum school leaving age.

Table 3.1 *Breakdown of School Pupils Who Had Been Involved in Child Labour, as a Percentage (School Pupil Survey)*

	Male	Female	Total	European	Non-European
Stayers	15	17	32	24	8
Leavers	39	29	68	63	5
Total (n = 140)	54	46	100	87	13

Table 3.2 *Breakdown of School Pupils Currently Working, as a Percentage (School Pupil Survey)*

	Male	Female	Total	European	Non-European
Stayers	21	13	24	26	8
Leavers	37	29	66	64	2
Total (n = 66)	58	42	100	90	10

As Table 3.2 illustrates, the greater significance of paid work for the leavers was again clearly evident among those pupils currently working. Sixty-six of these pupils (43 per cent) stated that they presently held paid jobs and this included a group of four boys who had what they described as two separate jobs; in each case a morning and an evening paper round. The discrepancy between those who had worked and those who were currently working also vividly illustrates the ease with which many of the young people moved in and out of work, 'job-hopping' in ways characteristic of school leavers during the 1950s and 1960s (Ashton and Field, 1976; Carter, 1962). Here, reasons for leaving jobs were dominated by considerations of pay and conditions: 'it [labouring] was shit really. The pay was crap and the work hard so I just decided to look for something else' (Derrick – MaC trainee), or their ability to endure often difficult work relationships: 'my present employer . . . treats me well and doesn't look down on me, like my last employer before, who did not care about her employees, only herself. That's why I left' (girl leaver).

Their willingness and ability to take full advantage of the fluid and informal nature of the demand for child labour meant that many could recall extensive work histories. Although the research did not specifically seek to investigate previous patterns of working, and therefore undoubtedly underestimates the overall depth of their work experience, eight (25 per cent) of the trainee child labourers provided spontaneous accounts of some of their previous jobs. This included seven who had managed two separate jobs at the same time, ranging from two paper rounds, combining a paper round with a weekend or Saturday job, to balancing an evening job with a Saturday job, and two who gave accounts of four or more different jobs in the last three years. Since the age of 13 these young people had been doing jobs like delivering newspapers and leaflets; they had experienced the routines of factory life, and had worked in hotels and restaurants and undertaken telephone canvassing.

A significant number of both the pupils and the trainees could therefore testify to having already experienced a diversity of the immediate social relations of production before even leaving school. Far from lacking those basic qualities necessary to locate work opportunities, these young people had already demonstrated a considerable eagerness to work and considerable success in finding it. Movement into and between jobs meant that many already possessed a considerable repertoire of the skills and knowledge involved in job-hunting, a know-how of employers' recruitment practices and where any job opportunities were likely to appear. These young people also knew how to successfully apply for jobs, had already succeeded in demonstrating to employers their potential as workers and had managed to hold down their employment over a relatively long period of time.

Limiting Choice: Discrimination and Child Labour

What is also immediately striking about Tables 3.1 and 3.2 is the already clearly differentiated experience of child working both between the boys and the girls, and between young people of European and non-European origins. Given that we are often led to believe that people from minority ethnic groups actively encourage their children into waged labour from an early age, possibly in a family or a friend's business (Head, 1988; Wilce, 1988), the low number of working non-European school pupils, mainly young people of Asian descent, is initially surprising. This is especially unexpected considering the importance of sweated work in Coventry's clothing industry for the local Asian community noted in the previous chapter, and the ways in which family and friendship networks provide important routes for informal recruitment.

However, care needs to be taken in not simply reinforcing stereotypes of black Asian entrepreneurs or small businesses as especially ruthless or particularly eager to utilize their children as a cheap and willing source of labour. The evidence as far as child workers go is far from conclusive. In its most recent study the Low Pay Unit found that white European and black Afro-Caribbean children were proportionately more likely, and Asian children only slightly less likely, to be working while at school. Furthermore, 'the myth that [Asian] children's employment is mainly concerned with Asian family business also suffers some damage' (Low Pay Unit, 1991, p. 12), as working in family businesses accounted for only 16 per cent of all child workers. A more likely explanation lies not with ambiguous references to the activities of black and Asian business practices or to the insularity of ethnic cultures, but with the wider barriers of discrimination that young black workers are forced to confront in the labour market each day.

Child workers are undoubtedly subject to the same discriminatory recruitment practices that disadvantage adult black workers. Research by the Policy Studies Institute has consistently found that black workers continue to face systematic forms of discrimination (McCrudden *et al.*, 1991; Brown, 1984). Many employers fail to recruit black workers and, where black workers are taken on, they tend to be in lower-paid and lower-status jobs:

> Every study to compare their prospects has found that black and brown school leavers are less successful than whites in the quality of jobs obtained and in avoiding unemployment (Roberts, 1984, p. 52).

Because Asian child workers ostensibly work in the same labour market as young adults, they are also subjected to the same processes of discriminatory recruitment practices. It is this which primarily explains lower levels of child working among Asian young people and it is this that goes some way to explaining their greater tendency to continue in full-time education, as they seek to escape the vicious circle of discrimination and low status that has continued to plague their parents (Craft and Craft, 1983).

Child working also involves a clearly gendered experience, with girls usually less involved than boys (Low Pay Unit, 1982, 1991; MacLennan *et al.*, 1985; Finn, 1984). Apart from that of Finn, other studies have tended to marginalize the importance of gender in influencing forms of child labour and have relegated tasks associated with domestic responsibilities below more directly visible types of waged labour (e.g. Roberts *et al.*, 1986a). The result has been that the relationship between domestic labour, family ideology and employers' demands for differentiated forms of labour power has been marginalized in considerations of subsequent occupational choice for young women, and therefore how later opportunities for paid employment are structured.

As Rees (1992) neatly summarizes, it is the interrelationship between the ideology of the family, the material constraints on women's choices and the exclusionary mechanisms operated by men that largely structures the position of women in the labour market. For working class young women, a growing maturity inevitably brings with it an increasingly prominent role within the immediate family economy (Lees, 1986; McRobbie, 1978). Opportunities for paid employment outside the family are therefore constrained in ways not experienced by brothers. Similarly, the constraints of family ideology mean that girls are subject to different forms of parental control than boys and, just as their leisure activities are policed in ways not experienced by any brothers (Frith, 1983), so too do girls have to endure greater constraints on their freedom to enter paid work.

Failure to recognize these constraints ignores an early facet of the sexual division of labour and fails to grasp the common connections between the work young women do both inside and outside the home. Thus baby-sitting and associated domestic tasks take on additional significance because they represent types of work both acceptable and accessible to young women. What is more, not only do they provide the rare chance to generate an independent income, but they also provide girls with the seldom-found opportunity to escape from the confines of family, home and estate: 'when I baby-sit she leaves me food and drink, no spirits, and I'm allowed a friend around' (girl leaver).

It is also this relationship between the family and waged labour, between the interrelated forms of patriarchal and capitalist social relations, which reinforces gender-appropriate notions of work and which limits the opportunity structures which many young women perceive to be open to them as adult women (Rees, 1992). Table 3.3 illustrates the pervasive sexual division of labour which structures patterns of child labour from an early age, with the girls working as sales assistants, supermarket workers, and assistants to hairdressers or cleaners. For the boys, work was more likely to involve delivering newspapers and leaflets, but also doing milk and egg rounds. Labouring appeared their prerogative too. They were also more likely to work as attendants or stewards, and where there was

Table 3.3 *Range of Part-time Jobs*

	Pupils			Trainees		
	Male	Female	Total	Male	Female	Total
Newspaper deliveries	13	2	14	8	3	11
Other deliveries	7	1	8	2	1	3
Retail/shop work	3	4	7	2	7	9
Baby-sitting	1	10	11	0	2	2
Cleaning	2	3	5	2	1	3
Catering/hotel	4	4	8	2	3	5
Labouring	3	1	4	7	0	7
Door-to-door sales	1	2	3	0	1	1
Steward/attendant	2	0	2	0	0	0
Printing/art	1	0	1	0	1	1
Engineering/electrician	2	0	2	0	0	0
Miscellaneous	0	0	0	1	1	2
Total	39	27	66	24	20	44

work in electrical or engineering jobs these too were occupied by boys.

Within the categories of Table 3.3, work was again strongly delineated by gender. In shop and retail work, the girls were more likely to work on check-outs or as sales assistants in high street shops, whereas the boys worked in 'Do-It-Yourself' stores, held Saturday jobs with butchers or worked on the forecourts of service stations. Cleaning work for the girls also meant jobs in offices, shops or as domestic cleaners, whereas the boys were car, warehouse or factory cleaners. Catering and hotel work meant waitressing or serving work in restaurants, cafes or snack bars for the girls and, for the boys, glass collecting in clubs or hotel portering work.

Child's Play?

Consistent with other findings (e.g. Low Pay Unit, 1986, 1991), Table 3.3 shows that around one-third of the school pupils and about a quarter of the trainees were working in jobs more traditionally associated with child labour; mainly baby-sitting or newspaper deliveries. Yet to conceive this as child's play, as a few simple chores to earn a few easy pounds, ignores its significance both as a source of work for the young people themselves and for the ways in which child labour has evolved as an important feature in the continuing profitability of some large-scale industries. Newspaper boys and newspaper girls, for example, play an often unacknowledged yet essential role in the multi-million pound newspaper industry they service. This was clearly exposed by the move to ban Sunday working among children in Gloucestershire in 1988 following the abduction and murder of a newspaper boy. The local authority's proposals met with such vociferous protests from the county's 400 newsagents that they were subsequently withdrawn and even the multinational media group, News International, was forced into the debate, declaring that while the group was 'extremely concerned about what happened . . . deliveries by newspaper boys and girls are an *essential* part of the industry' (*Sunday Times*, 14 February 1988, emphasis added).

The importance of newspaper deliveries also fits in with working class preferences for outside work and its associations with freedom and independence (Blackburn and Mann, 1979). Nonetheless, the young people's experiences of delivery work also testified to the fact that a newspaper round often meant anti-social hours and physically demanding work, regardless of the weather. It required an early start or a late finish to the day, often in darkness and 'hard work in all weathers' (Robert – engineering trainee), so that 'I was knackered sometimes and that was before I even got to school' (Joe – MaC trainee). It also meant working to the discipline of the clock, where it 'was sometimes really hard, especially when it was raining or cold. I used to hate getting up that early in the mornings [6.00 a.m.], especially during the holidays' (Jane – catering trainee).

However, child working also extends well beyond newspaper deliveries and baby-sitting, involving young people in a host of jobs more immediately associated with adult forms of employment. The Low Pay Unit has consistently pointed out that 'children undertake jobs across the whole range of adult employment, from shop work and cleaning through to work in factories and building sites, garages and offices' (Low Pay Unit, 1991, p. 14). Many of the jobs in Table 3.3 overlap with work more commonly associated with adult employment, albeit those jobs almost exclusively confined to the lower segments of the labour market and dominated by mainly manual and unskilled tasks. Here the school pupils worked as petrol station attendants, shop workers, waiters and waitresses, office cleaners and on milk rounds. Similarly, the trainees had also worked in shops, as building labourers, industrial cleaners and hotel and catering workers. As a first direct taste of the immediate social relations of production it was work devoid of much intrinsic value, where shop work meant 'tasks such as till operating, shelf stacking and serving delicatessen foods' (girl stayer), or 'menial jobs, mainly in stacking shelves and cleaning the shop. I never got to work on the till much' (Julia – clerical trainee). One pupil summed up much of the experience in relation to his work on a potato delivery round:

> We always have to say the right things, run all the time. He [the boss] does what he wants. He just sits there driving the van and Anthony, his full-time worker, just sits in the van making pre-packs and eating sweets. (boy leaver)

Some jobs may have required some skill and even possibly some rudimentary training or instruction. One pupil worked in his father's engineering firm on Saturdays 'drilling holes in jobs and deburring them' (boy stayer). Another also worked on Saturdays for a self-employed electrician, 'helping repair fridges and freezers' (boy leaver). Nevertheless, these types of jobs appeared few and far between and child labour was considerably more likely to thrust a young person into a first direct experience of waged labour involving hard work and sacrifice.

As such, their work was therefore often more likely to be physically demanding, 'having to be on your feet the whole time and constantly on the go [waitressing]' (Fiona – clerical trainee), or 'humping stuff around, cleaning up and helping with pot plants' (Richard – construction trainee). Labouring for a builder meant 'doing things like help fitting windows, bricklaying, roofing, cleaning up whenever he needed a hand . . . shovelling stuff into bags' (Derrick – MaC trainee). Even those employers much coveted by child workers for their relatively good rates of pay and desirable working conditions, the large high street retail stores, often provided hard and unrewarding work:

> Sometimes it [a chain store of stationers] was really horrible. Customers would often swear at you, some of the people were so ignorant. It was very trying and at times I really hated it. At work they didn't appreciate you or the work that you did anyway and you usually got all the rotten jobs. (Kath – clerical trainee)

For employers, child workers therefore represent a willing and flexible source of labour, and evidence suggests that certain trends in the restructuring of work and employment in recent years may lead to increased demand in the future. In spite of the fact that trends in child working are difficult to discern, Finn (1984) argued that the rise of mass unemployment during the early 1980s was accompanied by an increase in the willingness of employers to utilize such a ready source of labour. More significantly, a qualitative change in the restructuring of work and employment is also making child workers a more attractive source of labour for employers as increased economic imperatives are necessitating further cost-cutting measures. Privatization and the trend towards the contracting out of jobs and services, like cleaning and gardening work, has meant the only way for contractors to secure profitability is to drive down previous wage levels and erode existing working conditions. One consequence has been the increased use of child workers (Lamb and Piercy, 1987; TUC/UNICEF, 1985). The Trades Union Congress (TUC) has presented evidence of the use of child labour by contractors carrying out privatized services, and in the London Borough of Merton one private cleaning agency was found to be using child labour as young as 13. In 1984 one of the country's leading paediatricians resigned over the use of child labour by the contract cleaners in the Cambridgeshire hospital where he worked. It was claimed that 'the firm has used children because it cannot find adults to work for the pay and conditions it is offering' (TUC/UNICEF, 1985, p. 24). Here, too, some of the child workers had already been drawn into these types of work, either 'delivering post for a private firm' (boy stayer) or 'emptying bins, polishing tables and desks and hoovering floors' (girl leaver) for a firm of contract cleaners.

In emphasizing the overlap between jobs done by children and those more commonly associated with adults, it is not being suggested that child workers are directly displacing adult workers in any large numbers, although we have seen there is evidence that this does happen. However, they do represent a source of labour that is willing to work hours inconvenient for many adult workers, for example shop work at weekends, office cleaning for a couple of hours in the evening or labouring for a builder on Saturday mornings. Some of the hours worked by the child workers here would not even be considered by most adults, like delivering newspapers in the early hours or working early Friday and Saturday mornings when demand for milk deliveries is at its highest. It is precisely this flexibility that makes child workers an especially attractive source of labour.

All Work and No Play

Putting an exact figure on the amount of time child workers spend working each week is notoriously difficult, precisely because they are a mobile and flexible workforce. The majority of Finn's (1984) young people worked for under 10 hours each week although, significantly, over 40 per cent worked for longer. Similarly, the Low Pay Unit's 1985 study also found that the majority of child workers spent under 10 hours a week at work, but also that one in three worked longer and around 20 per cent worked for more than 16 hours a week. Assessing the implications of this they concluded: 'added to hours actually spent in school, . . . even a short working week may mean that a child is "at work" much longer than the average adult' (MacLennan *et al.*, 1985, p. 26).

For the child workers here, a picture similar to the one painted by Finn and the Low Pay Unit emerged. Of the 66 currently working pupils, 47 (71 per cent) indicated that they worked on a regular basis and another seven when needed. Of the 66, another 47 worked on more than one day a week and, of the 14 who worked on just one day, 10 held Saturday jobs. In 51 cases it was possible to establish the total number of hours worked each week and, in the remaining cases, it either depended on when they were needed or the information was not provided. On average both the boys and the girl pupils worked around seven hours a week, almost an extra working day, with the leavers working around seven and a half hours and the stayers five and a half each week. Hours spent working could be two or three a week collecting glasses, serving in a coffee or snack bar, or delivering newspapers. Others worked nine hours a week, helping out in a hairdresser's salon or a butcher's shop on a Saturday, as a petrol station attendant on a Sunday, or two hours every day cleaning offices after school. Of the 51 pupils for whom a weekly rate could be established, 19 (38 per cent) worked more than eight hours a week, 15 of whom were leavers and 11 of whom were boys. This included a very small number who worked a considerable number of hours each week, with one boy leaver working 28 hours each week on a potato delivery round.

Of the 32 trainees, 24 (75 per cent) could remember the hours they had worked in their last job before leaving school and overall they tended to work slightly longer than the pupils; around 10 hours a week. Interestingly, the girls averaged over 10 hours a week and the boys just over nine hours, and again the actual hours spent working varied widely. For the girls, two or three hours a week could be spent baby-sitting or delivering papers, nine hours could be spent in a newsagent or high street fashion shop at the weekend, or 12 hours could be worked on a market stall on Friday evenings and all day Saturday. For the boys, too, work could range from a couple of hours each week delivering newspapers, to nine hours at a garden centre, to 13 hours in a supermarket. Again, a small number worked extremely long hours, including four boys who worked for more than 13 hours each week and another who held two jobs simultaneously, working in a chemical factory after school and in a hotel at weekends, clocking up around 25 hours each week.

A Source of Cheap Labour?

The Low Pay Unit (1991) has rightly emphasized that child workers generally earn very little and that hourly pay is frequently less than half the Wage Council minimum rates for adults when they still applied. However, despite the often appalling rates that some child workers have to endure, low pay is a feature more generally experienced by the young working class as a whole. Consequently, the average rates that child workers are earning may be low, but they are also generally commensurate with the average levels of hourly pay they could expect if they were lucky enough to find jobs directly on leaving school.

Potter (1989) suggests that by any measure the majority of young adult workers are increasingly beginning to fall below thresholds of low pay and that the wages of the 16 to 18 age group have been particularly badly hit. He cites figures from the Department of Employment's 1987 New Earnings Survey which show average basic pay for 16- and 17-year-olds at around £74.50 per week. For a 38-hour week this means an hourly rate of approximately £1.96. As Table 3.4 shows, he also provides figures from a nationwide survey showing comparable rates of pay and, although they obviously obscure the wide-ranging variations between regions, they do provide a useful point of comparison.

Because of the often casual nature of much child working, hourly rates can be difficult to establish. Five of the school pupils here were paid on a commission-only basis, usually delivery work or selling door-to-door, so that hourly rates were impossible to calculate. Others were paid a variable lump sum which appeared to depend on how hard their employers had felt they had worked. An hourly rate could therefore be established for 47 of the 66 pupils currently working and this averaged £1.60 per hour. For the

Table 3.4 *1988 National Rates of Pay for the 16 to 18 Age Group (£s)*

Age	Rate per year	Rate per week	Rate 38-hour week
16	3406	65.50	1.73
17	3978	76.50	2.01
18	4922	94.65	2.49

Source: *Professional Personnel Consultants (PPC) Ltd (quoted in Potter, 1989).*

trainee child workers, hourly rates could be established in 31 cases and this averaged slightly higher at £1.66 per hour. Although these represented figures below both those of the 1987 New Earnings Survey and the 1988 PPC findings, they were not too incompatible and many of the child workers were already experiencing market rates of pay.

What is also striking is that hourly rates of pay, like other features of child working, clearly begin to prefigure likely future experiences of work. Just as young adult female workers tend to earn lower rates than their male counterparts (Potter, 1989, p. 15), so too do female child workers. Like Finn's (1984) child workers and those referred to in the findings of the Exeter University studies, the girls who took part in my research were already having to suffer consistently lower average hourly rates of pay. For the girl pupils this meant £1.62 per hour in contrast to the boys' £1.77, and for the girl trainees £1.39 per hour in contrast to the boys' £1.84. Furthermore, a similar differential existed between the stayers, who averaged £1.88 per hour, and the leavers, who averaged £1.55 per hour. The significance of this lies in the fact that the leavers are more likely to find themselves unemployed, on training schemes or in semi-skilled or unskilled work, with the stayers benefiting from those opportunities further up the employment hierarchy. Both Roberts *et al.* (1986a) and Hutson and Cheung (1992) have made a case for the importance of these 'brighter' pupils in filling many of the part-time vacancies among the larger, high-street-type employers, likely to offer better wages and conditions: 'Their ability to pick things up quickly and the up-market atmosphere they could help to create . . . made them attractive to the employers' (Roberts *et al.*, 1986a, p. 92). Here, gender and anticipated levels of educational achievement were already significant factors in constituting young people as specific and differentiated forms of labour power.

It must be further emphasized that this is not to claim that child workers are relatively well paid or that they earn comparatively good hourly rates, but that child working provides direct links with many of the features these young people were likely to experience in their initial years of adult work. It is clearly evident that direct attacks on the level of pay and working conditions for young people have been a central plank of government policy over the past 15 years (Potter, 1989; Finn, 1987), and that the concomitant attempts to deregulate the labour market for 16- to 19-year-olds 'has had spin-off effects on children at school' (Low Pay Unit, 1991, p. 23). The abolition of wages councils has removed minimum wage protection from young people under 21 precisely in those industries in which child workers feature most prominently, and successive pieces of employment legislation have also reduced the restrictions on the work young people can and cannot do.

Here the average rate obscured wide variations in their hourly earnings and it is here that the particular forms of exploitation child workers suffer are most visibly exposed. Baby-sitters were some of the lowest hourly paid workers, 50p to 75p per hour being the most common rates, but they were by no means the exception. Newspaper rounds could pay as little as 20p per hour, although more usually they paid between 70p and £1.25 per hour, and two girls who worked as a waitress and on a market stall earned 75p and 85p per hour respectively. For the boys, 'doing fucking hard work' (Richard – construction trainee plumber) in a garden centre meant 70p per hour, and labouring for a carpet fitter paid £1 per hour. Better-paid work included £1.47 per hour for a chain store of stationers, £1.50 in a supermarket and £2 per hour in a high street shop. The top earners tended to work for family or relatives, earning £3.30 per hour as a sales assistant for a sister, or £4 or £5 per hour in a father's business, although one young entrepreneur was making around £2.50 per hour on his 'self-employed egg, bacon and pop round' (Jim – construction trainee plumber).

The Importance of Their Income

Although child workers are on the whole low-paid, the importance of the income generated by them should not be underestimated. The persistence of mass unemployment throughout the past decade has meant that money earned in this way has become increasingly important for young people, especially where 'high levels of unemployment mean that a child may be the only breadwinner in the family' (Head, 1988, p. 20). Although young people still in full-time education rarely pay any 'board' or 'keep' money (Jones, 1991), an independent income, however small, represents an important addition to a low-waged family. This may well be in a direct way, as reports have consistently illustrated that among the notoriously low-paid agricultural communities of East Anglia, children are actively encouraged by their families to work in jobs like carrot-topping, for as little as 70p per hour: 'parents approved, and the mothers even put their children on the gang labour buses after school' (TUC/UNICEF, 1985, p. 27). But a young person's ability to generate any independent income will more likely ease pressure on the family to finance their growing involvement in sports, leisure and social activities (Frith, 1983).

While research is only just beginning to explore young people's role within the wider family economy (see Chapter 7; Jones and Wallace, 1992), paid employment clearly represented an important and often substantial source of independent income for child workers. For the 49 cases in which weekly income could be established among the school pupils currently working, it averaged around £13.70 per week, with the majority earning under £15. This ranged from £3 to £5 per week baby-sitting, delivering newspapers or washing up in a café, to £7 per week working after school in a shop or £8 per week waitressing. Sixteen (33 per cent) did, however, earn £15 or more each week, including seven who regularly earned over £20 per week. These included one girl leaver who earned £22 per week working in a cafe, another girl leaver who earned £36 each week door-to-door selling, a boy leaver who earned between £20 and £40 depending on how many deliveries he had to make that week, and another boy leaver who earned £40 per week as a cloakroom attendant.

Of the 32 trainee child workers, a weekly income could be established in 26 cases and these averaged out at £14 per week, with the boys earning slightly more than the girls. Again this obscured considerable variations, for the girls ranging from £8 for an eight-hour day in a newsagent's to £12 for a Saturday's work in a stationer's store, through to one young woman who earned £20 for eight hours on a Saturday in a rest home for the elderly. Among the boys the majority earned over £10 per week, with a small number earning over £20. Considering the low hourly rates that were generally on offer, this represented a considerable effort, with the highest-earning child worker having to put in over 20 hours a week in two different jobs to bring in his modest £42 per week.

The Experience of Work

As well as involving poor-quality, low-paid and arduous work, the vast majority of child working goes unregulated. In its latest research, the Low Pay Unit (1991) found that three-quarters of the child workers it surveyed were working illegally and that if this figure were applied nationally, around 1.57 million school-age young people would be involved in illegal work. Consequently, many are exposed to considerable health and safety risks, the most extreme form of which is the example of the murdered newspaper boy discussed earlier. Child workers are also involved in a host of more commonly reported work-related accidents, with over a third of the Low Pay Units reporting involvement in some form of accident over the previous 12 months. In response to the high number of children killed or seriously injured on British farms each year, the Transport and General Workers Union has long campaigned to raise the legal age at which children can drive tractors from 13 to 17. Again, a measure of how important child workers are to this industry is illustrated by employers' steadfast refusal to support these demands (TUC/UNICEF, 1985).

Despite these and the many other hazards child workers are exposed to, the significance of work for young people themselves should not be underestimated: 'Most school children look upon a casual job as a valuable asset – a source of independence, responsibility, financial freedom and work experience' (Head, 1988, p. 20). Research has consistently highlighted the 'eagerness and obvious pleasure with which some young people enter what are often referred to as "dead end" jobs' (Ashton and Field, 1976, p. 12), and the ways in which, at least among young males, they can actively condemn themselves to a life of manual labour (Willis, 1977).

Given the wide and varied experience of the young working class of wage labour while still at school, the expectation of arduous and intrinsically unrewarding work on leaving should come as little surprise. Working class school leavers appear satisfied with their jobs because they already know that most of the work that is on offer is unpleasant and generally alienating. They expect work to be hard, demanding and often dirty because many have already experienced these constraints at first hand and know that this is the price that is exacted for earning an independent wage. Most child workers therefore remain generally enthusiastic about their jobs and here only 10 (15 per cent) of the currently working pupils felt they had been unfairly treated by their employers. The main complaints related to the low levels of pay: 'I think we are not being paid the right amount of money for the consumer goods on sale today' was the comment of one girl stayer who earned £1 per hour waitressing. Nonetheless, there was also criticism about the content of the work: 'the job I do [delivering leaflets] is a bit of a slave labour job and gives me no experience' (boy stayer), or 'the jobs that we do [milk round] are a stage of slave labour and give no experience at all' (boy leaver).

However, 46 (70 per cent) of the working pupils expressed some form of general satisfaction with their work. One boy pupil even found his Saturdays at a screen-printer's rewarding: 'I enjoy the people I work with and find it satisfying that things I have worked on are seen all over the country' (boy stayer). However, this type of comment was the exception and the others were considerably more likely to express an assessment of their work in terms of 'fair hours and pay' (girl leaver), or 'good wages and hours' (boy leaver). The quality of work relationships was also considered important: 'my supervisor is very kind and polite and if things really need to be done she will ask you in the right attitude' (girl leaver), and 'my boss is OK, we can have a joke and he doesn't mind if I'm a few minutes late' (girl leaver).

The trainees were generally more critical than the pupils, but they too tend to express a general satisfaction with their work. In all, 22 (69 per cent) had felt: 'the boss was a good bloke. He treated me fairly and paid a good wage' (Frances – retail trainee), or 'they treated me fairly, it was nice and clean and the people were friendly. We had a good rest room and the meals were cheap' (Glenn – PSV trainee). Many of the trainee child workers were already developing clearly worked-out ideas about what was tolerable in their work relationships, where employers were considered 'decent', 'good' or 'bad' according to whether 'reasonable' wage was offered, and whether staff were treated with consideration. This meant a job was considered acceptable where: 'he was a good boss, the work was OK and the pay all right. If you worked hard you got paid OK' (Derrick – MaC trainee). Similarly, 'she was nice and considerate, and would always ask if it was OK before deciding what hours to give me' (Samantha – clerical trainee).

Failure to meet these criteria could meet with a swift and uncompromising response, as bad working practices and poor conditions were not easily tolerated. One young woman had reacted to an argument with her boss by failing to turn up again: 'I just didn't bother going back [to the restaurant] after that . . . I hope I landed him in the shit' (Fiona – clerical trainee). It could also mean 'finally I had to tell them where to stick their job' (Lucy – community care trainee) after work patterns and starting times were constantly changed at short notice. Altogether, 10 (31 per cent) of the trainees expressed dissatisfaction with their jobs, through being asked to do tasks which they felt were unreasonable or beyond their present capabilities – 'I was treated like a bloke, expected to shift heavy bags of fruit and veg., doing all the cleaning and stuff and getting paid rubbish for it . . . That's why I left' (Anne – community care traineee) – or because they were just being exploited: 'It was a rip-off, I don't know why I stuck it out so long . . . A pound an hour isn't much when you're expected to work really hard [labouring]' (Jim – construction trainee plumber).

Child Labour and Full-time Employment

Not only were the child workers clearly beginning to develop a discerning attitude towards employment relationships and an appreciation of what was tolerable and what was not, but child working also proved significant for future working in other, less obvious ways. Indeed, for some there appears to be little choice in the matter, as the persistence of mass unemployment has meant that few working class school leavers now have the possibility of directly obtaining a job on leaving school, let alone the ability to exercise any real choice. As a consequence, for those with few or no qualifications, 'time spent in a part-time job could seem more important to their chances of future employment than school' (Head, 1988, p. 21). Researching during the early 1980s, Finn (1984) found that the majority of his young people not worried about their future prospects had already been offered a full-time job by their school-time employers. However, among those still unsure about what they would be doing on leaving school, less than a quarter indicated that they would be prepared to continue in similar work to their child labour, pointing to the low pay and unpleasant working conditions.

As Table 3.5 illustrates, a small majority of the school pupils here were unwilling to continue working for their school-time employers after leaving school, and, considering the work they were doing, the hours they

Table 3.5 *Breakdown of Pupils Willing or Not to Continue Working for Their Employer after Leaving School, as a Percentage (School Pupil Survey)*

	Stayers	Leavers	Total	Male	Female
Yes	10	34	44	23	21
No	23	30	53	33	20
Don't know	0	3	3	2	1
Total (*n* = 61)	33	67	100	58	43

worked and the low levels of pay, this too was unsurprising. Yet what is more startling is that well over 40 per cent of the pupil child workers expressed a willingness to continue with their work, a figure well up on Finn's research at the beginning of the decade, and this figure reached over half among both the leavers and the girls. It is clear that as unemployment among the young has remained at such high levels, working class school leavers are increasingly seeing school-time jobs as a direct way into work.

The trainees were also asked whether their experiences of child working had influenced what they had wanted to do on leaving school, and 16 (50 per cent) stated decisively that it had not. For this group, working while at school had been a way to earn some extra money: 'a way of getting a few quid together. I had a few complaints but it was just for some pocket money' (Louis – construction trainee carpenter).

For the remaining 16, their school-time working had some clear impact in structuring their decisions about what to do on leaving school. For eight of this group, child working had given them a negative insight into work and an experience of the sort of jobs they did not want to spend the rest of their adult working lives doing. Experience of stacking shelves and cleaning the shop had meant 'I didn't want to work in a newsagent's again' (Julia – clerical trainee). For another, the routines of industry had meant 'it made me not want to do factory work again' (Chris – trainee). For the other eight, however, the relationship proved more direct and these young people had used their experience as a positive reference point: 'I found building work easier than I'd expected so I went for a construction scheme' (Derrick – MaC trainee). Similarly, growing up with the circus and working with machines meant a public service vehicle youth training scheme was 'a logical step' (Keith – PSV trainee) to take on leaving school. Others just valued the experience: 'it was good experience. It gave me confidence in meeting and dealing with people in their own homes . . . enough to try for an apprenticeship' (Thomas – construction trainee carpenter). Two of the trainees recounted stories which illustrate the increasing significance that many young people are giving to their school-time jobs but also the ways in which these have been affected by youth training. One had worked at a service station on Sundays and the other for a newsagent's at varying times of the week. Both had been offered full-time jobs on leaving school and both had eagerly accepted. Yet shortly afterwards, both young people were given the same ultimatum by their bosses, 'when he could no longer afford to pay me' (Frances – retail trainee), either to continue working as they were doing, but this time as youth trainees, or to leave and face the prospects of becoming unemployed. Much to their regret, they were forced to accept the former option.

Conclusion

It is through child labour that the young working class gain substantial knowledge of the world of work in an immediate form. Although child workers tend to look upon their jobs with the sort of satisfaction that comes with the freedom of a wage, they also know that such freedoms are not given lightly. Through child working many school pupils discover that paid employment means the discipline of the clock and the keeping of good time. They find that work means the management of fraught and tense relationships with employers, and the continued ability to do so throughout the duration of their jobs. Above all they find out directly that paid employment usually involves little more than intrinsically unrewarding and demanding tasks. Contrary to popular belief, child workers do not just walk the dog or earn a few easy pennies running errands, and even where they deliver newspapers, this involves early starts and late finishes, being exposed to the vicissitudes of the weather and carrying around heavy newspaper sacks. However, more often than not, school-time working involves a whole range of jobs more generally undertaken by adult workers, and child labourers can be found in a whole range of jobs from labouring to shop work, and from catering work to working in a rest home for the elderly.

It is through child working that young people also discover how to look for jobs, the ways in which they become available and how to apply successfully. Moreover, it is through such direct contact with employers that young people increasingly become aware that work is organized in racialized and gendered ways. Because they are involved in similar jobs, child workers are exposed to the same forms of discrimination that their parents have long been familiar with, so that Asian child workers have particular problems in securing paid employment beyond their own communities. Furthermore, the jobs open to girls are also heavily constrained by employers' demands for differentiated forms of labour power and by gender-appropriate notions of work. What is more, not only do girls undertake different forms of work from the boys, but these forms of discrimination are further institutionalized through lower rates of pay.

Clearly, in the light of this, the 'deficiency model' serves to obscure more than it illuminates. The young working class do not need to be told how to adapt to the demands of employment or what the world of industry, business and technology really involves, because they already know. Work does not become a reality for the young working class only when they are taught about it in school or when they actually leave to enter the labour market. It is a central organizing feature in their home and community lives, and many have spent a considerable amount of time and energy already working. Indeed, a fundamental dimension to the training state's form is its continuing attempts to deny and suppress the collective realities of being young and working class, a reality in which they have already proved themselves as capable workers. School leavers therefore know that it is not they who are the lacking in the qualities needed to find work, because many have already found jobs and managed to hold them down successfully. They know that they must work, that they can work, and given the opportunity this is what they want to do. It is precisely because the young working class are constituted as a distinct and emergent source of labour power that they can never totally acknowledge the validity of the 'deficiency model'. They are compelled to work and expend much effort in trying to achieve this, only to find that this means negotiating new barriers and obstacles in the movement from school to work. It is this knowledge and experience which forms one of the central points of opposition to the training state, and it is one important reason why the young working class will never easily tolerate its demands.

4 RELUCTANT TRAINEES: NEGOTIATING THE LABOUR MARKET

Now that we have established that the material realities of growing up young and working class mean that, from an early age, working class young people are constituted as distinctive forms of labour power, this chapter moves on to consider the implications of this for the movement out of full-time education into the labour market proper. In particular, the intention is to examine how young people's emergence as specific categories of labour power constantly comes into conflict with the ways in which youth training seeks to impose new forms of authority on the young working class. It is precisely through working class young people's recognition that youth training means subjecting themselves to new constraints and disciplines that the significance of the ways in which school leavers confront the scheme can be found.

An acknowledgement of problems with working class resistance to youth training have been a feature of the scheme's development. The initial surge in enthusiasm with which school leavers greeted the YOP quickly gave way to disillusionment and despair as it proved woefully incapable of providing anything but the flimsiest protection against the rising tide of unemployment. As the YOP's replacement, the YTS was therefore to be a qualitative break with these unemployment palliatives of the past and with the *ad hoc* and piecemeal development of Britain's postwar training infrastructure (Ainley and Corney, 1990; Finn, 1987). Depicted as part of a comprehensive manpower policy and as an attempt to modernize Britain's antiquated training system, youth training was to herald the beginnings of a new and permanent system of foundation training to give young workers the quality training they would need for a successful working life. It was to be 'a scheme so attractive to employers and to young people that a minority of people [would] enter jobs outside the scheme or remain unemployed rather than join the scheme' (Manpower Services Commission 1982, p. 4.8).

Proposals to bring all school leavers within youth training's framework were rapidly discarded, however, as it quickly became apparent that hostility from both employers and school leavers would make such a move unworkable. Now, with the problem of an even more explicit focus on unemployment, official pronouncements went about the considerable task of trying to convince new generations of school leavers coming into the labour market that the scheme was the quality opportunity so energetically advanced. After only eight months, ministers were already in congratulatory mood, proclaiming: 'young people have voted YTS a success. They know full well what the government have done and will be doing for them' (Peter Morrison, then Employment Minister, quoted in Kirby and Roberts, 1985, p. 1). Reviewing the scheme's third year in 1986, Bryan Nicholson, then chairperson of the MSC, announced: 'YTS has become an integral part of post 16 life for young people, who have responded with great enthusiasm and in great numbers' (*Youth Training News*, September 1986, p. 32). By the turn of the 1990s, with the scheme seemingly established as a two-year programme and with little if any obvious opposition, the government once again indulged itself in self-congratulation by claiming that youth training had revolutionized the British training system and had been a resounding success among the young. Testament to this, they argued, was the fact that over three million school leavers had already been through youth training, over two million of whom had trained on the two-year programme. In 1990–1991 alone they could point to over 300 000 young people having gone through the scheme (Conservative Party, 1992).

Taken at face value these claims seem highly plausible. Even towards the end of the 1980s, when a booming economy combined with demographic factors to create a short-lived up-turn in school leavers' employment prospects, around a quarter of all 16-year-olds were entering the scheme; or half of all minimum-age school leavers (Employment Gazette, 1991a). Although the numbers subsequently declined in the first two years after 1990, around 15 per cent of all 16-year-olds nationally are still beginning their lives as youth trainees (Maclagan, 1993).

Youth training was to have a similarly impressive impact in Coventry, as Table 4.1 illustrates. Having reached a high point in the mid-1980s, when over one in three 16-year-olds were entering the scheme, by the time of the research the figure was still around 20 per cent. In 1989, of the 2333

Table 4.1 *Destination of Final-year Pupils in Coventry between 1986 and 1992, as a Percentage*

	1987	1988	1989	1990	1991	1992
Full-time education	40	40	41	46	58	64
Work	17	21	29	26	12	11
Youth training	32	28	19	15	18	12
Unemployment	7	6	5	7	8	9
Unknown	4	5	6	6	5	5
Total	100	100	100	100	100	100

Source: Coventry Careers (1988, 1993)

young people who left school in the city, 741 (32 per cent) entered a training scheme compared to 51 per cent who went directly into work. Although the figures between 1989 and 1992 show a considerable drop in the number of participants, when taken as a proportion of all Coventry school leavers 34 per cent (388) were still entering a scheme in 1992, compared to the 30 per cent who got jobs (Coventry Careers, 1993). These figures are clearly testament to the impact youth training had, and continues to have, on the lives of substantial numbers of working class young people in Coventry and beyond. However, whether they can be construed as evidence of the great enthusiasm which youth training has generated, or as a vote of success for its training regime, remains considerably more doubtful.

The Pupils

Decisions at 16: the stayers
Despite the scope and scale of the youth training movement, the long-standing desire of minimum-age school leavers to enter directly paid employment at the earliest possible moment remains a distinctive feature of working class behaviour. Suggestions that 'in order to avoid the dole or government schemes' (Brown, 1987, p. 40) a greater number of young people tend to stay on in further education than actually plan to do so have proved only partially true. It has been well documented that rates of staying on in full-time education beyond the minimum school leaving age in

the UK have consistently lagged behind those of most other major industrial countries (Audit Commission, 1993; Cassells, 1990; House of Lords, 1990). Throughout most of the 1980s, when unemployment remained at unprecedented levels, large numbers of working class school leavers rejected sheltering in full-time education as an alternative to the uncertainties of a hostile labour market. No dramatic increase in staying-on rates accompanied the surge in unemployment at the beginning of the 1980s (Ainley, 1988), as many predicted would happen, and it was not until 1988 that the proportion of 16-year-olds staying on at school climbed back to its 1982 level (Employment Gazette, 1991b).

More recently there has been a considerable increase in staying-on rates, although Britain continues to lag behind many other major industrial societies. Between 1989 and 1991, the number of 16-year-olds remaining in full-time education grew from over 50 per cent to well over 60 per cent. Yet this was only after the economy had once again lurched into recession, unemployment among young adults had risen to around the one million mark and social security benefits for unemployed 16- and 17-year-old school leavers were withdrawn. Initial assessments of this expansion illustrate its delicate foundations, with recent figures from the government's own research revealing large-scale dissatisfaction and discontent among many further education students (Audit Commission, 1993). Over two in three 16-year-olds may now stay on in full-time education but this has been at the cost of over one-third of these either leaving their schemes early or failing to complete successfully their courses.

The hesitant nature of this expansion is all the more unexpected given that educational qualifications have taken on an increased significance for school leavers over the past two decades. As opportunities for direct entry into work have decreased, a reluctant process of trading down has taken place among first-time entrants into the labour market, whereby young workers have been forced to readjust their job expectations as increased competition for fewer places has allowed employers greater selectivity (Roberts, 1984). Although recruitment is never based solely on educational criteria, in times of high unemployment they tend to take on additional significance if only for screening purposes. For those with no or few qualifications there has been nowhere downwards to trade and, for both men and women, as levels of unemployment increase the lack of qualifications becomes more obvious (Department of Employment, 1990).

However, as many working class young people have found to their cost, staying on in full-time education does not guarantee later success in the labour market. Further qualifications may enhance employment prospects but they do not guarantee it, as the extra time spent in education may serve to exclude young people from certain forms of employment. A further education course may mean that a young worker becomes too old to be considered for an apprenticeship or a craft technician training place (Lee and Wrench, 1983). It may also fail to provide young people with the second chance often proclaimed since, for many working class young men at least, rather than opening up possibilities for occupational mobility, non-advanced further education has acted to reproduce class inequalities through effectively socializing them into a life of manual labour (Raffe, 1983). For black school leavers too, further education has acted to reproduce processes of discrimination: 'a second chance for ethnic minorities through further education when seen in the context of labour market structures and other experiences appears at best irrelevant, at worst obfuscating' (Dex, 1983, p. 178).

The tenacity with which the young working class seek to hold on to the labour market was immediately apparent among the pupils who took part in my research. As Table 4.2 illustrates, only 54 (36 per cent) of the pupils hoped to stay on after the minimum school leaving age, a figure lower than the proportion for Coventry as a whole at the end of the 1980s (see Table 4.1). Of these stayers, the vast majority wanted to study for A levels, either at college or in the sixth form, with the remainder opting for art college or more vocationally orientated options, like the Certificate of Pre-Vocational Education (CPVE), secretarial or business studies courses.

What is also noticeable is that almost half of the stayers were made up of young people of non-European origin, and almost all of these were of Asian descent. Overall, young black people, and Asian young people in particular, are significantly more likely to stay on in full-time education beyond the minimum school leaving age (Craft and Craft, 1983). We have already noted the widespread discrimination which black child workers face, as study after study has highlighted employers' discriminatory recruitment practices, their failure to take on black workers and, when they do, the ways in which those workers tend to be concentrated in lower-paid and lower-status jobs than their white peers (McCrudden et al., 1991; Brown, 1984). Research has also illustrated how many black young people actually choose to remain in full-time education as an active way of resisting the cycle of low status and low pay experienced by previous generations of black workers (Wrench et al., forthcoming; Craft and Craft, 1983).

Table 4.2 *What Pupils Hoped to Be Doing in 12 Months' Time (School Pupils Survey)*

	Male	Female	Total	European	Non-European
Full-time education	28	26	54	31	23
Craft apprentice/technician	21	2	23	20	3
Bank/finance/estate agent	4	1	5	4	1
Nursing	0	3	3	3	0
Acting/art/sport	5	3	8	8	0
Secretarial/office	1	4	5	4	1
Retail	3	2	5	5	0
Catering/hotel	0	3	3	2	1
Armed forces/police	3	0	3	2	1
Factory	4	1	5	5	0
Youth training	11	15	26	22	4
Any job	7	5	12	10	2
Total (*n* = 152)	87	65	152	116	36

Similarly, employers' demands for differentiated forms of labour power and their assumptions about the 'natural' attributes of women workers also explain the greater tendency for young women to remain in further education beyond the minimum school leaving age (Keil and Newton, 1980). As Table 4.2 illustrates, a significantly higher proportion of the stayers were girls, reflecting the more acute constraints placed on young women's post-16 choices. Because employers assume that women are not naturally committed to the labour market, that their careers will be broken and that their domestic role necessarily makes them short-term workers, young women tend to be drawn into highly segregated areas of work (Rees, 1992). The result is that, in the first year after school, more girls stay on than boys but more often than not this is to take business studies and pre-vocational clerical courses. Girls may stay on in greater numbers at 16 but this is largely explained by the high numbers who tend to join clerical and secretarial-type courses (Cockburn, 1987).

The leavers: prepared to work
The persistence of large-scale unemployment has had only a limited impact on the eagerness with which working class school leavers have

sought to enter waged labour at the first possible moment. Indeed, a long-standing feature of research into working class school leavers has been the characteristic ways in which boys develop a clear and realistic understanding of the good and bad jobs available to them (Clarke, 1980; Willis, 1977; Ashton and Field, 1976; Carter, 1962). More recently, research has also began to unravel the ways in which girls too show an appreciation of the barriers to occupational choice imposed by the ways in which processes of domestic and waged labour have been structured (Rees, 1992; Cockburn, 1987; Griffen, 1980; Sharpe, 1981).

Here too the leaver's refusal to forgo entry into the adult labour market in favour of further education or training was manifest in their aspirations for a narrow range of jobs more traditionally occupied by young workers. Like large numbers of male school leavers before them, the boys still desired skilled manual work, through apprenticeships or craft technician training, or were more ready to embrace manual unskilled work, labouring or in factories (Keil and Newton, 1980). The boys were also considerably more likely to aspire to those professional occupations with a more clearly defined career structure, like banking, finance and estate agency, areas which have traditionally tended to exclude young women as career workers. The boys alone wanted to enter the armed forces and the police, and, given the precarious nature of the local labour market these final-year pupils were destined to enter, it is significant that a large number of both the boys and girls in Table 4.2 longed for just 'any job'.

The contrast between the boys' and the girls' aspirations was startling, if sadly to be expected, given their experiences (as already detailed). Rees (1992) has clearly identified the external constraints and ascriptive factors which constitute often insurmountable barriers to young women exercising real choice in the labour market. We have already seen in the previous chapter that from an early age child labourers are drawn into highly gendered forms of work. Where they aspired to a job with training it meant hairdressing or beautician work, and elsewhere they settled for work in the service sector, doing hotel and catering work, or as carers in nurseries or medical nursing. The girls were also much more likely to want to work in offices or do secretarial work; the figures for this understate the number most likely destined to end up on full-time secretarial or office courses after leaving school. Within the occupational categories the girls also saw themselves working on check-outs in supermarkets or as sales assistants in clothes shops, whereas the boys were more interested in warehouse work or management training in a menswear shop. In the acting, art, sport category, the boys aspired to being professional footballers while the girls hoped to become professional dancers or actresses.

Because young workers continue to desire these types of jobs directly on leaving school, recent commentators suggest that there is 'an unbridgeable gap' (Hollands, 1990, p. 34) appearing between what school leavers expect and the brutal realities of the contemporary labour market. However, because the young working class continue to want to do the types of work previously done by school leavers, it does not necessarily follow that their expectations are unrealistic. A more convincing explanation points towards the ways in which the young working class have continued to look on emerging forms of post-16 provision as poor alternatives to the relative freedoms of a wage, and the ways in which the prospect of a job outside of youth training continues to exert a powerful motivating force.

One consequence of this, something considerably aggravated by the withdrawal of social security benefits for most young people in 1988, has been a worrying trend in young people disappearing from the labour market statistics completely. Youthaid puts the current number of 16- and 17-year-olds not in full-time education, without jobs or training and not in receipt of any benefit, at over 97 000 (Maclagan, 1993). Such figures suggest that on finding out that there is nothing really on offer to them after leaving school, significant numbers of young people simply 'drop out'. The latest figures from Coventry indicate that 590 young people have just disappeared from the statistics (City of Coventry, 1993).

Race equality and youth training

Although only a small number of black pupils took part in the research, Table 4.2 also begins to illustrate the often deep-seated hostility to youth training among young people from ethnic minorities. The ways in which black young people have attempted to use further education as a way of escaping employers' discriminatory recruitment practices has already been noted as widespread discrimination continues to obstruct their opportunities. Mock job applications sent to over 100 employers in the Nottingham area revealed that an Asian name or the suggestion of West Indian origin meant the chances of being called for an interview were severely reduced (Hubbuck and Carter, 1980). Lee and Wrench (1983) found that although young men from ethnic minorities were the most likely group to aspire to apprentice or craft technician training, they were considerably less likely to secure a place than their white peers. This was because employers were more likely to draw their new recruits from areas where few black people lived, felt their white workers would be unwilling to work alongside black workers and tended to give preference to the families of their existing workforces. The well-publicized case of Massey Ferguson Tractors found that black workers were effectively excluded from recruitment to its Coventry factory, where jobs went to family members of its already almost entirely white workforce (Commission for Racial Equality, 1982).

More specifically, the reiteration that youth training 'is an equal opportunities programme, and is open equally to all eligible young people regardless of race, religion, sex or disability' (Manpower Services Commission, 1986, p. 1) has proved little more than an empty gesture, unable and unwilling to confront the ways in which discriminatory practices have become embedded in the organization of training schemes (Pollert, 1986). A recent survey by the Runnymede Trust found that black people were over-represented on the waiting lists for training places. Furthermore, black young people were also more likely to suffer from the failure to honour the government's much publicized promise to all school leavers not in a job or full-time education course that they would be guaranteed a place on a training scheme by the Christmas after leaving school (quoted in Maclagan, 1993). Research in Coventry and the West Midlands has consistently exposed the extent of the problems faced by ethnic minority school leavers looking for training, where the more prestigious schemes, those with the guarantee of quality training and a job at the end, have failed to take on and train black young people (YETRU, 1988; REITS, 1985, 1987). This has meant that where they have entered youth training, black school leavers have become segregated into schemes run primarily by voluntary organizations and private training agencies, effectively reducing the chances of their training leading to a recognized qualification or directly into jobs.

This is not to deny the fact that some employers and managing agents have been more successful than others in recruiting and training black young people (Mizen, 1990a). Nevertheless, many continue to resort to pointing out that they cannot attract black applicants in the first place and then seek to explain this in terms of 'cultural' factors, for example the tendency for young Asian people to stay on at school or the unrealistic aspirations of Afro-Caribbean school leavers. However, such arguments merely serve to obscure the real obstacles encountered by black young people on leaving school, through equating the specific difficulties they face with their own limitations or failings. The result is that the focus of attention is shifted away from 'broader dynamics, social forces and structural factors when explaining social phenomena' (Wrench *et al.*, forthcoming) towards the intrinsic qualities of young black people themselves. Inner-city Afro-Caribbean and Asian young people are likely to be at least as well qualified as their white peers on entering youth training. They are also generally more enthusiastic about obtaining a skill, to the extent that they much more readily forgo short-term earnings for long-term benefits, and there is no evidence to suggest that they are less willing to travel to seek work or training opportunities. To explain the labour market position of black young people from such a perspective means:

> The result is perhaps the most tenacious and insidious of assumptions: that ethnic minorities in general . . . are disadvantaged in a way that is analogous to mental and physical disabilities. (Cross, 1987, p. 3)

It is to the discriminatory recruitment practices of employers, managing agents and the careers service that we must look in order to understand more fully the ways in which such forms of segregation are reproduced over time.

A recent survey of London's career offices found that 60 per cent reported that employers and managing agents had overtly refused to take black young people on to their training schemes (GLARE, 1989). The careers service itself has long been criticized for accommodating employers' and managing agents' discriminatory preferences and for stereotyping the needs and abilities of black school leavers (Pollert, 1985). More recently, extensive research among careers officers and their placement of young people into youth training found evidence of widespread discrimination (Cross *et al.*, 1990). Careers officers were far more likely to consider the aspirations of young people from ethnic minorities to be unrealistic when compared to those of white young people, and consistently underestimated the abilities of Asian young women. They also identified a tendency among black young people actively to prefer less desirable training schemes, motivated by a fear of hostile tutors and racist incidents on predominantly white schemes. Careers officers encountered regular discrimination by employers and training providers, so that some officers actively pandered to these practices by steering black young people away from schemes where it was felt they were likely to encounter a hostile reception.

Training for All?

What is also noticeable within Table 4.2 is the relatively large number of leavers, 26 (27 per cent), who saw themselves in training schemes after leaving school. Although this represents a figure well below the number eventually destined to start their adult working lives in this way, considering the deep ambivalence with which the working class young have continued to confront the prospect of youth training it represents a far from insignificant number.

As Raffe and Smith (1987) point out, little is known about young people's attitudes towards youth training across the school leaving age group as a whole. This is important because the original proposal for the YTS was that it would provide an opportunity for work experience-based vocational education and training for all school leavers under 18 (Manpower Services Commission, 1981). A major component of youth training's new deal was its stated intention of removing the traditional dichotomy between education and employment, with their concomitant associations of academic success and vocational failure, so that every school leaver would be in a position to take up the offer of a period of foundation training which combined both off-the-job and on-the-job training elements (Ainley and Corney, 1990).

As we have seen, the scheme's continuity with the unemployment palliatives of the 1970s and early 1980s meant that its promise of quality training immediately rang hollow (Finn, 1986). Following YOP, youth training's primary function in alleviating high levels of youth unemployment, and its association with corrective purposes for those unable to make the direct entry into work, constantly proved a barrier in convincing working class young people of its self-stated aim of providing school leavers with quality training for jobs. What working class school leavers wanted were real jobs. Jobs with employers outside youth training, and, for those who could offer employers the qualifications and experience they were demanding, the prospect of avoiding training schemes and moving into relatively well-paid work remained a distinct possibility. Shortly after its launch it was already being argued that youth training had become locked into a 'vicious circle of low status' and risked 'being stigmatised as a scheme for the less able, the less motivated and above all the less employable' (Raffe, 1987, p. 5).

Interestingly, Raffe's own solution to the problem of low status lay in the need to attract school leavers into the scheme from across the entire ability range, especially the more academically able, so as to strengthen its

Table 4.3 *Pupils Willing to Train on a Scheme, as a Percentage (School Pupils Survey)*

	Stayers	Leavers	Total	Male	Female
Willing	14	71	50	44	58
Unwilling	86	21	45	49	40
Don't know	0	8	5	7	2
Total ($n = 148$)	100	100	100	100	100

training credibility. However, far from it gaining wider acceptance his own research highlighted a growing intransigence, as 'a hardening of attitudes' (Raffe and Smith, 1987, p. 251) took place among those whom he saw the scheme as needing to attract if its training revolution was to become established among school leavers more generally.

This conclusion is further strengthened by Table 4.3, which highlights school pupils' feelings towards the prospect of youth training. At best, the table illustrates that severe reservations about the scheme remain across the population of school pupils as a whole. Here, their reactions were distinctly mixed, with exactly half expressing a willingness to train and just under half resolutely opposed. Moreover, as we would expect, pupil orientations to youth training should loosely reflect their assessment of its likely reward and, as Table 4.3 also graphically illustrates, for the more academically minded this amounted to very little. The hardening of attitudes noted by Raffe in the mid-1980s looked more firmly set by the end of the decade, with a clear contrast between the different groups of pupils' dispositions to enter youth training. Altogether, almost three quarters of the stayers indicated that they would be prepared to train on a scheme compared with only 14 per cent of the leavers. Far from endorsing the assertion of Lord Young, then Chairperson of the MSC, that the youth training certificate would become 'more important in employment prospects for young people than even "O" or "A" levels' (quoted in Finn, 1986, p. 62), these young people clearly had other ideas. Given that young people with a Youth Training Certificate are still considerably more likely to be unemployed than those with more traditional forms of qualifications, this reflects an accurate and realistic assessment of youth training's limitations (Department of Employment, 1990).

The stayers' low estimation of youth training was also clearly reflected

Table 4.4 *Reasons Why Pupils Would or Would Not be Willing to Enter Youth Training, as a Percentage of All Responses* * *(School Pupils Survey)*

	Stayers (resp. = 81)			Leavers (resp. = 143)		
	Male	**Female**	**Total**	**Male**	**Female**	**Total**
Positive reasons						
Training	1	6	7	18	17	35
Experience	1	4	5	6	9	15
Better job prospects	3	4	7	8	3	11
Negative reasons						
Better than dole	0	0	0	4	4	8
No choice	0	1	1	5	3	8
Slave labour	26	23	49	10	9	19
Scheme for 'thickies'	4	1	5	1	0	1
Prefer further education	10	6	16	0	0	0
Crafty government	1	3	4	2	1	3
Not interested	4	3	7	1	1	2
Total	**50**	**51**	**101**	**55**	**46**	**101**

*Pupils could give more than one reason

in the various reasons, given in Table 4.4, for their decision on whether they would be willing or not to train on a scheme. As the table demonstrates, the stayers were more adamant in their rejection of the scheme as 'something I'm just not interested in, I prefer further education to YTS' or 'it's not for the likes of me'. These pupils tended to see youth training as a low-level alternative to more traditional routes on leaving school because 'you learn more at college' and 'college gives you a much better way of learning than YTS'. For them youth training was clearly an inferior option because 'it's got a poor reputation among employers', 'it is a scheme for thickies', 'a scheme for those who don't know where to go' and 'only for people who can't get work'. Their association of the scheme with remedial functions was also clear: 'it's a waste of time if you want a good job' and 'because you end up being used by employers as cheap labour. Nothing else'. Here, it was the stayers who were more likely to express the opinion that youth training was 'slave labour' or 'cheap labour', offering only 'poor training', 'not much of a start in life' and, ultimately, 'poor job prospects'.

This wholesale rejection of the scheme by the stayers initially appears to be in stark contrast to the leavers among whom over eight out of 10 indicated that they would be willing to train. This willingness largely related to the scheme's perceived ability to open up an otherwise largely closed world of work through the leaver's emphasis on the 'training' dimension of the scheme. This meant that stress was put on 'the training opportunity YTS gives you', 'the chance of learning how to do a job properly', or 'training as a way to get skills'. It also meant 'you get trained' and 'you can get some training'. Beyond the importance attached to training, these pupils also expressed a readiness to train on a scheme in terms of its perceived ability to provide access to employers and the wider labour market, and through an assessment of the opportunities it offered in merely establishing a general presence in the workplace. This meant that youth training 'gives you work experience', 'experience in a workplace', or 'because you can get some experience in a working situation'. These young people appreciated that experience was important in this way because, ultimately, 'it could lead to the chance of a real job', 'you might get a job', or even 'it's possible you might get taken on at the end'.

The pupils therefore assessed the prospect of youth training through an evaluation of its freedoms and opportunities but these were also tempered somewhat by a deeper sense of unease about its disciplines and constraints. In all, over 80 per cent of the leavers indicated that they would be willing to train on a scheme but nearly two fifths of the reasons they gave for doing so focused on the negative implications of youth training. This apparently contradictory assessment of youth training was therefore indicative of a deeper-seated ambivalence which, in the context of their willingness to train, put considerable stress on the scheme's limitations and apparent failings. So, for this group of pupils, youth training was only 'better than the dole' or 'it beats signing on'. Some also felt they had 'little choice in the matter' or 'it's all that's available to me'. Yet like the stayers, they too were also ready to condemn youth training as 'slave labour', 'a cheap labour scheme', or 'you just get ripped off. Employers are out to take advantage of you'.

What this apparent paradox begins to demonstrate, therefore, are the complex and contradictory ways in which the young working class assess the prospect of youth training. First, a division exists between more and less academically minded school pupils, where the stayers are considerably more likely to reject, and the leavers more likely to accept, the prospect of training on a scheme. In this way the scheme would appear to have become further entrenched as a poor alternative to further education. Yet such a contrast between the two groups also risks ignoring the real continuities which become evident when the pupils' reasons for their decision whether or not to train are taken into account. Here pupil assessment across the groups focuses on an appreciation and awareness of youth training's relative freedoms and constraints. On the one hand, its freedoms are seen to offer training, experience, the ability to get into the workplace and eventually the possibility of a job. On the other hand, youth training's constraints are detailed by an awareness of the scheme as a low-status option, and possibly one over which the pupils see they have little real choice, and which involved exposing themselves to new forms of discipline associated with hard work, low status and little money. This is not to argue that each pupil evaluates the prospect of youth training in an identical or uniform way. Nevertheless, it does point out the collective basis to young labour, as many of the opportunities and constraints experienced by one individual or group of pupils are reflected in the experiences and reactions of many others.

Training for jobs

Other research has also highlighted the complexity of working class responses to the scheme. Data from the Scottish School Leavers Survey have illustrated that young people's attitudes towards youth training are at best contradictory, with school leavers likely to identify both advantages and disadvantages to training (Raffe, 1989; Raffe and Smith, 1987). Scottish school leavers too have been receptive to youth training's promise to make them more employable and they have been willing to agree that it provides different and interesting types of work. But these freedoms have also been closely associated with a realization that youth training involves sacrifices too. Any advantages are therefore simultaneously assessed in relation to its apparent disadvantages, including the cynical machinations of governments and their desires to reduce unemployment statistics, and an enduring feeling that the scheme continues to provide employers with a ready and limitless source of cheap labour.

Research has also exposed similar feelings among young people actually training in England and Wales. The government-funded Youth

Cohort Study found that trainees generally found the work interesting, enjoyed the training and appreciated the opportunity of working with colleagues and other workers. However, the level of pay, again (in an apparent contradiction) the training and the actual content of the work the trainees were given to do were all consistent sources of dissatisfaction. Similarly, the Economic and Social Research Council's extensive *16–19 Initiative* has more recently illustrated the ways in which working class young people perceive youth training as, in principle, a beneficial way to start an adult working life, while simultaneously remaining deeply committed to the view that it is nothing more than 'slave labour' (Banks *et al.*, 1992).

This contradiction was again readily apparent among the final-year school pupils in Coventry, as outlined in Table 4.5. Here, across the pupils as a whole, there was a considerable readiness to endorse the claim that youth training offered a young person a good opportunity to train. In all, over 80 per cent of both the boys and the girls agreed to the suggestion and, once again, the leavers were significantly more likely to agree than the stayers.

However, as Table 4.6 illustrates, their reasons for endorsing the scheme's training opportunity were again characterized by deeper-seated uncertainties and suspicions. Here the stayers' reasons were again more likely to highlight youth training as 'cheap labour', 'slave labour', or 'you're just a dogsbody on YTS'. They were also more ready to link the efficacy of training more directly to its chances of leading into a 'real job with pay and prospects'. For them, training for training's sake was illogical and made sense 'only if you get kept on at the end', 'if you get a job', or 'if your boss keeps you on'.

Table 4.5 *Does Youth Training Offer a Good Training Opportunity, as a Percentage? (School Pupils Survey)*

	Stayers	**Leavers**	**Total**	**Male**	**Female**
Yes	70	90	83	84	81
No	27	8	15	14	16
Don't know	3	2	5	2	3
Total (*n* = 147)	100	100	100	100	100

Table 4.6 *Reasons Why Youth Training Would or Would Not Offer a Good Training Opportunity, as a Percentage of All Responses* (School Pupil Survey)*

	Stayers (resp. = 78)			Leavers (resp. = 135)		
	Male	Female	Total	Male	Female	Total
Positive reasons						
Training	13	15	28	23	15	38
Experience	7	6	13	11	11	22
Better job prospects	3	6	9	7	3	10
Choice	4	3	7	4	4	8
Negative reasons						
Better than dole	3	2	5	3	2	5
Slave labour	11	6	17	3	1	4
If it leads to a job	6	6	12	4	2	6
Miscellaneous	4	5	9	6	1	7
Total	**51**	**49**	**100**	**61**	**39**	**100**

*Pupils could give more than one reason

For the leavers in particular, but also for the final-year pupils more generally, there was again a strong tendency to evaluate youth training's claims to offer a quality training opportunity in relation to an assessment of its ability to open up access to employers and to the world of work. This was most immediately apparent from the comments of those who evaluated the scheme's training opportunity in terms of the 'training' and 'experience' it offered. However, 'training' was rarely understood in terms of the opportunity to obtain specific skills or the opportunity to acquire new types of abilities or qualifications. In actual fact, references to skills and qualifications were totally absent from their comments. On the contrary, it was an appreciation of 'training' and 'experience' which actually debased traditional notions of skills training and which was significantly more likely to emphasize its instrumental, job-related benefits. Here training's value lay primarily in its ability to get a young person into the workplace and to bring them into contact with employers, and not as an opportunity to accumulate new skills, dexterities and work-related expertise.

Training in these pupils' views therefore primarily meant 'the chance of working with people who are trained', 'training in the workplace', 'on-the-job training with an employer', or 'an employer can train you how they want you'. Furthermore, 'experience' meant 'getting experience of the workplace', 'experience with an employer', 'the chance of learning the ropes at work', or 'giving you an idea of what it's all about'. These young people knew that 'employers want experience' and that 'employers want people who know how to work'. 'Training' and 'experience' therefore meant 'you can get your foot in the door', 'a chance to work your way up', and, ultimately, 'the chance of a better job'.

Other studies have also noted young people's 'pervasive instrumentalism towards the scheme' (Raffe, 1989, p. 130), together with their 'short-term instrumental orientation to training' (Banks *et al.*, 1992, p. 44). The generally instrumental orientation of the working class to work has long been noted (Blackburn and Mann, 1979), but what these recent studies of young people have failed to grasp more fully is that the significance of their instrumentalism lies not only in school leavers' appreciation of training exclusively in relation to its likelihood of leading into full-time paid employment – instrumentalism in a narrow or economistic sense of the term. More fully, this notion of instrumentalism also embodies an active process of resistance and negotiation in which school leavers are forced to confront the realities of youth training. Young people may attempt to use the scheme as a way directly into employment or the world of work more generally, but they never experience youth training in the ways in which it was construed. Indeed, school pupils' assessments of youth training are largely defined in opposition to and against youth training's claims and it is this that explains the distinctiveness of working class young people's complex evaluation of the scheme.

As Table 4.7 further illustrates, it is this instrumentalism, this appreciation of youth training's complex freedoms and disciplines, which accounts for the willingness of final-year pupils to endorse the scheme's claim to improve a school leaver's chances of getting a job. After all, this is what gives youth training its partial value in the eyes of many working class school leavers. However, even here significant opposition to the idea remains, with around 20 per cent of all pupils disagreeing with the suggestion that youth training could improve job chances. Moreover, two in five stayers disagreed with the proposition, reflecting these young people's

Table 4.7 *Does Youth Training Improve School Leavers' Job Chances, as a Percentage? (School Pupils Survey)*

	Stayers	Leavers	Total	Male	Female
Yes	58	89	78	81	74
No	39	8	19	18	21
Don't know	3	3	3	1	5
Total (*n* = 146)	100	100	100	100	100

knowledge that youth training has served to further entrench divisions within a labour market already highly structured by the exclusionary value of formal educational qualifications. These young people know that the possession of GCSEs and A levels still offers a way to avoid dead-end jobs and training schemes, and that work continues to be made available to those with these types of recognized and valued (at least by employers) qualifications (Banks *et al.*, 1992; Lee *et al.*, 1990).

The contrast with the leavers was again quickly apparent from their justifications for their answers, as Table 4.8 points out. Again, the leavers were more likely to place greater emphasis on the scheme's general 'training' and 'experience' opportunities, but training and experience linked to general ideas of work and not the ownership of skills: 'training for a particular job', 'training gives you more knowledge of work', or simply 'training gives you a chance in the workplace'. Again the emphasis was on 'experience of a job', 'experience in the workplace' and 'getting to know what it's like'. Indeed, the centrality of training and experience in finding work was clearly appreciated by these pupils because 'employers are looking for experienced people', 'you won't get work without experience of work' and 'YTS provides the employers with what they are looking for'.

A detailed examination of the ways in which working class school pupils more generally have sought to confront the possibilities of youth training quickly reveals the contradictory and complex nature of young people's perceptions of and responses to training. On the one hand, significant numbers of pupils continue to reject the prospect of youth training as inferior to traditional school leaver routes, particularly into further education, even though many pupils have also responded to the expansion of this

Table 4.8 *Reasons Why Pupils Thought Youth Training Would or Would Not Improve Job Chances, as a Percentage of All Responses* (School Pupil Survey)*

	Stayers (resp. = 71)			Leavers (resp. = 117)		
	Male	**Female**	**Total**	**Male**	**Female**	**Total**
Positive reasons						
Training	15	8	23	23	8	31
Experience	10	10	20	17	16	33
Possibly get taken on	4	7	11	8	5	13
Negative reasons						
You need to get qualifications	10	9	19	0	1	1
No jobs at end	5	7	12	3	4	7
Might help less able	7	4	11	2	4	6
Depends on the scheme	3	1	4	7	3	10
Total	**54**	**46**	**100**	**60**	**41**	**101**

*Pupils could give more than one reason

sector in an often hesitant and tentative way. On the other hand, large numbers of young people have remained committed to entering the labour market at the earliest possible moment, despite the likely consequences of being unable to find work directly. These young people also remain discerning in their attitudes towards training, assessing the prospect in terms of its likely opportunities and compulsions. They understand the chances it offers for opening up possible routes into the labour market and more specifically for bringing them into direct contact with employers. Nonetheless, they are also under no illusions that these promises are available only at the considerable cost of exposing themselves to new forms of authority and domination associated with the scheme, and that training for real skills has very little to do with youth training. It is this awareness of youth training's freedoms and constraints which lies at the heart of any explanation of pupil behaviour in relation to youth training and it is these issues which we will continue to explore through the experiences of a group of young people who have actually entered schemes.

The Trainees

Searching for a 'real job'

At best, youth training can therefore claim to have had a mixed impact on most school leavers, with many demonstrating an awareness of its possible use as a way of negotiating a troubled labour market. At worst, many pupils remain deeply suspicious of the scheme's promises and see training more as a stepping stone into jobs, a possible vehicle for their own aspirations and needs, but one which simultaneously involves the negotiation of a whole new set of obstacles and constraints. Yet considerable numbers of young people do enter training schemes, and so the remainder of this chapter examines how school pupils are propelled into youth training and how this relates to the experiences of the pupils already detailed.

Many of the issues the pupils here were concerned with in relation to youth training have been found to be of similar gravity to the issues concerning school leavers who have actually entered schemes. Wider research has found that prospective trainees also evaluate youth training in terms of its ability to lead to jobs but that this is not their only consideration. Failure to secure work outside the scheme also proves to be another powerful contributory factor propelling school leavers into training because most school leavers, despite sustained attempts to portray them as otherwise, continue to see the scheme as a better alternative to doing nothing at all. These studies have also found that a young person's desire to train and equip themselves with skills remains only a relatively minor consideration in training, so that

> implicit in most of [their] answers was the assumption that YTS was a second-best option, and that permanent jobs or alternative educational opportunities were to be preferred if possible. (Raffe and Smith, 1987, p. 246)

This caution in respect to youth training was undoubtedly a significant contributory factor in the eventual decision to make training effectively compulsory for unemployed school leavers: working class school leavers simply refused to join the scheme in the numbers anticipated. During its first year of operation, less than three-quarters of the available places were filled, and since then problems in attracting sufficient trainees to fill all the available places have plagued its expansion (Finn, 1987). Before its effective compulsion, it was conservatively estimated that one in 10 young people were refusing the offer of a place (Horton, 1986) and that 'refusers' were far more likely to see the scheme as cheap labour, workfare and a way to massage the unemployment statistics (Craig, 1986; Kirby and Roberts, 1985). We have already seen the latest manifestation of this opposition to youth training, as large numbers of 16- and 17-year-olds, rather than subject themselves to a period of enforced training, have reacted to the withdrawal of social security benefits by disappearing from the labour market completely.

It is a measure of young people's determination to resist the pressure of youth training that none of the trainees here had wanted to enter the scheme on leaving school. As Table 4.9 clearly illustrates, every one of the trainees had wanted to enter paid employment outside youth training (a small number mentioned two or more jobs they had been contemplating) and even where they had no specific ideas, the desire for work

Table 4.9 *Trainee Aspirations on Leaving School (YTS Trainee Interviews)*

	Male	Female	Total
Shop/retail	3	2	5
Driving (lorry and coach)	2	0	2
Secretarial/office	0	5	5
Nursing/care	2	1	3
Electrical/engineering	5	1	6
Armed forces/police	2	1	3
Gardening/horticulture	1	1	2
Hairdressing/beautician	0	3	3
Building/painting and decorating	6	2	8
Catering	0	3	3
Miscellaneous	3	1	4
Didn't know	2	3	5
Total	**26**	**23**	**49**

remained emphatic: 'I wanted a *real job*, not a YTS' (Clive – clerical trainee).

Thirty-seven (88 per cent) of the trainees did have specific ideas about what they had wanted to do on leaving and, like those of the pupils, their aspirations for 'real jobs' (i.e. a job outside youth training) reflected the types of work which had previously been open to working class school leavers, and the clear sexual division of labour this entailed. Only four young people, the 'miscellaneous' category, had anything like unusual aspirations: one wanted to be a snooker coach, another a publican, a third a computer programmer and one young woman aspired to become a social worker. Seen in the context of their wider experiences and expectations, however, even these aspirations could not be labelled as wildly unrealistic. The would-be snooker professional was already playing illegally on the local pub and club circuit (an apparently lucrative alternative source of income from side-bets and wagers) but was too young to be considered for a coaching course. The aspiring publican had started helping out in his father's pub but had moved away from the area when his parents separated. The computer programmer was already heavily involved in computers as a hobby, and for the last the idea of becoming a social worker had been:

> the highest thing I could aim for . . . They [her teachers] told me to get real considering the level of qualifications I'd need to get to university, so I agreed that my best bet would be a Community Care YTS . . . I was told I had no chance of passing my exams but came out with nine O levels at the end! (Lucy – community care trainee)

What emerges, therefore, is a picture similar to the hopes of many of the final-year pupils; the trainees had desperately wanted to leave school and enter the sort of real jobs that working class school leavers had been doing for decades. What is noticeable, however, is that in contrast to the pupils' aspirations in Table 4.2, the trainees made no direct references to youth training as a possible option on leaving school. It is doubtful that this reflected a greater willingness among the pupils to enter youth training. A more plausible explanation is that many of the leavers had already resigned themselves to the prospect of youth training, as the harsh realities of the Coventry labour market became increasingly apparent. Twenty-two of the 26 pupils who actually saw themselves as youth trainees on leaving school identified the type of training scheme they saw themselves as entering. It is therefore probable that, as they were so close to leaving school, rather than risk the uncertainties of unemployment many had already succeeded in lining up a training place.

Getting experience

The prospect of youth training had therefore not really been seriously considered by the trainees until they were getting close to leaving school. It has been suggested that one of the major reasons for their enduring antagonism, and one of the major reasons why Britain has failed to produce a durable training culture, has been the existence of 'substantial personal ignorance of the scheme' (Raffe and Smith, 1987, p. 256) among working class school leavers. That a partial and often hostile knowledge of youth training exists among the young working class is beyond dispute (Hollands, 1990), but blaming school leavers in this way fails to appreciate the real value and significance of their knowledge. On the contrary, it is precisely because young people know that youth training involves low-paid, insecure and arduous work that they have remained reluctant to commit themselves fully to the sacrifices these programmes demand.

Thirty-eight (90 per cent) of the trainees readily accepted that their knowledge of youth training while at school amounted to 'hardly anything' (Bob – engineering trainee), 'not much' (Clare – horticulture trainee) or 'not a lot' (Sarah – clerical trainee). Indeed, only four (10 per cent) claimed 'I knew everything about it (Derrick – MaC trainee). Yet even here a closer examination revealed that this 'everything' corresponded to much the same knowledge as the other trainees possessed. What knowledge this latter group possessed, however, tended to come from a variety of different sources. Eleven (26 per cent) of the trainees mentioned information about training schemes received from careers officers at school, an unexpectedly low number given the decentralized system of careers advice in operation in Coventry at the time. Also, where careers advice was mentioned it was exclusively referred to in coercive terms: 'the careers teacher really pushed YTS' (Bhovinder – clerical trainee), or 'they would rather force you into YTS than help you find a job. That's what I wanted, a job not a YTS' (Clive – clerical trainee). This is hardly surprising given the already noted ways in which careers advice has taken on an increasingly functional role in relation to youth training's requirements for trainees, and, for the young people here, careers advice had been little more than another factor pushing them ever closer towards a training scheme.

Interestingly, only four (10 per cent) of the trainees mentioned the MSC or Training Agency (TA) as a significant source of information about the scheme. Considering that the early years of youth training were dominated by extensive advertising campaigns and that prior to the research the MSC had launched another attempt to persuade school leavers that 'the best advertisement for YTS is the people who've done one' (Youth Training News, July 1987), they were obviously getting poor returns for the large sums being expended. Exciting graphics, clever packaging and sophisticated advertising techniques had failed to have a positive impact on these young people at least and, paradoxically, it was just as likely to reinforce their negative impressions as to provide youth training with the glossy image intended: 'they [the TV adverts] were pretty depressing. They just made it even clearer that the YTS was the only thing open to me when I left school' (Terry – PSV trainee).

This 'personal ignorance' has also been used to explain the emergence among school leavers of a 'folk mythology or demonology' (Raffe and Smith, 1987, p. 256) regarding youth training, whereby tales of exploitation and ill-treatment had 'created a kind of "folk lore" about its "slave labour" qualities' (Bank et al., 1992, p. 44). It is the durability of these 'demonologies' over time which, in part, is seen as responsible for the continued hostility towards youth training and the inability to create a lasting commitment to training among British school leavers.

The fact that working class young people continue to refer to youth training in this way is undeniable and it featured heavily in the school pupils' responses examined in more detail earlier in this chapter. Among the trainees too, perceptions of youth training while at school had been dominated by the belief that it was 'slave labour . . . the money was shit, [and] you got treated pretty badly by employers' (Colin – community care trainee). In all, 33 (75 per cent) of the trainees stated that they had known 'the pay was lousy and the work was hard and boring' (Wendy – clerical trainee), and 'you got paid peanuts for working your back off' (Joe – MaC trainee). For another: 'I had heard that it was slave labour, that you got given all the shitty jobs and that the money was poor' (Neil – community care trainee). As one of them phlegmatically put it: 'it was very unpopular at school' (Glenn – PSV trainee).

To see these reactions as part of an enduring playground 'demonology' or 'folklore' is to miss their significance and risks locating young people's resistance and opposition to youth training in the inability of the state to communicate effectively the training message. Rather, working class young people's continuing antagonism to youth training is grounded in their already intimate knowledge of work and a growing realization that youth training may represent an alternative to unemployment but that, in doing so, it also involves submission to new forms of discipline and authority. We have demonstrated at length that working class young people have a sound, if incomplete, understanding of local labour markets, and one which immediately stems from their own direct experience of child labour. Blackburn and Mann (1979) have argued that the working class tend to form relatively accurate assessments of the structure and organization of local labour markets and that this knowledge is firmly rooted in the direct experiences of family, relative and friends. It is from these immediate origins that an understanding of the demands of different jobs, contrasting rates of pay and differing working conditions are primarily obtained.

Here too, family and friends were reported as a significant influence, with 18 (43 per cent) of the trainees mentioning that they had learnt about different training schemes in this way. This included eight (19 per cent) trainees who stated that they knew family, friends or relatives who had actually been on different youth training schemes and it was this that gave them the authority to claim: 'I knew it was rubbish . . . My cousin had been on one and he said, "whatever you do stay well clear"' (Clare – horticulture trainee). These types of network provided a powerful source of information which most of the trainees considered reliable and which they saw as entitling them to describe youth training 'as a way for them [employers] to get cheap labour' (Louis – construction trainee). Similarly: 'I knew that you were used as a skivvy and that you got all the dirtiest and worst jobs to do' (Terry – PSV trainee) and 'people at school said if you get on one then don't do any work. You're getting shit money for hard graft' (Neil – community care trainee). This was not part of some mythology but knowledge, however partial, accumulated from family and friends, and from those who had already experienced the reality of youth training.

This is not to argue that such information had led these young people to dismiss the scheme out of hand before they had even left school; after all, this is where they had eventually ended up and none of these trainees had been forced, physically or as yet through benefit sanctions, to train. Although they did not want to begin their working lives as trainees, their initial understanding of youth training as something harsh and alienating was also moderated by the knowledge that there were also possibilities to negotiate and alleviate these disciplines. Seven (17 per cent) of the trainees therefore knew: 'you could go to college and that could have been good. You could get some extra qualifications as well' (Clare – horticulture trainee). For others too:

> I'd never thought much about it before I left school . . . but I'd been told it was slave labour and the money was poor . . . I wasn't very good at school so I needed to catch up after leaving. YTS was a way for me to help improve my reading and writing and help me get some qualifications. (Derrick – MaC trainee)

These young people were also willing to concede that youth training could offer possibilities of getting training and experience, despite such references not being as prominent as may have been expected. Only six (14 per cent) of the trainees described what they had known about the scheme in relation to the opportunity to train: 'it could give you some training and that's important because it would make my chances of getting a job more safe and secure' (Samantha – clerical trainee). It could also offer 'training for a job because a job is something you can't get now without training these days' (Thomas – construction trainee carpenter). Similarly, six (14 per cent) more discussed their knowledge of the scheme in relation to the possibilities it offered for getting some direct work experience. These young people recognized the importance of experience in securing a real job: 'I knew it was good experience-wise. You can't get a job without experience these days' (Lucy – community care trainee). Also: 'I knew YTS meant the chance to get some training and some experience because that's what employers are demanding now' (Niki – clerical trainee).

Like the pupils, these young people had faced up to the prospect of youth training through a consideration of possible opportunities and rewards, weighed against the heavy price they knew it could also exact. While they freely admitted that their knowledge of the scheme's detailed workings was shallow, on closer examination they did have a wider appreciation of the scheme's relative freedoms and constraints. This meant that they approached leaving school with an informed and realistic impression of youth training and one which emphasized the antagonisms that being a trainee would most likely generate. They knew the scheme meant the prospect of exposing themselves to new forms of demands associated with youth training's discipline of hard work and low pay. Yet they also knew that the lack o opportunities for real jobs outside the scheme meant that training and experience took on increasingly important meanings. These were not necessarily the meanings which the scheme's proponents had intended or even desired, but nonetheless they conveyed an understanding of the scheme in which its opportunities and demands stood in uneasy opposition: 'I knew that it was slave labour, but at least you get experience. That's what you need today' (Clare – horticulture trainee). Similarly

> I knew that it was a rip-off, you spent most of the time messing about and doing nothing. But I needed experience and youth training was the only way of getting it. I thought it would be a way into full-time work. (Joe – MaC trainee)

Like the school pupils, the trainees had therefore developed an assessment of youth training which attempted to grapple with its competing demands and emphases. On leaving school, all 42 had hoped to make a direct entry into paid employment outside youth training, yet, regardless of the deep-seated reservations they obviously felt, youth training had become the great leveller and all were beginning their adult working lives as trainees. How, then, had these young people come to find themselves reluctant trainees and what factors had propelled them into schemes?

Reluctant trainees: negotiating the labour market

Sociologists have long argued that the structural constraints faced by working class young people mean that it is largely a misnomer to talk about occupational *choice* on leaving school. In contrast, early theories of occupational choice tended to view adolescent patterns of behaviour among school leavers as the result of individual socio-psychological decision-making processes, whereby physical maturity and psychological development evolved in relation to the formation of a greater understanding of the world of work (Roberts, 1968). It was through the creation of a rounded self-identity and the development of a stable relationship with the external world that young people were seen to make rational decisions regarding their future occupations.

The onset of mass unemployment, however, questioned the validity of these assumptions, as the constraints that governed young people's entry into the labour market became increasingly obvious.

> Sociological studies drew attention to how stratified patterns of family
> life, education and occupations interlocked to present different groups of
> school leavers with contrasting opportunity structures, and thus set
> definite limits to their scope for genuine choice. (Roberts, 1980, p. 16)

Throughout the 1980s, research progressively focused on the implications of these 'opportunity structures' for working class school leavers, often concluding that many were taking any available jobs out of desperation and necessity rather than out of any sustained notion of choice or vocation (West and Newton, 1983). As school leavers' job opportunities continued to deteriorate, by the beginning of the 1990s even these limited notions of choice were being jettisoned and it was increasingly being argued that for very large numbers of young people any talk of choice on leaving school had little, if any, meaning in reality (Roberts and Parsell, 1990). It was argued that a young person's career trajectory was increasingly being determined by their social class, gender, ethnicity and region (Banks *et al.*, 1992).

Looking for jobs

While the structural constraints operating on a school leaver's job choices have been well documented, how these actually impact on the lives of young people as they seek to negotiate their way through a hazardous labour market remains less clear. For the trainees here, being pushed along a path towards a training scheme meant having to confront a whole host of barriers and obstacles which appeared as directly contrary to their desires for 'real jobs', the most immediate and pressing of which was the plain and simple absence of available opportunities for work.

It was this sheer pressure of unemployment which meant that 17 (40 per cent) of the trainees had not seriously applied for jobs before or after leaving school, although most admitted 'I tried to keep an eye open to see if anything came up' (Sarah – clerical trainee). This in no way represented a lack of commitment or motivation to find work on their part, or an endorsement of youth training as a desirable way to start their working lives. Rather, it represented a progressive awareness through the last year at school that direct entry into paid employment was an increasingly elusive process and that, in the short term at least, a training scheme represented a necessary if not strictly desirable alternative.

Experiences of school often conspired to reinforce these views as teachers and careers advisers sought to channel what they saw as unrealistic aspirations away from the demands for 'real jobs'. This often meant being told in no uncertain terms that youth training was the only practical option considering the state of the labour market and that talk of anything else was unrealistic: 'they [her teachers] told me it was what I had to do if I wanted to get into caring work' (Lucy – community care trainee), or 'I was told this would be the most effective way into doing what I wanted to do [working with young children]' (Colin – community care trainee). Others received similar advice, often bordering on ultimatums, frequently pointing out that staying on in school was a waste of time and that finding a job directly was simply out of the question. This usually provoked a bitter response and merely compounded the hostility towards youth training that many already felt. However, the trainees increasingly came to accept that a training scheme was a more appropriate alternative, even if it proved a bitter pill to swallow:

> I said I'd never go on one but YTS is the only way into things now. Everyone at school said it was slave labour and that you got treated like rubbish but when it came to it I didn't have much choice really. There wasn't much else available. (Kath – clerical trainee)

The experience of the remaining 25 (60 per cent) trainees was similar, the major difference being that this group had all made committed and sustained attempts to find work 'in a proper job' (Thomas – construction trainee carpenter), before reluctantly submitting to the pressure to train. Getting them on to schemes proved no easy task, however, and many had gone to considerable lengths to find work which did not involve youth training. We have already outlined the familiarity of the young working class with local labour markets and, as the last chapter revealed, the young people here had already gone some way towards demonstrating their ability to find paid employment while still in full-time education. For many, these job-search efforts had grown more intensive as school leaving approached, and visits to 'the Careers Service, looking in local [news]papers, following up suggestions from my mates and my family, asking local places if they had anything and just asking employers on the off chance' (Bhovinder – clerical trainee) had all formed part of their regular job-search routines.

It was therefore neither a lack of motivation nor an insufficient appreciation of the ways in which work became available which explained these young people's inability to find paid employment. On the contrary, the possibility of unemployment was solely the effect of employers' reluctance to take them on. Accounts of unwelcome job enquiries, sharp rebuttals and unacknowledged application letters were common, and in all only seven (17 per cent) had managed to get as far as an interview. We saw in Chapter 2 that careers advice while at school could have meant a young person being lined up for a youth training scheme without their prior knowledge, and two of these interviews could well have been for youth training places. Nevertheless, as we have already seen in the previous chapter, only two trainees had actually been offered jobs and both of these had subsequently been forced onto schemes.

The trainees' desire for work outside the scheme also involved a reluctant process of trading down as it became apparent that employers were demanding levels of work experience and/or qualifications well above what these young people could offer:

> In the end it's not easy getting a job. I didn't have much choice in the matter. My exam results weren't very good and that's what you need to get a job these days. YTS was the only thing I could do. (Julia – clerical trainee)

For these young people already at the bottom of the pile there was little further downwards to trade and, as the unsuccessful enquiries and applications grew, a training scheme became an increasingly likely option: 'at our school if you didn't get a job you would go on a YTS' (Clare – horticulture trainee). Also 'I thought it was rubbish, the pay was lousy and you still weren't sure of a job at the end but I just couldn't get a job' (Bob – engineering trainee).

Significantly, nine of the young men (21 per cent of the total) had wanted an apprenticeship on leaving school, and one which did not involve youth training. However, two had found places on an Engineering Industrial Training Board (EITB) recognized apprenticeship and technician training courses, which had been subsumed within youth training's framework (see the next chapter), and another was currently finishing a 36-week qualifying period before he too hoped to be upgraded to apprentice status. Another five of these had entered the first year of the city council's construction youth training scheme and had formed part of a larger pool of recruits from which second-year apprentices were later selected.

Youth training, even with the prospect of apprenticeship status, had not been the preferred choice for these young men and all had applied to the 'cream' of local employers still running their own apprenticeship training programmes independently of, or alongside, youth training. These young men knew that employers like the car-markers Jaguar and Rover, or the tractor firm Massey Ferguson, still paid their apprentices trade union-negotiated rates of pay, provided their workers with good working conditions and guaranteed their apprentices a job at the end of their training programmes. Nevertheless, their growing sense of disillusionment and disappointment had only been aggravated by the fact that not one of them had managed to get as far as an interview.

For these trainees, youth training had only been considered a realistic alternative because 'I got desperate' (Robert – engineering trainee). This desperation had led them to reconsider their initial hostility to the scheme and begin to explore its possibilities. Eventually they had all been offered places on schemes which at some point would pay the rate for the jobs and which offered the strong possibility of a job at the end, but their suspicions lingered on: 'I was wary at first but I knew I'd have trouble getting something any better' (Patrick – engineering trainee). Similarly:

> For me the YTS has just been a way into an apprenticeship, if I hadn't have got taken on [as an apprentice] I wouldn't have stayed for the second year. (Harinder – construction trainee carpenter)

For the others:

> I wanted a job without going on the YTS but the only way I could get a job was by going on one. I knew that if I was lucky enough I'd be taken on at the end. (Louis – construction trainee plumber)

However, this young man's 'luck' had not held out and like many of his colleagues he was to hear shortly afterwards that no apprentice plumbers were to be 'taken on' that year.

Avoiding unemployment

Many of the trainees showed considerable tenacity in trying to find work and in their attempts to confront the often insurmountable obstacles they faced. Closely related to these problems of finding work, and another powerful reason for entering a scheme, was the deep-seated desire to avoid starting their adult working lives as unemployed. For the young people here, it was this sense of dread about becoming unemployed which again influenced many of them to reconsider their initial hostility towards youth training.

Contrary to some of the more popular myths which have been sustained in relation to young people and unemployment, the trainees were uniformly hostile to the idea of signing on as unemployed. At the time these young people became trainees it was still possible for unemployed school leavers to claim social security benefits from the September after leaving school but this had been an 'option' which only five (12 per cent), four men and one woman, had taken up. For three of these their experience of registered unemployment had lasted for under two months, for a fourth four months and for a fifth almost a year. For the last of these, the bulk of this time had been spent unsuccessfully applying for real jobs and further education courses involving work with cars, and as with many other unemployed young people the strain of filling his 'spare time' (Coffield *et al.*, 1986) with little or no money had begun to show: 'It was boring being on the dole . . . You can't really do much with the money you get so there's nothing really to do' (Rajesh – MVM trainee). It was the boredom of unemployment combined with the lack of money and a feeling that 'I was going nowhere rapidly' which eventually wore down this young man's opposition.

However, shorter periods of unemployment were also experienced as a distressing and negative ordeal, and after only eight weeks' unemployment one young woman's desperation for work had led her to apply for 'loads of jobs . . . local hairdressers', beauty parlours', only to find that they all meant youth training. Even her short spell on the dole had produced a deep sense of unease: 'I was just lying around the house all day, doing nothing and getting bored in the process.' For her, life signing on the dole quickly acquired a dull routine of staying at home owing to lack of money or passing the time between her own and a friend's house. It was this that eventually persuaded her to abandon a school leaving resolution not to submit to youth training: 'At least it offered a chance to meet people and to get out and have a laugh at the same time' (Elaine – catering trainee).

However, it was not just the direct experience of unemployment that precipitated a motivation to train, as the mere threat of the dole was enough to provoke serious bouts of anxiety. In all, nine (21 per cent) other trainees explicitly stated the fear of unemployment as a reason why they had eventually opted for a training place: 'I took no notice of them [his friends] at school, anything would be better than the dole' (Derrick – MaC trainee). Similarly:

> With YTS there's some chance of getting a job or at least keeping you busy until you can find one. Unemployment is just a dead-end . . . I know you've got no guarantee of a job at the end but its more of a possibility than being on the dole. (Bhovinder – clerical trainee)

'Staying on'

The possibility of staying on at school for minimum-age school leavers had been considered and dismissed by 12 (29 per cent) of the trainees; nine women and three men. The intention had mainly been to retake failed exams or pursue vocationally related courses in search of secretarial or clerical qualifications in the hope that it would improve their future job chances. But this had been decided against because the unsavoury taste of compulsory schooling was still fresh and these young people were unwilling to surrender to 'more of the same. I hated school, the last year was piss-boring and a waste of time' (Anne – community care trainee).

A further period of full-time education was equally likely to be rejected on the grounds that it entailed prolonging a period of dependence with little or no regular income. A training allowance might have been pitifully low but the desire, or indeed the need, for a wage meant that £29.50 per week was better than nothing at all. In all eight (19 per cent) had felt that 'more of the same' was not a realistic possibility because of a further enforced period without an income: 'I hated being at school, so I thought college would be the same and I could earn more money from going to *work* [i.e. youth training]' (Wendy – clerical trainee). For another: 'School was a laugh, well some bits of it, but I wanted to get out and earn some money so I could start enjoying myself properly' (Sarah – clerical trainee). Not only did more studying mean forgoing a much-needed wage, but also the possibility of having to find relatively large sums of money for equipment for a hairdressing or beautician's course: 'Neither me or my parents could really afford it' (Elaine – catering trainee).

The pressure to do something

The last significant factor in their eventual decision to train stemmed from the pressure exerted by parents. Research has already began to highlight the stress that unemployment can place on family relationships, especially where parents themselves have not experienced unemployment directly (Jones and Wallace, 1992; Wallace, 1987b; Coffield *et al.*, 1986). In one study it was found that parents frequently 'nagged' their children into visiting the Jobcentre or insisted on the importance of maintaining the 'right' attitude towards work while unemployed (Hutson and Jenkins, 1989). In another the significance of parental pressure was acknowledged, where 'in the background was often a parent who, though superficially sympathetic, was showing at a deeper level mistrust and alarm' (Cockburn, 1987, p. 46) at the prospect of their offspring becoming unemployed.

In all, 13 (31 per cent) of the young people, six men and seven women, mentioned the importance of their parents in the eventual decision to train. Although some had initially pledged that they would 'never go on youth training', pressure from parents, e.g. 'It was mum that really kicked my arse' (Fiona – clerical trainee), lack of money and bleak immediate prospects demanded a reconsideration: 'It was my mum and dad that were really keen for me to go on YTS' (Clare – horticulture trainee). Similarly: 'My mum suggested the idea' (Samantha – clerical trainee) and 'They said at least it would be better than the dole' (Chris – PSV trainee). For one young man his parents' concerns extended to their insistence that they accompany him to his training scheme interview, 'to make sure I got a place' (Derrick – MaC trainee).

Conclusion

From an early age, working class young people are increasingly con-stituted as specific and direct forms of labour power. They grow up in working communities, they must work to survive and they themselves express a desire to work; and through child working many gain immediate and direct experience of work before they reach the minimum school leaving age. One important consequence of the centrality of work to the lives of the young is that working class young people leave school with a strong and evolving understanding of the freedoms and constraints inherent in wage labour. What is more, it is alongside this understanding of work that an appreciation of the demands of youth training emerges. Child labour may involve an essentially harsh and alienating experience but it is one which most working class young people know, and it pales into insignificance against the disciplines and rigours required by youth training.

It is precisely this knowledge, derived from a direct experience of the social relations of production, that contributes to the desire of the young working class to enter real jobs. School leavers want to work, despite the unrewarding work usually on offer, and they continue to search for those jobs which have been occupied by school leavers for generations. They have therefore not taken easily to youth training's attempts to push these types of work increasingly beyond their reach, and many continue to struggle to resist its continued desire to do so. However, working class school leavers are equally aware that even these modest aspirations are no longer being met and that being young and working class now means new and bigger obstacles to the search for real jobs.

Where real jobs are not forthcoming, working class school pupils assess the prospects of youth training through a clear evaluation of its likely benefits and constraints. One the one hand they know that it can offer limited longer-term opportunities, in a labour market more intent on excluding them from employment. They also know that it can be instrumental in getting into the labour market in the first place, provide limited access to the workplace and give them an opportunity to demonstrate to employers that they are able and competent workers. Nevertheless, they also know that there is another, less compelling, side to these instrumental considerations. They know that youth training is not the quality training opportunity they are repeatedly told it is and that youth training demands their subjection more directly to the imperatives of employers. It is in this way that working class young people's instrumentalism towards youth training also contains a rejection of its values and objectives, because they are all too well aware that these values and objectives ultimately lie in stark contradiction to their own needs and aspirations.

For some groups of working class young people these tensions are more acute than for others. For black school leavers in particular, it means having to confront the ways in which youth training has further institutionalized processes of discrimination so that they find themselves constantly channelled into poorer-quality schemes. It also means having to face the reality of employers who do not want to take on and train young black people, and it means encountering the hostility of a careers service which does not respond to their needs. Because there are fewer alternatives for these young people, many are forced to bow under the weight of these discriminatory pressures only to find themselves ghettoized in certain training schemes. Many others just refuse to participate in the scheme at all and prefer to take their chances of eventually finding work in other ways.

For all working class school leavers, the decision to enter a training scheme is not taken lightly and many continue to resist its increasingly influential pull. Trainees are as likely as any other school leaver to appreciate the freedoms and constraints a scheme will ultimately bring. Yet those who eventually enter a training scheme do so only reluctantly and after it has become clear that finding a 'real job' directly is nearly impossible. The direct pressure from mass unemployment, fruitless searches for jobs, refusals from employers, a deep-seated fear of doing nothing, pressure from the family and an intense dislike of school all proved increasingly compelling reasons for young people to enter schemes.

Working class school leavers have therefore not taken lightly to the imposition of youth training. The need and desire to work are defining aspects of growing up and leaving school. Yet all around them, school leavers increasingly face major barriers to even this basic aspiration, let alone the opportunity to begin their working lives proper in rewarding and beneficial forms of work. It is what it actually means to be in and against youth training that will be considered in more detail in the following chapter.

5 PARTICIPATING IN A SKILLS REVOLUTION OR AGAINST LOW-SKILLED WORK EXPERIENCE?

In outlining its commitment to provide quality skills training for school leavers, the New Training Initiative (NTI) reflected underlying changes within the social relations of production which increasingly sought to tie young workers more closely to the imperatives of a changing labour process. From the beginnings of the 1980s, an overt and highly politicized critique of notions of craft-based skills and apprenticeship training appeared, arguing that it was increasingly anachronistic, out of touch with the needs of industry and more concerned with restrictive practices and outmoded methods of collective bargaining than with the direct and genuine needs of the British economy (Finn, 1987). As such, it suggested traditional notions of craft skills needed to be replaced with 'competencies', as determined by the specific needs of employers and the more general demands of the future economy, and that traditional methods of time serving should be superseded by training to standards.

This theme of generalized and transferable skills was vigorously taken up by the NTI through its advocacy of a new and modern apprenticeship system in the form of youth training. Such a system of youth training would, it was argued, embody a new approach whereby the development of 'portable' skills, transferable within and between occupational boundaries, would replace the inflexibility of the old craft system (Ainley and Corney, 1990; Pollert, 1988). This flexibility needed for a modern and internationally competitive economy was therefore to be obtained through the classification of training into 11 'occupational training families', with each 'family' supposed to represent an area of the economy within which an individual trainee could acquire a general set of related skills and attitudes (Ainley, 1988). The intention was to separate young workers from the idea that skills training would tie them to specific work for life and instil in them the view that youth training was a foundation for subsequent flexibility towards different jobs and tasks (Roberts *et al.*, 1986a). Although the concept of training families subsequently lost favour, it was later replaced with TOCs which continued to organize youth training along similar generic lines (Ainley, 1988).

Youth training was therefore given radical status by its advocates, who claimed that it represented a major turning point in the history of British industry:

> We are moving rapidly towards achieving the kind of high quality permanent training provision that young people, industry and the country need and deserve. The training process has been part of an evolution, I would say revolution, in which work-based learning linked to periods of off-the-job training has proved to be popular and successful. (Bryan Nicholson, then chairperson of the MSC, *Youth Training News*, September 1986)

We have seen in some detail that the popularity of youth training has remained largely open to question. Plainly put, working class school leavers have refused to relate to youth training in ways which its planners deem desirable. Furthermore, this claim for revolutionary status also merits careful examination. Critics have argued that, far from representing a radical move, TOCs, with their focus on developing transferable skills, have essentially been concerned with preparing large numbers of working class young people for a life of low-skilled, insecure work, and for coping with periods of intermittent unemployment (Finn, 1987; Benn and Farley, 1986). Similarly, it has been argued that the emphasis on flexible attitudes has been more to do with creating an easily disposable workforce than with meeting either the training needs of workers or the real demands of employers (Pollert, 1988). They argue that, beyond the surface impressions of youth training's claim to be a modernized system of apprenticeship training, there is a scheme

> not concerned with training for real skills in the traditional or craft sense. A few traineeships involve real skill training but most centre on experience of semi- or unskilled work. (Ainley, 1988, p. 105)

It is this assessment of youth training as a low-skilled work experience programme that this chapter seeks to examine in more detail. Through the accounts of the trainees themselves, it specifically seeks to explore the extent to which youth training is dominated by the demands of semi-skilled or unskilled work, or whether it lives up to its claims to be a period of quality foundation training. Moreover, it also draws out the ways in which these forms of training constantly come into conflict with the trainees' desires for jobs. Through an examination of those experiences which define being a youth trainee, we explore how the scheme's organization constantly comes into conflict with these aspirations, further propelling the trainees in an against youth training.

Training for Skills?

To begin with, before we can assess the content of youth training it is necessary to outline in more detail what we actually mean by skill. The notion of defining skill, and what constitutes skilled work, is a highly problematic one[1] but for our purposes it is useful to follow Cockburn in unpacking an understanding of skill which focuses on both its individual and sociological content (Cockburn, 1983). For Cockburn, skill has, first, a specific dimension which relates to the abilities of individual workers. In this way, skill refers to the actual capacity of each worker to do a particular job, for example how well a worker is able to undertake tasks involving differing levels of hand–eye coordination, and how the stock of these individual abilities is added to over time as each worker adds to the totality of skills he or she possesses. Secondly, she argues that skill also relates to the imperatives of the task a worker is required to perform, whereby different tasks require different levels of ability and demand the learning of new types of specialities. And thirdly, she argues that there is a political dimension to skill, one that is defined in relation to the ability of different forms of collective labour to protect their control and influence over the immediate labour process, both in relation to attempts by capital to deskill them and through the ways in which some sections of labour are brought into conflict with other parts of the workforce. It is through such an appreciation of skill that we can now move on to a detailed consideration of youth training on a scheme-by-scheme basis.

The Further Education College

The public service vehicle scheme

The first group of schemes researched was run by a local further education college which also acted as a managing agent. The college was a large tertiary organization which at the time ran a mixture of A- and O-level provision, together with a rapidly expanding number of courses in non-advanced further education and youth training. In total the college operated five youth training schemes which offered around 105 places for first- and second-year trainees. About average for the size of a training programme, the public service vehicle (PSV) scheme provided places for around 21 young people, all of whom at the time were young men. Its publicity claimed that 'training is given in a wide range of heavy vehicle maintenance and clerical skills related to the bus and coach industry', that trainees had the opportunity to pursue Parts I and II of the City and Guilds Certificate in Motor Vehicle Craft Studies and that there were possibilities of moving towards taking a PSV driving licence. As such, applicants with O levels or CSEs were preferred, but the scheme's broad-based emphasis meant that 'any applicant keen to work in the industry will be considered'.

Owing to the specific nature of the training, the PSV scheme recruited nationally, offering work experience placements throughout the West Midlands and beyond. The trainees therefore came to the college for off-the-job training from a variety of different work experience placements, and this was reflected in both the types of work they were doing and the diversity of the areas in which their training was located. Because of this geographical dispersal, the scheme was structured so that the off-the-job training provision was organized into two 10-week blocks during the first year and one 10-week period during the second. This meant that trainees from outside the area had to find temporary lodgings during their off-the-job training, staying mainly with local families or in bed and breakfast accommodation.

During training off the job, the scheme's time was divided between the technical classrooms and workshops at the college's main site and, about three-quarters of a mile away, a garage/workshop which in a previous incarnation had been a government training centre. While at the college's main site, the trainees spent most of their time in and around the technical workshops and classrooms, where they were required to attend classes for their City and Guilds courses. The bulk of the more practical off-the-job training took place at the garage/workshop, which appeared to be relatively well equipped, with tools and engine parts littering the floor space and the work benches, and which had a couple of old coaches in various states of disrepair on which the trainees undertook different aspects of their work.

The importance of small, private sector employers in providing the bulk of work experience placements has been a distinctive feature of the development of training schemes for the unemployed (Ainley and Corney, 1990; Finn, 1987). With YOP, around two-thirds of placements had been with small private sector firms employing fewer than 10 people, and as many as 75 per cent of trainees were to be found in non-unionized workplaces. Similarly, with youth training it has been estimated that near half of all trainees are placed in workplaces with fewer than 10 employees, and nearly all of these workplaces were to be found in the private sector. As a result, training with a small, private sector employer meant that trainees received only a nominal commitment to standardized and systematic forms of training. During the mid-1980s, a Department of Employment-sponsored survey of training providers found that

> two thirds of trainees mainly spent their work experience time assisting other people to do their normal jobs or doing work similar to that of other employees in the work place. (Employment Gazette, 1985)

A similar picture emerged here, as all the PSV trainees were based with small, private sector coach firms, with the result that their training bore only a passing resemblance to training for skills. For the bulk of their training time, this meant that trainees were compelled to endure long periods of unsupervised work with only minimal instruction or direction: 'I do any work they want me to do, really . . . I'm told what to do and get on and do it. You have to pick things up as you're going along' (Keith).

> This could mean an assortment of general work all over the coach. Both mechanics and body work . . . rubbing down and filling body work and responsibility for checking the oil and water levels of the coaches after they've returned. (Terry)

It also meant tasks like 'wheel work: you know, changing tyres, fixing punctures and helping check the brakes, that sort of stuff' (Keith).

Like most of the trainees interviewed, all of these young people had been training for around a year, yet these were hardly the accounts of skilled workers in the making. One of the trainees on the scheme recounted a particularly sorry tale where his training had begun with him being given 'responsibility for checking and refuelling the coaches each evening and morning . . . cleaning them out, making sure they are OK to go out on the road'. However, after such a 'promising start', instead of the trainee progressing on to more sophisticated and demanding tasks, the situation had begun to deteriorate and by the time of the interview he had completely lost direct contact with any of the vehicles he was supposed to be training to service. Now, to his considerable resentment, 'sweeping up and making the tea' was dominating his training:

> I've complained to my boss, . . . here at the college, the MSC but they haven't taken much notice . . . They told me things will get better but they haven't . . . I've now just resigned myself to bearing the situation until either something else comes up or the boss starts to rely on me more. (Glenn)

Rather than moulding these young people into the skilled mechanics of the future, their training consisted of little more than semi-skilled and unskilled work experience routines, which made only minimal demands on their capacities and abilities, and which offered few opportunities for their individual progress and development.

The horticulture scheme

This picture of training led by the demands of low-skilled work continued with the college's horticulture scheme, which offered training to around 20 young people in a variety of agricultural settings. The trainees spent four days a week out on work experience placement, either at the scheme's garden project or with a small local employer, such as a golf course, nursery or landscape gardener. The fifth day of each week was spent at the college's main site, where trainees were encouraged to follow a City and Guilds Phase I in Horticulture or the more general City and Guilds Skills Horticulture, with the possibility of Phase II in the second year. There were no formal entry requirements for the scheme, although the publicity demanded that 'applicants must have an interest in horticulture'.

The majority of the trainees were eager to get outside work experience placements with employers, but where these were in short supply training would centre around the college's garden project. Located across the other side of the city from the college, the project consisted of a large area of land surrounded by a high perimeter fence, chiefly aimed at deterring the vandals who had recently given the project the focus of their attentions, and which contained a number of different horticultural settings. This included a large greenhouse, some plots for vegetables, a number of flower beds, lawns and two prefabricated huts. One hut was used as the project office and the staff room, and the other contained the tools and equipment, together with an area which the trainees used for their breaks.

While at the project the trainees recounted experiences of training largely directed at mainly manual jobs: 'preparation for planting, loads of weeding, digging and general plant care . . . making sure they don't get diseased or spraying for bugs and insects' (Lorraine). The specifics of these tasks depended on the seasons and the weather but during the winter, or when it rained or snowed, the trainees recalled 'long periods huddled up in the hut . . . drinking tea, smoking, chatting and having a laugh; trying to keep warm' (Adam). It was therefore difficult to ascertain any structure to their training beyond the general maintenance and plant care familiar to even the most reluctant gardener. Work with garden machinery, such as mowing lawns or trimming hedges, was kept to a minimum, and many of the tasks they described were repetitive, with little real depth or skills training content. This was not lost on some of the trainees, who felt:

down at the Project they have difficulty in finding work to keep us occupied. We're doing things just to pass the time. The supervisors end up giving you the jobs they don't want to do themselves so you end up learning nothing. (Clare)

These trainees would also describe themselves as 'lucky to be out with an employer' but once they were out on placement the limits of this good fortune quickly became apparent as they too were quickly exposed to a period of essentially low-skilled work experience. Training at

a large fruit farm . . . [meant] general gardening work really, like weeding, digging and planting out, pruning fruit trees, cutting back . . . I also assist the public to pick their own fruit and serve in the farm shop. (John)

Training at a nursery involved

> moving trays around, that sort of stuff. Planting out flowers, pricking out
> and labelling the plants . . . tending to the stock, keeping the nursery
> clean of leaves and weeds. (Lorraine)

and at a landscape gardeners it was little more than manual labouring:

> I help with digging, planting and laying lawns . . . loading the van with
> turf or trees or whatever, and helping the gaffer get on with what he's
> got to do. (Adam)

These trainees' accounts of their training revealed a pattern of simple and repetitive tasks, which required very little proficiency on the part of the trainees and which allowed few openings for future progress and development.

The community care scheme

The community care scheme was the college's largest programme, offering around 40 places each year training in work with children, the elderly and those with physical and learning disabilities. First-year trainees were required to spend four days each week out on placement and one day a week at the college, with a stipulated minimum 39 hours a week at the scheme. Again, the scheme emphasized opportunities for certification, with trainees offered the chance to pursue courses leading to a City and Guilds Caring Certificate, the British Red Cross Certificate and the Home Nursing Certificate. There were no formal entry requirements but, as with the horticulture scheme, the community care literature also recommended that 'applicants must have a general interest in caring work'. During the first year of the course, trainees were required to spend three periods, each of three months, out on placement in different areas of caring work with possibilities for specialization later. Unlike with the horticulture scheme, work experience placements were usually located in the public sector, primarily in local authority rest homes or facilities for the disabled, but there had been a recent move towards accepting placement offers from the private sector. The trainees had one day a week training off the job with the morning being spent in facilities owned by a nearby secondary school before the trainees were bussed to the college for the afternoon sessions.

The emphasis on a broad-based approach to training meant that in theory the trainees had the opportunity to experience a number of different working environments and work-related situations. In practice, however, it meant rotation through a series of work placements which brought little variety and no real challenge to extend their existing low skills training. Experiences at a rest home for the elderly, at a day nursery and at a school for children with learning difficulties were recounted as involving repetitive and mainly domestic tasks:

> It's easy to pick up, you know what you're doing after a while, then the training doesn't come into it. You keep the clients entertained, help them with their food or take them to the toilet. (Colin)

While it is crucial to point out that this was training in no more than name, it is equally important to note that it often involved hard, arduous and unpleasant tasks. It has been pointed out elsewhere that becoming a 'care girl' on youth training necessitates 'physically and emotionally stressful tasks such as coping with violence, dealing with incontinence and laying out the dead' (Bates, n.d., p. 1). It could also mean being given considerable responsibility for the welfare of others, especially at weekends or evenings when there were few other full-time members of staff to on call for assistance. However,

> Most of the time involves supervising the clients, keeping them occupied or entertained, making sure they can feed themselves properly and sometimes cleaning and bathing them . . . but once you get into the swing of things and you've learnt the ropes, the training doesn't really come into it. Off you go and do your job. (Lucy)

The similarities between the work experience placements were often remarkable. Work experience at a nursery school could involve 'playing with the children or helping them with projects like painting . . . playing with water, organizing the sand pit . . . keeping them occupied' (Colin) and being called upon in similar ways at a school for children with learning difficulties:

> We spend a lot of time just being with the kids, playing with them, helping them with their food, getting them to the toilet and back, and things like talking to them. Keeping them occupied.

At a rest home for the elderly, training meant

washing, ironing and cleaning the toilets. Spending time with the old people . . . They really did rely on you there. There was no one else to do the washing up! (Anne)

The last point in particular emphasizes the ways in which the community care trainees were primarily involved in little more than domestic labour. Much of their training involved drawing on capacities many already possessed from their own family experiences, and even when they were brought into contact with new domestic or child-caring situations these too involved routine tasks which gave little opportunity for future skills development.

The Centre

The second group of trainees were drawn from three schemes run by a local authority-funded training centre, located in an older working class area of the city and housed in a large, single-storey factory building that stood testament to Coventry's manufacturing heritage. Now showing distinct signs of wear and tear, the building had been converted for use as a training centre some years earlier when the shopfloor had been partitioned into a large number of discrete units which housed the centre's office, workshop and other training facilities. The centre provided a large number of work experience and training opportunities for different groups, ranging from work experience placements for school pupils to schemes for unemployed adult workers on the New Job Training Scheme, then in the process of becoming Employment Training. According to the centre's staff, a number of the 150 youth trainees based in the centre came with learning or behavioural difficulties and most of the youth training places on offer were designated premium places. The centre also boasted a Developmental Skills Unit, one of the few facilities in the city which catered for special needs training and provided a sheltered working environment; this was seen by the staff as epitomizing the centre's community-based training ethos of giving young people who needed it the opportunity for a staged entry into the labour market.

To a newcomer the centre had a lively feel, generated in no small part by the large number of school pupils who visited regularly as part of their work experience programmes. Because of its special needs emphasis, the centre accepted trainees on a roll-on roll-off basis and, after an initial period of six month in-house training and assessment, attempts were made to find outside work experience placements. This emphasis on gradual entry into the labour market was under threat, however, in the light of its resource implications. Cuts in local authority expenditure had recently been announced and the centre, against the better judgement of its staff, had been reluctantly forced into finding trainees outside placements as rapidly as possible. The cumulative effect of these pressures now meant that 'morale among the staff is at an all-time low and I'm afraid it's rubbing off on the kids' (the centre's director); many of the staff were contemplating their own future job prospects in increasingly bleak ways.

The catering scheme

In addition to the Developmental Skills Unit training scheme, the centre ran three other training programmes, the largest of which was the 40-place catering scheme. This scheme offered training in kitchen practices, hygiene, nutrition, menu planning, the use of the cash till and the preparation of food for restaurants, with the possibility of trainees taking a City and Guilds Food Service Assistants Certificate. The scheme's publicity stated that no formal qualifications were required but it was emphasized that 'trainees should be neat, clean and show a genuine interest in catering. A willingness to work unusual hours will also be necessary.'

The bulk of the initial training took place in and around the centre's canteen and catering service, which served up snacks and meals each day to its large number of users. The canteen area consisted of seating accommodation for about 50 people at any one time, a large service section, a well-equipped kitchen and an adjacent storeroom, but like the rest of the centre it was also beginning to show its age. The training was organized between these different sections, with trainees having the opportunity to spend time in each. Training in the canteen would therefore involve

> general kitchen work like the preparation and serving of hot and cold food, and the washing and cleaning of kitchen utensils . . . in the storeroom we can do inventory work, like ordering food and making sure we've got enough for the menus the following week. (Jane)

Trainees also had the opportunity to take responsibility for 'menu planning and taking money on the cash register, and we do things on food hygiene practices' (Sue). They also spoke eloquently about the importance of health and safety practices in the canteen and I was regularly informed that 'kitchens can be really dangerous places' (Sue).

Through no fault of its own, budgetary constraints meant that the centre was increasingly being pressurized into finding outside work experience placements for its trainees quicker than it would have liked, and the increasingly market-orientated nature of youth training was progressively coming into conflict with the centre's attempts to retain some sort of trainee-centred approach. A number of the young people on the catering scheme had already spent time with outside employers, where a similar pattern of on-the-job training driven by the demands of semi-skilled and unskilled work emerged. For example: 'seven weeks on placement at a cafe . . . [meant] cooking, counter work, serving food, a bit of food preparation and washing up' (Sue). Also: 'six weeks out on placement at a delicatessen [included] shop work really, not catering'. This meant primarily 'washing and cleaning, and serving the customers'. A second placement for this trainee at a rest home for the elderly confirmed this pattern of low-skilled and repetitive work experience:

> six weeks of washing and drying up in their kitchen . . . It got a bit much in the end. They just tended to use trainees there . . . I don't think [the Centre] is going to send us there any more. (Jane)

The motor vehicle maintenance scheme

The centre's second largest youth training programme was a motor vehicle maintenance (MVM) scheme, which ran places for 24 young people, all of whom were young men. The scheme offered trainees a period of on-the-job training primarily involving hands-on work with a range of motor vehicles and components. This included the maintenance and service of a range of motor vehicles, preparation of vehicles for MOT testing, including minor welding, mechanical and body repairs, and some component renovation. Trainees were also given an off-the-job period of training, again also based at the centre, which offered the chance to take the City and Guilds 381 Motor Vehicle Craft Studies or the City and Guilds Motor Vehicle Servicing.

The bulk of the training was located around the centre's well-equipped and relatively spacious motor vehicle workshop. Here trainees were introduced to basic vehicle maintenance and servicing before being allowed to progress on to work involving engines, gearboxes and axle components. They also had the opportunity to do repair and reassembly work on steering, braking and electrical systems, as well as spraying and welding in the renovation of body work. However, the centre's rapidly contracting resources meant that even these introductory tasks were beginning to feel the pinch and increasingly the types of on-the-job training were being determined by the availability of vehicles. As a result, the MVM instructors had taken to encouraging other members of the centre's staff to bring in their own or their family's vehicles for servicing or preparation for their MOT. The workshop did have its own small number of cars which had either been donated or bought and these were used mainly as renovation projects or, if beyond redemption, taken apart for their components and eventually sold for scrap.

Training was therefore restricted to tasks related to servicing cars and MOT work, and although this may have represented a sound introduction to motor mechanics, the limited resources meant that trainees got very little more. Training therefore consisted mainly of

> getting to know how cars work . . . doing things like changing the oil and spark plugs, checking the timing of the engine and examining the vehicle's electrical systems.

It might also mean

> a bit of body work. Checking for corrosion and wear, popping out dents, filling them, sanding them down and giving them a quick spray with the paint gun. (Rajesh)

None of the trainees had yet been on work experience placements outside the centre, although one young man had recently been for an interview at a local garage and was looking forward to starting on a placement. But in terms of individual skills development, the external constraints on the centre meant few, if any, trainees had enjoyed the opportunity to sustain the development of their personal mechanical skills.

The maintenance and construction scheme

Training for 14 young people was also available on the centre's maintenance and construction (MaC) scheme. Based around the construction workshop, the scheme comprised three programmes which emphasized different aspects of the work: access and scaffolding, painting and decorating, and carpentry and joinery. Most of the training, however, was concentrated around the painting and decorating programme, with some bricklaying, plumbing and electrical maintenance available on an *ad hoc* basis, via in-house placements that were subject to the centre's own building maintenance requirements. No formal qualifications were required from potential recruits and it was not expected that many trainees would look for qualifications from their training. However, the programmes did offer opportunities to do Skills Testing for Painting and Decorating, a purely practical component of the general range of City and Guilds construction courses.

As much of the on-the-job training was dictated by the maintenance requirements of the centre itself, this was reflected in the young people's training. Training here involved painting and decorating in and around the centre: 'I've helped erect some boards for a wall partition and recently did some work removing a window for painting and repair' (Joe). Where their training was concentrated in the construction workshop, trainees were set basic introductory tasks. One had recently taken an office door from its hinges, stripped it down, primed the exposed wood and painted it, and he had recently been involved in wallpapering one of the offices. This meant that opportunities for specialization were extremely limited, although one young man had

> spent six or seven months helping to rewire the Centre. I enjoyed it. I'm thinking about becoming an electrician or at least concentrating more in that area. (Joe)

Work experience placements for these trainees were rare, but this young man had spent a short time out on placement at a YMCA hostel, where he had assisted the caretaker with the building's general maintenance and repair requirements: 'I enjoyed it, it was nice to see somewhere else, but it's good to get back here' (Joe).

Despite the fact that they desperately needed access to quality training, and despite the centre's genuine desire to go as far as it could to provide it, for all the trainees at the centre youth training had delivered little in the way of quality skills training for jobs. What innovations the centre had made through its trainee-centred approach could not go far in alleviating the scheme's broad-based training emphasis, with the result that most of the young people who went through the schemes could boast few of the skills they had been promised. Like the trainees from the college, they too had largely been fed a diet of semi-skilled and unskilled work experience, dominated by undemanding tasks and offering few opportunities for individual initiative and progression.

The City Council

The construction scheme

The city council ran two large youth training schemes with places for about 90 young people. The smaller of the two, the 30-place construction scheme, offered young people the opportunity to train as carpenters, painters and decorators, plumbers or electricians; year one of this was spent mainly in the Apprentice Training School with day release to the local technical college for a City and Guilds Craft Studies. Like many other employers (Roberts *et al.*, 1986b), the council used the first year of the scheme as an internal pool from which it could later select suitable candidates to go on and train as full apprentices, and eventually enter the council's workforce proper. Those unsuccessful in getting on to apprenticeships were encouraged to stay on for their second year as trainees. Competition for places was therefore extremely stiff and all applicants were required to be able to measure accurately and do basic workshop calculations. A CSE in mathematics was also considered desirable.

The Apprentice Training School was located at one of the council's main engineering and maintenance depots and had been purpose built some years ago as part of its then independent apprentice training programme. The first year of this had now been fully incorporated within youth training but it meant that trainees had access to impressive facilities, which included two classrooms and several workshops. The trainees shared the canteen facilities used by the rest of the depot workforce, something they clearly appreciated: 'it gives us a chance to get out of here [the School] and meet some of the others' (Thomas – trainee carpenter). Restrictions on their movement around the depot had recently provoked a dispute about smoking inside the school. Much to the trainees' delight, during their first year each trainee also spent short periods of time with craft workers in the depot's various workshops before moving on in the second year. For those picked to continue training as apprentices this meant going in to one of the other engineering and maintenance depots, where they were allocated to a craft worker on an almost permanent basis, punctuated by spells back in the training school. For youth trainees the second year also meant being allocated to an engineering and maintenance depot, where they would spend most of their time moving between its various departments.

Three of the five young men interviewed were trainee carpenters and the other two trainee plumbers. All the trainees were currently approaching the end of their first year and, for both groups, the routine of training required day release during college term time and six-week spells 'out on site with a tradesman. Getting a feel of what it's all about'. The first year had been spent doing 'mainly routine things in the workshops . . . getting familiar with the tools, materials and the ways to do the job'. During this time, the carpenters had also been introduced to

> general carpentry . . . like learning the different types of joints and their uses, hanging doors, doing casement work, general shuttering and an introduction to plumbing. (Thomas – trainee carpenter)

Significantly, only two of the trainees had been selected to continue their second year's training as apprentices and were eagerly anticipating the increased specialization this would allow: 'It will give us the chance to do something a bit more exciting than just hanging around the workshop and spending time in class.' As apprentices they would

> spend three months at a time in different parts of the Building Services Department . . . the first year is basic stuff, you know, getting to know your way around. The second year is the real thing.
> (Harinder – trainee carpenter)

The trainee plumbers described their first year's training in similar terms:

> We do basic plumbing skills . . . we work with different materials, spend time in the workshops getting familiar with the tools and we've done some basic plumbing and ventilation work. (Jim – trainee plumber)

Their first-year training had centred around the plumbing workshop and was occupied mainly with the type of task which

> familiarizes us with the tools and materials, as well as some heating and ventilation work. A lot of the stuff's common sense really. And we spend a lot of time in the classroom. (Jim – trainee plumber).

For this intake of trainees, however, the council had decided that it did not require any apprentice plumbers so that, much to their disappointment, instead of moving into a second-year apprenticeship place, with the guarantee of a job and trade union-negotiated rates of pay, all the trainee plumbers were facing the prospect of a second year of youth training.

The clerical scheme

The clerical scheme was double the size of the construction scheme, offering places to 60 trainees, only two of whom were young men. The scheme offered work experience and training in a variety of council departments, involving the young people in reception work, typing, basic accounting, work on telephone and switchboard systems, keyboarding work, correspondence, filing and photocopying. During the first year trainees were required to attend a local college one day a week, for either BTEC National or BTEC First Certificates depending on their level of entry qualifications, and it was stressed in the scheme's publicity that applicants were required 'to have a good level of general education particularly in English Language and Maths'.

The clerical trainees' accounts were dominated by the demands of general secretarial and office work in a variety of local authority settings:

> We were just doing routine jobs like filing all the time. The first six months were a drag. The work was boring and it was sometimes difficult to motivate myself to get in on time. (Clive)

For another, a four-month placement at a comprehensive school meant:

> mainly typing, filing and answering the telephone . . . It was pretty straightforward really, after a few days you just picked things up. I learnt to type a bit while I was at school and I quite enjoy it, so they just got me to type out letters and memos and stuff. (Julia)

Interestingly, one of the young people interviewed was in the process of leaving the clerical scheme after successfully applying for a clerical job with the council proper. She too described her recent training as being preoccupied with 'mainly personnel filing, receptionist work, dealing with the public and I remember a lot of photocopying at one placement. Lots and lots of it' (Kath). Now, speaking as a council employee, she argued:

> If you're on YTS you can't do a clerk's job. YTS is more like general training . . . getting to know your way around and filling in for other people . . . It's a big relief to get a job, I can tell you. I didn't know what I was going to do after leaving here. (Kath)

The Chamber of Commerce

The clerical scheme

The chamber of commerce was one of the largest training providers in the area, offering six schemes with places for around 260 trainees. It had recently cancelled its optical grinding and beauty/reception schemes owing to lack of demand and was in the process of offering applicants for the latter course a place on its hairdressing programme. As the third largest of its courses, the clerical scheme offered training in modern office procedures, including keyboard skills, word-processing and reception work, with possibilities for day release to follow a General Clerical Course, a Certificate in Pre-Vocational Education Business Studies module, or a BTEC National Certificate in Business and Finance.

The actual content of the clerical training was broadly similar to that experienced by the city council's clerical trainees, the major difference being that all work experience placements were located with private sector employers. The scheme ran places for 50 young people, all of whom were women, with four days a week at their work experience providers. All the young people took their off-the-job training at the chamber's own 'college', where most were given the opportunity to pursue general clerical courses or modules for a CPVE.

The clerical trainees' experiences at their work placements were again dominated by low-skilled and repetitive office tasks. This included

> basic admin. stuff in the accounts department for a firm of distributors [involving] typing and filing and anything to do with office work. I've also done some receptionist work, answering the telephone and dealing with the public. (Sarah)

Another had trained in

> general secretarial skills . . . constantly on the move between different departments and doing different things . . . Where I'm working now, the morning's usually spent doing typing or word processing, and possibly some book-keeping. Most afternoons I do general office and telephone work. I've also done some typing, filing and word processing. (Niki)

The retail scheme

Although it has been recognized that youth training has been dominated by the demands of low-skilled work, it has also been argued that one of its progressive features has been its role in introducing formal training structures into previously neglected sectors of industry. To this end, it has been claimed that the garage, engineering, hotel and retail sectors have all benefited in this way, particularly the latter two sectors where 'some firms did not have formal training schemes before the introduction of YTS' (Deakin and Pratten, 1987, p. 496).

Just how successful youth training has been in imposing new and effective forms of training in more than name remains open to question, if the experiences of the trainees on the chamber's retail scheme are anything to go by. The scheme, the second biggest of the chamber's six programmes, offered places for 60 young people for training in retail, warehouse and distribution work. It too was organized with trainees spending four days each week at work experience placements, usually small, private sector retail outlets, with the fifth day spent at the chamber's own college.

Retail training for these young people meant

> [working] at a newsagent's doing . . . shop work, cleaning, working on the till, organizing the displays, that sort of stuff . . . Doing the [news]paper bills, sorting them in the morning . . . keeping the shop ticking over. (Frances)

Training with a small local chain of DIY stores included

> loading delivery vans, pricing up goods on display, helping with stock checks and working on the till. Sometimes if I'm lucky I get to go out on deliveries with one of the lads. (Tony)

A third trainee undertook his work experience with a small, local menswear shop:

> training as a sales assistant . . . it wasn't what I expected really, . . . it's a bit more difficult. I help in the shop serving, helping customers, taking deliveries, sorting the stock . . . I also have to do things like hoover, dust, tidy and polish the shop at the end of the day. My sister does stuff like that at home. (Luke)

Indeed, despite the chamber of commerce's intention to provide quality training for school leavers, the experience of most of its trainees again questioned this commitment. On the whole, their training was dominated by the demands of their employers, which necessitated the trainees undertaking low-skilled and repetitive shop- and office-based tasks. Beyond some basic skills and competencies, such as filing, typing or shelf-filling, little of what they did could genuinely be identified with the acquisition of real skills in the traditional sense. Rather, they were forced to occupy their time by undertaking work-related tasks which were rapidly learnt and which subsequently made few other demands on their abilities.

The engineering scheme

While the trainees' accounts confirm much of the critical analysis aimed at youth training more generally, little research has been directed at how youth training has influenced traditional forms of apprenticeship and craft provision. The number of available apprenticeship places suffered heavily during the early 1980s as employers became less willing to continue bearing the costs involved in the supervision of young workers, especially the consequent disruptions to production, and the waste of materials that training was seen to involve (Roberts *et al.*, 1986a). Many firms reacted by cutting back their existing apprenticeship training provision or axing it completely, so not only was youth training intended to reform the craft and skills training infrastructure, but it was also hoped it would breathe some life into what was left of it.

Despite these 'radical' intentions, however, youth training's reforming zeal appears to have had little specific impact on the form and content of apprenticeship and craft training for skills. Across all sectors of the economy, employers have largely refused to recast their apprenticeship training along the lines of youth training's generic emphasis, as broad-based training has been considered inadequate for their skills needs and wasteful of valuable resources (Roberts *et al.*, 1986a). More specifically, evidence from Coventry points to employers in the engineering industry participating in the scheme more out of notions of social responsibility and community involvement than from any real commitment to youth training as a serious attempt to train their next generation of skilled workers. Many of the city's remaining engineering employers have therefore avoided bringing their own demand for apprentices within the remit of youth training, in an acknowledgement of the scheme's ability actually to deter potential recruits (Dutton, 1987). Coupled with trade union resistance, these firms had primarily become involved with youth training as a method of supporting or maintaining their existing training provision via the youth training grant, so that, paradoxically, 'it appears that apprenticeship has influenced the content and quality of the engineering YTS rather than YTS innovating apprenticeship' (Dutton, 1987, p. viii).

The ways in which youth training could actually deter possible recruits to apprenticeships was well illustrated towards the end of the last chapter, where it became clear that even an apprenticeship fully incorporated into a youth training scheme would be considered by a prospective trainee with measured caution. This was in spite of the fact that the chamber of commerce's engineering scheme prided itself on offering training to the 'highest standards of industry', paid its trainees apprentice rates of pay and, once they were on the scheme, for the trainees meant dramatically improved prospects of subsequent employment. Although some of the young people on the engineering scheme would begin as youth trainees, by the end of the first year the majority of the 35 trainees would quickly gain full apprenticeship status and would most likely be working at small engineering firms in and around the Coventry area. These firms did not have the commitment, ability or resources to run their own programmes and, as with many other small engineering employers (Roberts *et al.*, 1986a), the chamber's scheme was allowing these firms to support existing training provision and to recover from earlier cut-backs.

The engineering scheme was based in the purpose-built Apprenticeship Training Centre of a UK subsidiary of a large multinational corporation, which had itself recently gone through wholesale corporate restructuring. The corporation still ran its own now much-reduced apprenticeship training programme, for what the trainees themselves recognized as the 'top lads' (Robert), physically separate from the chamber's own engineering scheme. It was from the training centre's relatively well-equipped and modern workshops and classrooms that the chamber's scheme offered training in mechanical engineering skills, including machining, fitting, design, fabrication and welding, and the opportunity to achieve relevant City and Guilds certification. Applicants were encouraged to have O levels or CSEs, although this was not essential, and all had to sit a selection test to ensure that they could cope with college-based work. College in practice meant either day or block release to the training centre's workshop and classroom facilities.

In contrast to the other schemes already outlined, the chamber's engineering scheme had a more clearly demonstrable commitment to skills provision, even though these young people were also required to do their share of generalized work experience during their first year. One trainee had spent his first 'three months in assessment at [his firm] before they would take me on as an apprentice'. Much of this time had involved 'doing most things on the shopfloor. I did the lot: swept up, cleaned, made the tea, went down the shop. You name it, I did it', before he was released to the training centre, where 'things definitely got better'. Two months into his nine-month block release, he was now 'learning loads of different things, like milling, grinding and turning work on the lathes. Stuff to EITB standards' (Robert).

Another apprentice spent four days a week at an engineering firm and he too talked of his training in terms of 'good skills . . . inspection work, milling and turning work on the lathes' (Patrick). Unlike any of the other trainees, this young man also talked about his training in terms of the more abstract skills he was learning. He felt that in addition to the technical requirements of the job he was training to do, his training had also begun to equip him with problem-solving capabilities and the confidence to apply this across a range of industrial contexts. For another, due to move on to apprentice status in the next few weeks, training also had meant 'good skills for life . . . machining, milling, welding and some drawing board work' (Frank). A fourth engineering trainee was training as a laser cutter, working four days a week on placement with a firm which 'specializes in precision cutting and the application of laser technology to industry'. His training had so far introduced him to

> working with state-of-the-art CNC [computer numerically controlled] lathes and the installation, servicing and application of cutting machines using laser technology across manufacturing industry . . . I go out to firms with the boss, help with machine installation, learn about its uses, sit in on training sessions, do all sorts of different things. (Bob)

The experiences of the trainees clearly illustrate that youth training rarely involves equipping the young working class with training for skills in any sustained and recognizable ways. The move towards a system of training 'competencies' has been embedded in the demands of semi-skilled and unskilled work, and together with a broad-based emphasis, has provided the rationale for new forms of training which reinforce these low standards. For the majority of the young working class, the tasks performed on youth training call for little dexterity or individual initiative, and opportunities to accumulate and develop any real skills throughout the course of their training are few and far between. Instead, youth training is dominated by the experience of mundane, repetitive and unrewarding tasks which require little real ability, can be quickly learnt and which generally debase more precise understandings of what training and skills have traditionally meant. Indeed, much of the everyday training undertaken by the vast majority of trainees reflects poorly on Blackburn and Mann's somewhat earlier assessment of the skill content of semi-skilled and unskilled work: 'using technical notions of "skill" . . . almost all workers use less skill at work than they do, for example, in driving a car' (Blackburn and Mann, 1979, p. 12). When looked at in this context, it is therefore unsurprising that an emphasis on generic skills and worker flexibility has reinforced training driven by low-skilled work experience, rather than providing an enriching and developmental skills training process for school leavers.

This point is further underlined by the experiences of the engineering trainees. Although they too spoke of the generalized and repetitive nature of their work experience during the first year, the engineering training had retained much of its craft skills emphasis and as such they were enjoying the benefit of training to a much higher standard, both in terms of the capacity to develop new capabilities related to the work they were doing and through the ways in which the tasks they were set to do made new demands upon them. Employers' concerns over maintaining the ability to recruit suitably qualified young people and trade union resistance to the introduction of youth training into apprenticeships (Dutton, 1987) have ensured the persistence of greater job-specific training to recognized standards. It is in the context of the latter that Cockburn's (1983) political dimension to skill is most clearly visible, since it is through organized labour's resistance to processes of de-skilling that the historical links between craft skills and training have survived the onslaught of the training state.

Training for Him and Training for Her

The form of training institutionalized through youth training has another dimension that needs to be explored more fully: its gender dynamic. The classification of work as skilled 'has much more to do with the sex of the person who does it than the real demands of the work' (Cockburn,

1983, pp. 116–17), whereby gender assumes a central importance in determining the value of the skills perceived to be involved in different types of work. Men tend to dominate work categorized as skilled, but even where men and women are found to be doing similar jobs men retain a higher status (Coyle, 1982). Similarly, where a feminization of a particular occupation or profession occurs, a concomitant de-skilling effect takes place. Moreover, as Rees (1992) points out, where women have been admitted to professions from which they were previously excluded, new patterns of gender segregation have arisen between specialisms.

The rise of state training programmes has further served to direct young women into specific occupational areas, reinforcing and reproducing stereotypes of gender-appropriate work (Stafford, 1991). From containing an explicit commitment to extending young women's access to quality training in all areas of the economy, 'in the process of realizing the Youth Training Scheme the Manpower Services Commission dropped the commitment to positive action for women' (Cockburn, 1987, p. 73). From its beginning it was recognized that young women training in areas of non-traditional work were 'VERY difficult to find' (Fawcett Society, 1985, p. 6, original emphasis) and that they were more generally confined to narrow areas of training.

> These places tend to be in large employer-based schemes, the traditional employers of low-paid, unorganized female work forces, where "high street" distribution and other non-union work places predominate.
> (Marsh, 1986, pp. 161–2)

Cockburn's (1987) extensive study of how and why working class young women 'choose' youth training placements in traditionally 'feminine' jobs reveals the extent to which a distinct sexual division of labour exists throughout the scheme. She too found that youth training was 'highly sex-segregated' (Cockburn, 1987, p. 8) and that young women were concentrated into a small number of training categories, mainly in areas such as caring, clerical, personal services and sales work. Only in the area of food preparation and service work were there anything approaching equal numbers of young women and men. Furthermore, gender segregation occurred within schemes and placements so that in office and clerical work placements, male trainees were much more likely to occupy general administrative posts whereas young women tended to be involved in typing and general clerical work.

Since Cockburn's study, other research has also illustrated the ways in which such forms of discrimination have become embedded in the social relations of youth training. Bates (n.d.) and Hollands (1990) have sought to uncover the ways in which youth training acts to reproduce gender-appropriate forms of training and work, and more extensive research has also concluded that

> overall, MSC's lack of power to influence the pattern of schemes in the surrogate labour market and to radically change employers' behaviour in hiring young people could be seen most clearly in the persistence of gender stereotyping in placements. (Lee *et al.*, 1990, p. 71)

Here too, rigid gender divisions characterized the provision of youth training with the young men and women clearly segregated into 'masculine' and 'feminine' areas. Across the schemes, all the catering trainees were young women and only a small number of trainees on the city council's clerical scheme were young men. Interestingly, the one young man interviewed on this scheme liked to refer to himself as 'future management material' (Clive – clerical trainee) and had already worked as a temporary replacement in the community charge division, covering for a permanent worker who had suddenly left. In contrast, the young women clerical trainees tended to train in more general clerical and secretarial areas. Similarly, all the chamber's clerical trainees were young women and all but a very small number of the retail and community care trainees were also young women. For the former, only eight of their 60 trainees were young men, and for the latter only two out of 40 trainees were men. Only four of the 20 horticulture trainees were young women and only two of the 20 community care trainees were young men. In contrast, the engineering, construction, MaC, MVM and PSV trainees were all young men.

A slow but noticeable trend for women to enter areas of work previously barred to them has occurred in recent years but a high price is exacted in doing so and the few who succeed are still very much 'pioneers' (Cockburn, 1985). Young women stepping outside traditional occupational areas have to confront long-established barriers defining men's work and women's work, and the forms of submission and domination on which they rest. At one level these power relations manifest themselves through ranking jobs according to gender, and for young women moving into traditionally male areas of work this means a move upwards while carrying the ascriptive baggage of lower female status (Rees, 1992;

Cockburn, 1987). To survive, young women have both to confront directly and overcome the exclusionary mechanisms previously encountered, and simultaneously to perform as well as if not better than those males already entrenched in the same types of job.

The cost of failing to do so can be high and the sacrifice involved is illustrated at another level which presents many young women with an additional daunting contradiction. Some young women tend to anticipate a conventional move into work and family life on leaving school, and developing sexual relationships is crucial in this domestic/waged labour process (Lees, 1986; Griffen, 1985). Work can offer the opportunity to meet prospective partners but a move into traditionally non-female areas of work risks undermining ideas of femininity during a crucial stage of life. As Cockburn (1987) points out (see also Stafford, 1991), for young women working or training in non-traditional areas the penalties may mean having to endure being labelled as a maverick, a tomboy or a 'lezzie', rather than having the desire to experience new forms of work, or wanting to resist the pressures of conformity, recognized and supported.

For young men too, stepping outside conventional areas of work and training can also generate considerable social sanctions through the perception that they are taking an occupational step downwards. Such a move is often deemed 'irrational' and therefore explained in terms of their inability to cope, or their failure to succeed in 'masculine' occupations, or, where caring work is involved, it can become an indictment of their sexuality. This was clearly appreciated by the two young men who were training on the community care scheme. For one:

> a lot of people aren't too sure about men doing it [caring work]. Society doesn't bring up lads to do this sort of work. It makes it much more difficult if you want to succeed. (Neil)

Similarly, for another:

> when it was known that I was coming on the scheme, people at school thought I was a poof or something . . . I want to work with children, I like children, I get on well with them . . . I was lucky, both my parents agreed it would be a really good thing to do . . . but people still give you funny looks when you tell them what you're doing. (Colin)

Interestingly, such pressures had clearly influenced these young men and although both were determined to succeed in working with young children, both had also recently opted for further education courses for Nursery Nurse Education Board (NNEB) certificates: 'It'll give me the credibility I need to succeed' (Neil).

The Flexible Worker

One of the key concerns of youth training was to promote the idea of labour flexibility as both a means to enhance skill transferability and as way to get young people back into employment. A key aim of youth training was therefore the promotion of the 'ownership' of transferable rather than occupationally specific skills among young people, so that they would be able to move freely between employers throughout their working lives. The idea of 'occupational training families' itself was in large part motivated by the intention of creating a mobile workforce suited to movement around an open labour market, despite the widespread unpopularity of these aims among employers, who wanted their young workers to fit in with their own organizational structures and job-specific tasks.

However, we have seen that in reality this emphasis on broad-based training has been largely driven by the demands of semi-skilled and unskilled work. Furthermore, the preoccupation with flexibility during the past decade has been driven more by the state's desire to undermine the power of organized labour and by the need to manage spectacularly high levels of unemployment (Pollert, 1990). So, did the young people here see themselves as flexible workers with flexible attitudes towards both their work and their training?

If by adaptable workers is meant trainees willing and able to see themselves as capable of moving between different jobs, then they clearly saw themselves as a flexible labour force. Forty of the 42 trainees (95 per cent) thought that their training would be useful in another job, while the two others were unsure; the range of jobs they saw themselves as capable of doing reflected youth training's emphasis on flexibility between semi-skilled and unskilled work.

The chamber of commerce's clerical trainees felt confident that their training 'would be useful for other sorts of general office work' (Sarah), or 'answering the telephone, word processing, dealing with the public. The sort of things you do in most secretarial or receptionist jobs' (Samantha). The council's clerical trainees agreed: 'I think I could do any job doing general clerical duties . . . typing, filing, receptionist work' (Wendy). Only one young woman thought beyond the immediate confines of work with the council: 'possibly working in banking or finance work as a cashier' (Fiona).

Both the MVM and the PSV trainees thought their training appropriate to other types of mechanical work or to jobs related to working with vehicles. All four PSV trainees felt that they would be able to work in coach firms other than the one they were currently doing their work experience with, or they more generally saw themselves working as car mechanics, with heavy goods vehicles or buses. The two MVM trainees were equally sure that they could secure a variety of jobs related to work with cars, even though neither had yet been out on work experience placements.

The horticulture trainees again saw their flexibility in terms of semi-skilled and unskilled work related to the existing content of their training: 'I could work in a florist's or greengrocer's' (Clare). Indeed, there were obvious doubts about whether their training had equipped them to step outside these types of work: 'I could work in a florist's but I'm not sure about anything else' (Lorraine). For the community care trainees it was 'other forms of caring work' (Lucy) that they saw themselves as capable of doing although, as already mentioned, the two young men on the scheme were already thinking of specializing in nursery nursing. All four of the catering trainees thought their training would be useful 'in other types of catering work; canteen work or working in a food shop' (Elaine), or 'I think I could work in a café because I've done serving and working on the till at the Centre' (Carol). Another was slightly more adventurous: 'It might [i.e. her training] come in useful if I got a job in a bakery because I've done things like food preparation and cooking' (Jane).

The MaC trainees felt that their training would be useful for 'building work maybe . . . [but] at the moment I'm not too sure how useful it'll be' (Derrick). The council's construction trainees also felt they might be able to utilize what they had learnt 'in jobs like carpentry, plumbing or general building work. Beyond that there isn't much else I'll be able to do' (Jim – trainee plumber). The engineering trainees were also confident that the skills they were developing would be useful in a range of jobs: 'engineering or drawing-board work . . . Quite a number I would imagine' (Frank). Similarly, 'across the whole area of engineering work' (Patrick), or, for another: 'I've done some computer programming and there isn't going to be a shortage of computer programmers in the future' (Bob).

This latter contrast between the skill-specific training of the minority and the training in general work-related tasks of the majority, highlights what is in effect an attempt to impose a system of training on the young working class which effectively prepares them as a pool of adaptable, semi-skilled and unskilled workers. We have seen that the trainees have not taken lightly to this but in their desire for real jobs beyond youth training many are clearly prepared to embrace a more permanent move into low-skilled work. The trainees clearly felt that their training would be useful in other jobs and to that extent they constitute an adaptable source of workers for the future. Nonetheless, any closer examination of the types of work they felt their training had prepared them for served to reinforce the notion of youth training schemes as preparation for semi-skilled and unskilled work.

Antagonisms between 'Theory' and 'Practice'

An important dimension to youth training which is sometimes ignored by research is the significance of the off-the-job training element. The ability of the MSC to get the scheme up and running so quickly was in large part secured by the inclusion of a period of structured off-the-job training, which had been a central feature of the TUC's long-standing demand for a period of integrated work experience and training for all employed school leavers (Ainley and Corney, 1990; Ainley, 1988; Finn, 1987). Youth training was therefore to go beyond the YOP's piecemeal off-the-job provision by giving young people a period of structured instruction and tuition which would address literacy and numeracy problems, involve work with computers and other forms of work-related technology, allow discussions about work and personal effectiveness and, increasingly, orient trainees towards achieving a recognized vocational qualification.

Employers have remained deeply pessimistic about the merits of off-the-job provision and have proved continually reluctant to allow trainees their full rights to participate. With YOP it was reported that only one-third of participants were being given their full off-the-job entitlement (Finn, 1987) and youth training has faired only slightly better. Detailed research in contrasting local labour markets found that:

> some employers disagreed with enforced, irrelevant schooling that disrupted the working week. They rated off-the-job training as another imposition on industry . . . Some turned a blind eye to absenteeism.

They did not believe that the trainees would be taught anything useful, or that the firms would benefit. (Roberts *et al.*, 1986a, p. 58)

More importantly for our purposes, trainees too have steadfastly resisted the imposition of periods of day and block release to college, with less than a quarter of YOP trainees entitled to off-the-job training regularly attending (Finn, 1987). Youth trainees too have remained deeply reluctant to embrace their entitlement to periods of off-the-job training where its immediate relevance to their work experience placements has not been directly apparent (Lee *et al.*, 1990).

As we saw in Chapter 2, absenteeism from the off-the-job provision was extensive at the schemes researched and the importance of this was appreciated by a number of the training tutors. At the chamber of commerce's own college, the training supervisor acknowledged that 'the trainees hate their schemes. Particularly this bit at College'. This was explained as 'the product of poor experiences of school and their preoccupation with work [*sic*] and money'. She also felt that the trainee's aspirations were frustrated by the college's lack of facilities and by the fact that the trainees felt there was no direct relationship between what they were taught and what they did out on placement.

This turned out to be an accurate and astute assessment of both the chamber's clerical and retail trainees' feelings about their off-the-job training. Both sets of trainees intensely disliked the fact that they had to learn book-keeping, as it was considered to have little direct relevance to the types of tasks they were required to carry out on placement. This was recognized by the appropriate tutor, who deliberately taught book-keeping 'in the morning when there's a better chance of it sinking in. During the afternoon sessions it's often difficult to hold their attention.' The unpopularity of the off-the-job training was further underlined by the high rates of absenteeism, despite the chamber's move away from subcontracting out its off-the-job provision to running most of it in-house.

The ways in which the off-the-job training was consistently portrayed as an obstacle to their primary concern of securing a 'real job' continually surfaced throughout the research. It was this division between the off-the-job training and the work experience, between 'theory and practice' (John – horticulture trainee), that at some stage was mentioned by every single trainee. At one level, the experience of going to college served to reproduce some of their earlier feelings about schooling, something which they had already explicitly rejected in favour of work. These young people therefore spoke with contempt about how they were treated as

> school kids . . . doing ridiculous things . . . I don't do a lot here, it's painfully boring . . . Sometimes it's just a waste of time and we end up doing stupid things. Things which kids do at nursery school. (Luke – retail trainee)

That very morning Luke had been required to produce colour pie charts as a mock exercise in the presentation and analysis of sales figures. He had considered this 'a stupid exercise' because it bore no obvious relation to the demands of his work experience in a menswear shop, and because it merely evoked comparisons with picture colouring at school, rather than training for 'real jobs'.

For the community care trainees also, the work they had done on 'health studies, physical growth and the ageing process was similar to what we did at school' (Colin). It too bore little resemblance to what they were required to do at their placements and they felt it was more like 'school work . . . [which] was pretty easy to do on the whole' (Lucy). Others also made comparisons between their compulsory education and off-the-job training:

> They treated us like kids, it's like being back at school. From the very first day of the induction week they treated us like school kids. Sat us there and lectured us. (Julia – clerical trainee)

For another:

> During the last year at school we spend a lot of time filling in, doing nothing in particular. Just passing the time and now as a trainee I'm doing exactly the same sort of thing . . . This morning we were doing work on computers, doing typing and word processing. But tell me, when do you use computers looking after little old ladies? . . . I just think college is shit. (Anne – clerical trainee)

These comments stood in stark contrast to the importance they attached to their work placements, and time at college was recalled with little enthusiasm: 'college is just a waste of time' (Frances – retail trainee). As a consequence Frances had recently given up on her City and Guilds studies because 'I just can't be bothered with it any more.' Just like Frances, another trainee 'prefer[red] to be at work. It's more enjoyable, the staff are better fun and at least you can have a laugh' (Tony – retail trainee). It was being on placement that was important and time spent in a training centre or college was boring. More importantly, it had little relevance to the demands of working out on placement:

> The college bit isn't very good . . . we are shown one thing in here and then we go out on site with a tradesman where we are shown something different . . . It's confusing, sometimes you're not sure which way to turn. (Thomas – construction trainee carpenter)

Others echoed this divide between what the trainees saw as theory and practice, where college was experienced as unresponsive to, and possibly at odds with, their needs, in contrast to the job, which they considered to be really important:

> It gets on your nerves after a while, just sitting and listening and writing . . . What we learn in college you don't really need on site. You learn to do it one way and then when you get on site you end up doing it a different way. (Louis – construction trainee carpenter)

It was out 'on site' through working that the importance of youth training rested, where you had to know the job and where any training really counted: 'You don't really need it once you get on site. I don't really see much point to it' (Jim – construction trainee plumber)

Lack of Provision

The form of the off-the-job training clearly came into conflict with what many of the trainees saw as their primary objective of getting a 'real job', and this feeling that their aspirations were continually being frustrated in this way was often compounded by the poor quality of the off-the-job facilities the trainees felt they had to endure. Some of the trainees were more concerned with their facilities than others but, in some way or other, most of the trainees expressed the belief that their needs were not being met by the provision of the off-the-job training.

On the chamber of commerce's retail and clerical schemes, for example, the trainees were unanimous in condemning their facilities and were especially critical of the chamber's move from subcontracting its off-the-job training from a local further education college to providing its own training in-house. The switch to in-house provision meant that those young people following BTEC courses still had to attend the further education college, with the remainder of the trainees attending the chamber's own college one day a week.

The college's rationale for this move had been a mixture of measures, from cost-cutting and efficiency, to a concern with policing more directly the trainees' attendance. The college had therefore been housed in the top floor of an old converted workshop, the ground floor of which was still used by a small engineering company. The noise from downstairs would occasionally vibrate through the four or five rooms in which the teaching took place and, although the classrooms were new and relatively well equipped, apart from complaints that the keys kept falling off the typewriters, the confines of the college gave it a crowded, almost claustrophobic feel. The trainees had no direct recreational area of their own and during breaks tended to just sit around the classes and stairwells, or hang around the front entrance to the building. These problems were compounded by the closure of the tuck shop some weeks earlier when large amounts of stock had gone missing. Because the college was situated in an older working class area of the city, there was very little to compensate for this lack of amenities other than a 20-minute walk into the city centre. If a trainee did not bring their own lunch, it meant a walk into the city to a chip shop or settling for the limited selection from a local corner shop.

The community care trainees were also unanimous in their criticism of their off-the-job facilities. These young people were required to do their off-the-job training based in the annexe of a nearby comprehensive school, which again fuelled the belief that they were getting a second-rate deal. Their persistent complaints about the annexe's facilities had recently resulted in their being bussed to the college's main site for each afternoon session, with morning sessions staying at the school. The annexe had not been purpose built for teaching, its main function being to house a youth club and community centre run by the school during the evenings, so that there were no proper classrooms and only limited support facilities for the teaching staff. None of its facilities for food or drink were available during the day, although the coffee bar did open for a short period during the morning, and there were no local amenities to compensate for this lack of provision. Before their move to the college, not bringing their own lunch again meant a long walk to a local store or chip shop.

The community care trainees felt strongly about being 'hidden away in a corner of the college where nobody can see us . . . sometimes they probably forget we even exist' (Colin). Being located at the school's annexe had compounded the feeling that they were not considered as students or trainees proper. Furthermore, this feeling of being housed in second-rate facilities also acted as a barrier to their developing aspirations as young workers: 'The school environment is disgusting. We're supposed to be training, not be back at school' (Colin). This was reinforced by the fact that at the school annexe, they were segregated from the pupils, their movements in and around the buildings were highly restricted and accounts were given of incidents with pupils where they had been subject to verbal and physical intimidation. While spending time at the annexe, the school's pupils regularly came up and taunted the trainees through the windows: 'They call us thickies, morons, that sort of stuff' (Lucy).

Training for Qualifications: 'I Won't Be Around Long Enough'

The young people's training was dominated by the demands of semi-skilled and unskilled work, bearing little relation to high-quality training for skills. For most, it was not the promise of training that gave youth training its legitimacy, but its role in providing them with an opportunity of getting into the workplace and possibly finding a 'real job'. Furthermore, these demands for work also generated deep-seated antagonisms between the work experience and off-the-job provision elements of their schemes. It was the former that was crucial, giving the trainees a foot in the door, access to employers and the chance of a job, with the latter relegated, at best, to an inconvenience, and at worst, a major obstacle to this aspiration.

A major aspect of attempts to revitalize youth training has rested on a further promise to working class school leavers that training would get them qualifications and thus jobs. In 1985 a White Paper, *Education and Training for Young People* (Department of Employment, 1985), reviewed developments in education and training provision, emphasizing that the skills and qualifications of the UK's workforce lagged far behind those of most of its competitors. It argued that vocational training to increase the supply of better-qualified young people was crucial for a modern and internationally competitive economy, and therefore proposed the extension of the one-year YTS by a further year. As a consequence of the two-year scheme, all unemployed school leavers were given a 'guarantee' (Department of Employment, 1988b) that they would have a place on a training scheme by the Christmas after leaving.

Enshrined in the two-year scheme was a greater commitment to quality which was encapsulated in the provision of broad-based foundation training to give 'all trainees the opportunity to obtain a vocational qualification related to competence in the work place, or to obtain a credit towards such a qualification' (Manpower Services Commission, 1985, p. 2). Although youth training did not have its own standard, national form of certification, beyond the much derided Youth Training Certificate, each trainee was to receive a training plan which would outline the 'competence objectives' they would be expected to achieve. The training plan sought to tie trainees to the idea of achieving a recognized vocational qualification or a credit towards one, by the time they were due to leave. From a previous concern with the content of training schemes, the emphasis was increasingly shifted to the level of outcomes.

This development was taken a stage further and, in May 1990, the YTS finally ceased to exist when it was replaced by the innovatively named Youth Training (YT), hailed as the next phase in the reinvigoration of the British training system. Falling numbers of school leavers and a relatively buoyant economy had provoked fears that, as more semi-skilled and unskilled work became available, young workers would be attracted away from youth training by higher wages and the prospect of a 'real job'. As a result, youth training's original commitment to a structured period of foundation training was further watered down in the name of increased flexibility and responsiveness to a rapidly changing labour market (Ball, 1989a). Schemes no longer had to run for two years and the mandatory commitment to providing a minimum 20 weeks of off-the-job training was also scrapped. Further emphasis was given to training-related outcomes, as managing agents were to be funded according to performance levels related to the number of young people leaving schemes with a recognized vocational qualification or credit towards one. In an effort to encourage more employers to come within its training remit, it was hoped that an increasingly market-led youth training programme would consolidate the 'training revolution' already set in motion.

Linking quality to accreditation and certification, however, has not generated the response among trainees that was hoped for. The state's own figures show that between April 1988 and March 1990 only 42 per cent of youth training leavers gained a qualification (Training Agency, 1990). The figures for Coventry show a similar, if slightly more encouraging, pattern with just over 48 per cent leaving their schemes after gaining a qualification. However, the most recent information to emerge from the post-TEC leavers survey has found a substantial decline in the number of trainees securing a vocational qualification or a credit towards one before leaving their schemes. From April 1991 to December 1991, only 35 per cent of trainees nationally left after gaining a recognized vocational qualification or a credit, with young women (37 per cent) slightly more likely to gain a qualification than young men (34 per cent). The poor deal offered to black trainees was further illustrated by the fact that only 27 per cent of young people from ethnic minorities did likewise (Unemployment Unit/Youthaid, 1993a). Over the same period, the Coventry TEC fared only slightly better, with 39 per cent of leavers gaining a recognized vocational qualification or a credit towards one.

The fact that only just over four in 10 Coventry trainees were leaving their schemes with a recognized qualification or credit was reflected by the trainees, who generally looked on the prospect of further certification with little enthusiasm, measured indifference and even outright hostility. In all, 11 (26 per cent) of the trainees indicated that they were not the slightest bit interested in obtaining a qualification or credit towards one. For some, their associations with school remained a powerful disincentive, as the decision to leave had often explicitly been linked to the desire to escape the routines of formal study and exams. For example, the motivation of one young woman doing a BTEC First Certificate in Distribution had vanished early in her scheme and she was now totally indifferent to the idea of a qualification: 'I haven't done anything for my course work for a couple of months now. I can't really be bothered' (Frances – retail trainee). Another retail trainee also commented, 'this is just a waste of time. I'd rather be out at work' (Tony). Significantly, another six (14 per cent) indicated that they did not even know whether they were following a course for a qualification but commented, anyway, 'I don't think I'd bother even if I had the chance' (Sue – catering trainee).

These attitudes did not necessarily spring from a distaste for qualifications *per se*. Importantly, a number of the trainees did not see themselves as staying on their schemes long enough to have the opportunity to get a qualification and, between April 1988 and March 1990, just over 75 per cent of those who completed their training gained a qualification or a credit. This figure fell to only 29.3 per cent among those who left early

(Training Agency, 1990). The ways in which youth training tends to compound existing inequalities were further illustrated by the fact that those entering training already in possession of a qualification were considerably more likely to leave with another one, 56.4 per cent, compared to the 24.8 per cent who received their first qualification through the scheme. Similarly, for Coventry over the same period, just over 67 per cent of those who completed their training secured an additional qualification, falling to just over 26 per cent for those who left early. Around half of those who entered youth training with a qualification gained a further one, but for those who entered with no qualifications at all just over one in five managed to leave with one.

Most of the trainees who did not see themselves as staying on their schemes long enough to get a qualification generally were the more reluctant participants and for them youth training was no more than a temporary stop-gap between school and a 'real job'. They felt they would not actually be training long enough to merit the time and effort they would have to put in to get a qualification: 'I won't be around long enough to get one!' (Anne – community care trainee, her emphasis). Simply stated, these trainees were just not concerned: 'I'm not interested really, and anyway I don't plan to be on the scheme long enough to get another one' (Clare – horticulture trainee). Similarly, when the two trainee plumbers had heard that they would not be taken on as second-year apprentices, the rationale for qualifications had been totally removed:

> If I was staying then I might think about it but there's no point to trying for one now, I'm looking to get out of here . . . I've just applied for a job on the bins [refuse collecting] and I'm waiting to hear right now.
> (Richard – construction trainee plumber)

The remaining 25 (60 per cent) were either following a course leading to a credit or a qualification, or had already taken one. Some appeared genuinely enthusiastic: 'if I can get it [BTEC] then it should stand me well if I don't get taken on here' (Clive – clerical trainee) or 'if I don't get me [apprentice] papers then it'll be just a waste of time' (Frank – engineering trainee). Yet others remained unconvinced about the merits of qualifications, whether because 'It's just part of the training . . . You've got to do it' (Adam – horticulture trainee), or 'It might help in getting a job at the end but if one comes up before then, that's it. I won't bother any more' (Julia – clerical trainee). Sixteen of the trainees therefore reported that they were following various City and Guilds courses or collecting units towards one, and one had already unsuccessfully taken a City and Guilds Phase I for General Kitchen Assistants, failing the 'theoretical bit' (Jane – catering trainee). The others were mainly pursuing typing qualifications and four had taken the BTEC First Certificate in Business Studies and Finance. One of these had already failed: 'I wasn't very good at college . . . I'm not really interested in all that' (Fiona – clerical trainee). She was now concentrating on a typing and word-processing course but was unsure whether it involved leading to a qualification or not.

Conclusion

Behind the appearance of youth training as a revolutionary phase in the restructuring of Britain's training infrastructure lies a more complex reality. Attempts to reform and modernize training provision through the scheme have been driven by a focus on equipping working class school leavers with a set of generic skills, transferable across specific sectors of the economy. Moving away from the idea that training would tie a worker to specific tasks for life, the intention has been to provide a new flexibility in the workforce which would both facilitate young people's movement between different jobs and enable them to undertake a range of different tasks throughout their working lives.

In reality, however, such a form obscures a content defined primarily by the demands of semi-skilled and unskilled work experience. Across the majority of schemes, the emphasis on giving young people generic skills gave rise to training dominated by on-the-job training with employers, exercising little of a trainee's existing capabilities and giving them scant opportunity to develop new work-related strengths and abilities. On the whole, training on a scheme involves repetitive and unrewarding tasks directed by the existing demands of each employer's organizational structure and immediate labour process, without any real commitment to provide quality skills training. As a result, most trainees find that they are set to work doing similar tasks to other employees and that this involves essentially mundane and repetitive tasks, which are quickly and easily picked up. Only in the area of previously existing apprenticeship provision does there appear to be any real and sustained commitment to provide working class school leavers with quality foundation skills for life.

It is significant that apprenticeships remain an important source of skills training for school leavers. Apprenticeship and craft technician training has suffered heavily in the restructuring of work and employment but where it has survived this has often been in spite of youth training's 'modernizing' intentions. Many employers have been reluctant to bring their apprenticeship programmes within the remit of the scheme, knowing that it will deter many potential recruits, but even where the youth training grant has been used to maintain or expand previous provision, this has been at the expense of the scheme's emphasis on general skills. Paradoxically, existing apprenticeship training in the engineering industry, for example, has influenced the pattern of skills training available through youth training, rather than the reverse, and trainees continue to benefit from skills training to recognized standards.

This fact has not gone unacknowledged by large numbers of trainees themselves. In their own accounts, most young people have difficulty talking in anything but the most generalized ways about the content of their on-the-job training because it includes such little skill-specific content. Consequently, they tend to provide accounts which contain no recognizable commitment to direct and tangible skills and which paint a picture of themselves being used as just another pair of hands, rather than young workers enjoying a period of quality foundation training. Youth training for school leavers has therefore actually debased notions of skills training, as working class young people have reacted to periods on the scheme as an imposed form of work experience bringing few new challenges and making only cursory training-related demands on their abilities. Furthermore, instead of producing multi-skilled or polyvalent workers, youth training's emphasis on flexibility has been used by school leavers in the more general hunt for work. Youth trainees have shown a willingness to take their training into different areas of work related to their schemes, so to that extent the scheme has been successful. However, closer examination illustrates that the 'real jobs' the trainees see themselves doing repeat youth training's preoccupation with semi-skilled and unskilled forms of work.

Training on the scheme also entails being exposed to a form of training which attempts to impose a strict sexual division of labour on school leavers. Youth training has largely served to reproduce young women's marginalization from access to skills training, through further segregating them into narrow areas of training characterized by even lower-skilled work. Where they do train in the same general areas, young women also still suffer being directed into generalized areas of work and training, in contrast to young men's greater access to occupationally specific forms of work and training with all their concomitant career-related benefits. Those young women who risk entering 'non-traditional' areas pay a high price for doing so through having their aspirations for 'real jobs' stigmatized as 'irrational' or 'abnormal', rather than having their desires to try new and different forms of work recognized and supported. Young men moving into what are considered 'non-masculine' forms of work also have to endure strong pressures to conform.

Not only has the off-the-job training failed to live up to its promise of quality foundation training for life, but the scheme's commitment to provide young people with a period of off-the-job training has also brought with it new tensions and contradictions. Many employers have resented losing their trainees for one day a week and have seen it as irrelevant to the demands of their existing work practices and organizational structures. Moreover, many trainees remain, at best, unconvinced of the merits of off-the-job training and, at worst, display considerable hostility. In particular, the form of the off-the-job training means that many trainees fail to see any direct relevance between the tasks they are required to do at their work placements and those they have to suffer at college. This does not necessarily mean that young people reject the idea of off-the-job training in general, but that most experience a clear division between youth training's theory and practice elements. What they learn at college is considered to be of little direct relevance to the demands of work and, more importantly, to the longer-term aspirations for real jobs. Similarly, its continuities with schooling and adolescence constitute a powerful barrier against taking the offer seriously through working towards a recognized vocational qualification. Indeed, with respect to the latter, significant numbers of young people remain deeply ambivalent towards youth training's offer of qualifications or further accreditation.

Note

1. For a more detailed review of the arguments surrounding skills, see Thompson (1989), especially Chapter 4.

6 YOUTH TRAINING FOR JOBS

Although presented as a revolutionary solution to Britain's long-term inability to stem the relative decline of its skills base, youth training has manifestly failed in its promise to provide working class school leavers with access to quality skills training. Beyond the rhetoric of training for skills, the scheme has attempted to put in place a form of post-16 training provision driven largely by the imperatives of low-skilled and mundane types of work, and one concerned more about creating a mobile and easily disposable workforce than meeting the real training needs of working class school leavers. More importantly, youth training's primary concern with imposing this form of discipline on the young working class has generated a new set of antagonisms and oppositions. Because working class young people's experiences of the scheme are likely to be characterized by long periods of low-skilled, repetitive and intrinsically unrewarding work experience, new confrontations in and against the scheme's explicit commitment to provide quality foundation training for jobs have thus been established.

More precisely, it is the experience of youth training as a contradictory and unresponsive form of social life which increasingly proves a direct obstacle to working class young people's primary objectives of securing 'real jobs' on leaving school. It is the driving need to find work which forces school leavers to face up to a fundamental contradiction at the heart of the youth training movement: the plain and simple fact that youth training has never primarily been about training school leavers for jobs. A new generation of working class school leavers have therefore repeatedly been forced to come to terms the hard way with the fact that youth training has evolved as the state's main response to the social and political problems arising from mass unemployment. This has meant that many trainees have found themselves on training schemes which are neither geared to the demands of securing future employment, nor primarily concerned with establishing the conditions from which they can pursue a successful and fully rounded working life.

The result has been that youth training's promise of quality training for jobs increasingly rings hollow for large numbers of trainees. The intention of this chapter, therefore, is to assess the ways in which this fundamental contradiction manifests itself, through exploring the extent to which youth training has actually provided a successful stepping stone into work. It will also examine the ways in which trainees assess the benefits of their training and how this relates to its usefulness as preparation for future working life. The chapter also examines how trainees perceive their subsequent ability to find work after youth training, before finally considering the significance of training for jobs in the context of the large-scale and sustained tendency of trainees to leave their schemes early.

Training for Whose Benefit?

We saw in the last chapter that youth training largely consists of a diet of semi-skilled and unskilled work experience, involving mainly repetitive and unrewarding jobs. Yet when asked how beneficial they thought this was, the trainees here tended to assess their schemes in terms of a ready mix of latent enthusiasm for the possibilities they held for getting into work, and a cooler assessment of the extent to which their schemes could actually help to achieve this. Indeed, there was a fairly general belief among the trainees that their training was benefiting them in some general way, with only one trainee displaying outright hostility: 'It's useless, slave labour . . . for the benefit of the MSC not me.' However, when pushed for a little more detail, even he was willing to concede that his work experience placement at a do-it-yourself store was enjoyable and had been generally worth undertaking: 'It's taught me how to get on at work, meet people and talk to customers' (Tony – retail trainee).

Like this young man, all the other trainees discussed the general benefits of their training in ways which more or less expressed an awareness of its usefulness and limitations. To a greater or lesser extent, each trainee agreed that their training had been of some general benefit but this was always qualified by an examination of some of its more obvious limitations. For a group of four (10 per cent) trainees this amounted to going as far as conceding that their training had provided them with 'some, but not a lot [of benefit] . . . it gets you into work and gives you a chance of working but not a lot more' (Sarah – clerical trainee). However, even this grudging recognition had to be seen in terms of other more pressing limitations and constraints: 'It's been of some benefit but not much when you sit down and add it all up . . . long hours, low money and boring work.' This largely negated any deeper enthusiasm, where only the stigma of unemployment – 'I'm not a lazy person' – convinced them that it was 'better than the dole, just about' (Frances – retail trainee). Similarly:

> It gets me outside into the fresh air and gives me something to do . . . I knew nothing about horticulture but needed the money. If I was actually interested in horticulture then it might benefit me more . . . but it's pretty useless really. (Clare – horticulture trainee)

Another 14 (33 per cent) trainees also recognized these same tensions, again contextualizing their more explicit enthusiasm for the benefits of work experience-based training with an appreciation of its limits in terms of the quality of training, the work and the money they were being paid. In contrast to the first group of trainees, these young people were more generous in their assessments of their training's usefulness, speaking of it as an opportunity to try out new tasks, to experience different work contexts and to get direct access to employers. Nevertheless, almost in the same breath, they too would point out that these benefits needed to be judged in the context of the often mundane and repetitive nature of the tasks that they were required to perform and the overall lack of depth to the content of their skills training. Their schemes were therefore

> benefiting me quite a lot . . . [but] it takes time to learn and sometimes people haven't the time to tell you . . . They just tell you what to do and let you get on and do it. I don't think things will change but you've got to make the best of it. You have to learn as you're going along. There's nothing else you can do, really. (Neil – community care trainee)

Others in this group also discussed the benefits of their training in similar ways: 'quite a lot, although most of it's common sense'. This was understandable given that this young woman's training had been dominated by little more than simple domestic chores:

> Sometimes you get all the shitty jobs, the jobs that nobody else wants to do. Once they [the permanent workers] know you are a trainee you get all the worst jobs. The hardest and the dirtiest ones. (Anne – community care trainee)

Similarly:

> It's benefiting me quite a bit, but it's easy to pick up. I feel trained, I know what to do . . . After a short while you know what you are doing but you do get experience of working and you need experience to get a job these days. (Colin – community care trainee)

This struggle to negotiate youth training's contradictory demands and opportunities was not restricted to the community care trainees. Others too commented that their training 'was enjoyable and I think it was benefiting me quite a bit to begin with', as the possibility of getting into the workplace and working with others had clearly been appreciated. Yet this young woman continued by outlining how the first month's novelty had now worn off and she too was forced to lament that 'it's all right sometimes . . . It's just become a bit repetitive' (Samantha – clerical trainee). Interestingly, even two of the engineering trainees, who had previously spoken at length about the skills content of their training, assessed the benefits of their training in terms which again located these advantages in relation to other, equally pressing constraints:

> They don't always give you the support and training you need . . .
> there's not enough training and the instructors won't respond to you.
> Sometimes they treat us rotten . . . I've tried complaining to my
> boss [at his placement] but he just told me to get on with it.
> (Bob – engineering trainee)

For the remaining 23 (55 per cent), youth training had much more tangible benefits but these again were closely linked to an awareness of their training's limitations. Significantly, for a number of these trainees the benefits of their schemes were linked to their assessment of the schemes' ability to lead them directly into 'real jobs' or apprenticeships. One young woman, who had recently secured full-time work with the city council, was willing to concede that her training had

> initially involved boring and repetitive jobs . . . [but] the placements were interesting and I learnt a lot from them. They prepared me well for going into full-time work. (Kath – clerical trainee)

Similarly, the two trainees who were just about to begin their second year as apprentices at the city council also felt their

> training has been good, the instructors are helpful and I've been lucky enough to get some high quality training. I've learnt a lot since I've been here and there's a good standard of instruction. (Thomas – construction trainee carpenter)

Three of the four horticulture trainees also assessed the general benefits of their schemes in relation to similar instrumental considerations. Again: 'The first six months were just general stuff and we didn't seem to be getting anywhere' (Adam – horticulture trainee). Since then, he had 'learnt a fair bit' and was 'confident of being kept on at the end' (Adam – horticulture trainee). Similarly, another trainee felt that the benefits of their training had been

> a lot . . . It's been a good opportunity to get some work experience . . . at least on the YTS you get good experience which is better than being on the dole. (John – horticulture trainee)

The majority of the centre's trainees also felt that the benefits of their training had been considerable, and these young people had clearly appreciated the centre's trainee-centred approach and the opportunity of a gradual entry into work. These trainees had liked the centre's relatively good working conditions and the friendly and informal relations with the staff: 'They treat you like adults . . . it's not like being at school' (Mick – MVM trainee). They also appreciated the intimate environment that the centre sought to cultivate:

> The staff here are good. They've got time for you and they are willing to explain things. I'm confident to do the stuff on my own without anybody watching over me, telling me what to do . . . that's what I like about this place. (Joe – MaC trainee)

One young catering trainee who had been at the centre for ten months summed up much of the general feeling:

> It's benefiting me a lot, I'm getting better all the time. I like the friendly
> atmosphere in the workshop; the staff call you by your first name and
> the people here treat you like adults and I like that. You learn useful skills
> . . . A lot of people talk about YTS as being no better than the dole but
> at least on the YTS you're getting experience. That's why I came on
> YTS, to get experience. (Elaine – catering trainee)

All the trainees, in some way or another, clearly appreciated that their training opened up real and discernible benefits. This included its ability to get them into the workplace and put them in touch with employers, while giving them some interesting things to do. However, alongside this appreciation of its benefits lay an awareness that youth training could only go so far and that beyond its claims to offer quality training for jobs lay the reality of repetitive work, little skills content and tasks that were easily and quickly learnt.

Moreover, despite the different institutional training contexts in which they found themselves and the clearly gendered nature of training, many of the young people shared similar training experiences. This is not to argue that each trainee experienced and assessed their schemes in identical or uniform ways. But what the preceding discussion points out, as does much of what follows in this chapter, is that many of the assessments by individuals or groups of trainees, in more or less varying degrees of intensity, corresponded to the experiences and reactions of others. What constituted an opportunity for one trainee was therefore likely to be perceived in similar ways by other trainees across the entire range of schemes and, conversely, a problem for one was likely to be felt as a problem for all. It was in these ways that the collective basis to these trainees' lives became clear, through their constitution in and against the training state.

In Search of Real Jobs

The common basis to youth training and the collective ways in which the trainees assessed its benefits and constraints were also clearly evident from their evaluations of how useful they felt their training was in preparing them for subsequent working life. Considering that most had been subjected to generalized forms of work experience, it was unsurprising that they talked in only the most generalized ways about any benefits and that, directly related to the specific demands of possible future work, they were deeply uncertain about how useful what they had been doing would be. Here the generalized nature of youth training proved to be both its greatest asset for the trainees and, at the same time, its greatest weakness. Only 14 (34 per cent) expressed with any commitment the belief that their scheme had been 'a lot of use, I think . . . it's given me good training and experience' (Joe – MaC trainee). Like the benefits, this usefulness was largely assessed in relation to its ability to provide 'general training, experience and knowledge of work that employers are looking for . . . all-round training' (Lucy – community care trainee). For these young people, their training's usefulness was evaluated not so much in the ways in which they had acquired distinct and readily identifiable skills but, more importantly, in its ability, whether potential or real, to open up a range of opportunities related to their general chances of work and employment. As one trainee commented: 'It gets you into work, gets you in the right frame of mind . . . it gives you a range of skills which you can then take to an employer' (Joe – MaC trainee).

For another group of 10 (24 per cent) trainees, youth training's perceived use in preparing them for work was even more elusive. This group of trainees felt that its relevance had been 'quite a bit I suppose' (Wendy – clerical trainee) but, when pushed to elaborate, many also reverted to generalized considerations of the scheme's ability to open up opportunities for 'the training and experience it gives you . . . YTS will contribute quite a bit because at least I'll have some qualifications and experience' (Wendy – clerical trainee). Yet in contrast to the first group, these young people were also considerably more likely to recognize that experience or qualifications would not necessarily lead them into jobs and that, ultimately, they would have to face competition from many other school leavers also competing for the same limited vacancies:

> It gives you experience of working that employers want . . . because you need experience before you can get jobs now . . . [but] there are lots of kids who've been on YTS so maybe it won't help that much at the end of the day. (Derrick – MaC trainee)

Similarly: 'quite a bit . . . but I suppose there's lots of other kids coming off YTS and they'll all have experience too' (Colin – community care trainee).

A further group of nine (22 per cent) were even less sure of their scheme's usefulness as a preparation for work. They too appreciated the 'training and experience you get from training . . . but when it comes to getting a job I don't really know. A bit useful, I suppose' (Tony – retail trainee). Like the others they hoped that the training and experience would eventually improve their chances of work but were inclined to assess their 'job chances [as] about fifty-fifty . . . it'll definitely give me more of a chance than if I hadn't been on YTS' (Lorraine – horticulture trainee). Others, too, recognized that

> the training might not be brilliant but I'll have more chance [of a job] than if I'd have gone on the dole . . . At least on YTS you're working with other people and that gives you a head start. (Elaine – catering trainee)

A final group of eight (20 per cent) trainees expressed similar sentiments but they were considerably more likely to emphasize that the very generality of the training was also its biggest weakness: 'I don't know. I suppose the training will give me an advantage over somebody who hasn't got any . . . but that's really it, isn't it?' (Sarah – clerical trainee). This group of trainees was also more likely to stress the realization that their training had not really been about preparing them specifically for jobs and that its motivation lay primarily in other directions. Its usefulness had therefore been 'practically nothing at all', where

> youth training is about giving employers cheap labour for a couple of years, so there's no reason for them to take you on. Its not about giving kids jobs . . . its not really helping that much. I meet new people and that may lead to a job . . . but I mean I meet people outside of YTS all the time. (Frances – retail trainee).

Similarly:

> Employers need to show more commitment to their trainees . . . if your placement were made to pay more for your training, to contribute or make some form of investment in you, then I think they would have more incentive to keep you on . . . At the moment, its just the government paying for it so there's a good chance that you'll be taken on and then shoved off at the end of two years. (Glenn – PSV trainee)

The trainees here all more or less agreed that their training had some use as preparation for work but these opportunities were heavily circumscribed by a realization of its limitations as a preparation for jobs. These uncertainties identified by the trainees were further underlined by data from the *Two Year YTS 100 Per Cent Follow-Up Survey*. Three months after leaving their schemes, all trainees are asked to assess how useful they feel their scheme has been, both in general terms and as preparation for any jobs they may have secured. The results for both Britain as a whole and Coventry are contained in Table 6.1 and they demonstrate the same contradictory, if slightly more optimistic, assessment.

In both Britain and Coventry, around 80 per cent of trainees indicated that their scheme had been very or fairly useful/helpful, with the remaining one in five considering it of little or no use at all. However, when trainees were asked to rate their scheme's usefulness/helpfulness since leaving, the numbers indicating it as useful drop to around two-thirds, with the other one in three indicating that their schemes had not been of much help. Interestingly, among even those trainees who had made

Table 6.1 *Responses by Youth Training Leavers in Britain and Coventry, between April 1988 and March 1990, to Questions about Their Scheme's Usefulness/Helpfulness, as a Percentage*

	Very useful	Fairly useful	Not very useful	Not at all
Britain				
The scheme as a whole	37	43	13	8
Since leaving youth training	25	43	17	18
As preparation for current job*	39	29	12	20
Coventry				
The scheme as a whole	40	42	13	6
Since leaving youth training	26	41	17	17
As preparation for current job*	40	29	11	19

*Number in job who answered

Source: Training Agency (1990)

the successful movement into work after leaving their schemes, one in three employed trainees were still rating their training as not particularly useful preparation for the current job they were doing. Clearly, even large numbers who have used youth training as a successful springboard into work are still reluctant to endorse the benefits of their scheme as a useful period of foundation training.

The Chances of a Job

These reservations about the scheme's usefulness as preparation for work have a sound foundation because the extent to which youth training actually makes a school leaver more employable remains open to question. Data from the government's own Youth Cohort Study paint a distressing picture, with the study's finding that youth training had virtually no impact on young people's employment chances and that they 'were just as likely to be unemployed as those who had not been on the scheme' (*Times Educational Supplement*, 27 January 1989). Another study also using data from the Youth Cohort Study was only slightly more encouraging, concluding:

> that the employment probabilities of those undertaking YTS were substantially higher than those of persons who experience unemployment but who chose not to participate and were slightly higher than those of all school-leavers who chose not to participate. (Whitfield and Bourlakis, 1989, p. 10)

More recently, large-scale survey research has also raised questions about the effectiveness of youth training in leading young people into jobs. It was found that not only was youth training one of a whole host of factors influencing the likelihood that a school leaver would get work but that 'the best way to ensure oneself a job at age 18 is to obtain one at age 16 if possible' (Roberts and Parsell, n.d., p. 9). Trainees were therefore more likely to be unemployed than young people who had made an uninterrupted movement into work and, where a trainee had succeeded in finding a job after leaving, they also had to endure work of consistently inferior quality.

The trainees, however, remained generally optimistic about their job chances after leaving, although this upbeat assessment was again mixed with considerable caution. Despite the short-lived relative upturn in employment prospects for school leavers at the time of the research, only four (10 per cent) of the young people here were willing to rate their employment chances as 'very good'. Even here, however, they were likely to express some clear reservations and, like many of the other trainees, their assessments of their job chances were closely tied in to the hope of being 'taken on' by work experience providers: 'If they don't take me on then I know that I'll get a good reference from them' (Samantha – clerical trainee). A young man in this group also felt that he would

> get taken on by the Council. They've given me an apprenticeship so I'm hoping it'll be in their interest . . . if I don't get taken on then [my chances will be] quite low. (Louis – construction trainee)

Another 18 (44 per cent) trainees were still quite optimistic, if more cautious than the first group, summing up their job prospects as 'a pretty good chance' (Chris – PSV trainee) or 'a pretty good chance in my trade' (Glenn – PSV trainee). For them youth training had succeeded in improving their job prospects, through its role in getting them access to the workplace and employers, but they were under no illusions that it would mean an easy passage into work: 'better than when I started . . . YTS does help you find work but it's not going to be easy, nobody would say you're going to walk straight into a job' (Wendy – clerical trainee). The importance of work experience providers as sources of future employment was once again evident, even if sometimes a little premature: 'I think I'll get taken on by the boss, although it's too early to tell at the moment . . . I've only been here three weeks' (Adam – horticulture trainee).

Despite the importance attached to work experience providers, many of the trainees retained considerable reservations about their job chances, with a further seven (17 per cent) entertaining more serious doubts. These young people felt that their job chances were still in the balance – 'it could go either way' (Bob – engineering trainee) – and that the line between employment and unemployment for leavers was thin. 'In the middle at the moment' was how they tended to describe their chances of finding work, but 'you just don't know. If I'm lucky I'll get something I want, if not, then who knows?' (Richard – construction trainee plumber). Even so these trainees were still willing to concede that youth training had helped even up the odds, which had been heavily stacked against them on leaving school: 'My job chances are about fifty-fifty at the moment, but they're better with the YTS than without' (Rajesh – MVM trainee).

Another six (15 per cent) were not so optimistic and although they were holding out for the possibility of work, they generally felt their chances were

> not very good. Probably better than when I left school but still not very good . . . whatever happens I'll make sure I don't go on the dole. I'll start a little business rather than go on the dole. (Tony – retail trainee).

Indeed, trainees consistently comforted themselves with the belief that youth training was a better option than the dole, a reasonable assessment given the available evidence discussed earlier:

> I'm not really that optimistic . . . if I don't get a job at a placement then my job chances won't be very good, then maybe I'll have a hard time . . . [but] I'll have a better chance than somebody who's been on the dole. (Jane – catering trainee)

One young man could not even bring himself to be this generous, and felt that being a trainee also meant bearing a stigma which he would carry for some time to come:

> Everyone says you've a better chance of finding work when you leave YTS than if you had not been on one in the first place. I don't think so . . . You're seen as not as good as the other person if you've been on a YTS and they haven't. In a way it's work experience, but that's all it is. (Joe – MaC trainee)

Finally, there was a group of six (15 per cent) who confessed that they were deeply uncertain about what their chances of a job were on leaving. They too placed a great deal of faith in their work experience placements but recognized that in reality they represented an easily disposed of source of labour: 'they could quite easily kick me off at the end of my training course and then get another trainee to do my job' (Helen – retail trainee). This did not mean that they had given up hope, but they recognized that finding a job had become something of a lottery: 'Getting jobs is all about knowing people and some people are lucky that way . . . I'm not' (Carol – catering trainee). Another had also resorted to 'keeping my fingers crossed . . . I think things are beginning to pick up in Coventry again . . . I only hope it turns out good for me' (Mick – MVM trainee).

Youth Training for Jobs

The trainees here were clearly uncertain about youth training's ability to lead to jobs. The bottom line was that they remained committed to the belief that youth training had made them more employable than they would have been if they had remained unemployed, but many were still haunted by deep uncertainties and reservations. Yet at first sight these reactions are surprising, because if we take the public claims for youth training at face value, we would encounter a formidable picture of its successes in leading school leavers into jobs. After its first full year of operation, ministers were already quick to extol the scheme's virtues as a route into work, claiming that over 70 per cent of leavers were either going into jobs or embarking on further programmes of training. By the time the two-year scheme was up and running and the first trainees had gone through, official pronouncements were even more celebratory, claiming that '74 per cent of young people leaving youth training go into jobs, or take up further education or training' (Department of Employment, 1988, p. 6.9). Whether this was due to the scheme's real ability to make school leavers more employable, or whether the temporary upturn in the economy combined with falling numbers of school leavers gave a small number of young people a short-lived relative advantage in the labour market, never seriously entered the wider debate. Nevertheless, going into the 1992 general election the government was still in complimentary mood, claiming that '82 per cent [of leavers] go into jobs or further education when they complete YT' (Conservative Party, 1992).

Most of these official claims have been based on the government's own data from the *Two Year YTS 100 Per Cent Follow Up Survey*, where every trainee receives a follow-up questionnaire three months after leaving his or her scheme (a fuller discussion of this survey can be found in Chapter 2). As with many other official sources of data, successive Conservative governments have consistently chosen to use the information from the Survey in an *ad hoc* and selective manner, so that obtaining an accurate picture of the real trends in leavers successfully finding work has been difficult. However, any sustained examination of the Survey quickly reveals that the scheme's successes in leading trainees into work has been more partial and complex than described in official pronouncements, and that youth training has remained severely limited in its ability to help working class school leavers into work.

Independent estimates have always been less sanguine about the scheme's successes in setting up school leavers for subsequent employment. In contrast to the state's initial claims that over 70 per cent of young people were going into jobs after youth training, other estimates suggested that a figure of 55 to 60 per cent was closer to the mark. It was also claimed that specific groups of young people, for example ethnic minority school leavers and the disabled young, were losing out particularly badly (Finn, 1987), and certainly any fuller inspection of the survey would confirm that ministers and others have been economical with the truth. Taken from the last comprehensive set of figures to emerge, Table 6.2 reveals that between April 1988 and March 1990 only 66.5 per cent of trainees in Britain as a whole were leaving for work, whether as employees, self-employed or part-time workers. Table 6.2 also reveals that the comparable employment rates for leavers in Coventry were slightly better at 70.8 per cent. What is not contained in Table 6.2 but what the survey also shows is that

Table 6.2 *Destinations of Youth Training Leavers for Britain and Coventry between April 1988 and March 1990*

	Britain	**Coventry**
Total leavers	745 748	12 116
Early leavers	492 589	7 589
% Early leavers	66.0	62.6
In work		
Same employer	33.1	35.3
Different employer	28.5	30.3
Self-employed	1.5	1.3
Part-time	3.4	3.8
Total	**66.5**	**70.8**
Not in work		
Unemployed	13.9	11.1
Another YTS	11.3	9.7
On a full-time course	3.8	4.3
Doing something	3.6	3.3
Total	**32.6**	**28.4**

Source: Training Agency (1990)

national employment rates for young men and women were approximately equal but that the employment figures for both Afro-Caribbean and Asian young people leaving youth training were around 48 per cent, with only four in 10 disabled leavers finding work (Training Agency, 1990).

It is also interesting that this last full set of figures from the survey corresponds with the ending of the late 1980s 'boom', during which time there was a steady increase in the general number of young people finding work. Since then, however, the situation has once again deteriorated but this has largely been ignored and, more worryingly, obscured by changes in the collection and presentation of official data, pointed out in Chapter 2. Although it may be overly cynical to suggest that the failure to provide comprehensive data has had something to do with the rapid decline in the fortunes of many trainees leaving the scheme, it is indisputable that leavers have been forced to confront the scheme's rapidly deteriorating ability to set them up for subsequent employment. The situation is well illustrated by the fact that between April 1990 and March 1991, only 57 per cent of leavers found work compared to 67 per cent in the previous year (British Youth Council, 1992). Data from the post-TEC survey which have recently begun to emerge also point towards a serious decline in the number of trainees leaving their schemes to enter work. The latest results provide figures for the period between April 1991 and December 1991 (well before current unemployment levels peaked in January 1993), and show that only 50 per cent of leavers were finding employment both nationally and in the area covered by the Coventry and Warwickshire TEC (Unemployment Unit/Youthaid, 1993a). What is more, only 30 per cent of leavers from ethnic minorities were finding jobs over the same period, a figure only slightly bettered by the 31 per cent of disabled leavers who could claim to be in work three months after leaving their schemes.

Youth training has therefore clearly failed to make the significant inroads into levels of mass unemployment among school leavers which its advocates have claimed it would do (and has done). With as little as one in two trainees nationally finding work during recent years, unemployment remains a distinct probability on leaving school. Table 6.1 also illustrates that even during a period of relative prosperity, 14 per cent of trainees nationally were becoming unemployed after leaving their schemes and over one in 10 were finding their way onto the dole queues in Coventry. Furthermore, these general unemployment rates hide the fact that, both nationally and locally, black leavers were almost twice as likely to end up unemployed than white leavers, and that for disabled young people the figure was almost two and a half times greater (Training Agency, 1990). However, youth training has not even been able to maintain this sorry state of affairs, and the most recent post-TEC figures show that over 23 per cent of all trainees nationally and more than one in five in Coventry are leaving their schemes only to sign on as unemployed. The contrast with an official national unemployment rate of around 9 per cent for the population as a whole (Unemployment Unit/Youthaid, 1992b) shows that the trainees' uncertainties regarding the ability of youth training to set them up for working life continue to be well-founded.

Youth Training and Early Leavers

What is clear from the above is that trainees remain deeply concerned about the ability of youth training to provide a springboard for future employment success. Many regard the benefits of their training in more general and ambiguous ways and have difficulty in assessing any real or direct impact it has had on preparing them for subsequent work. The trainees do, however, remain firmly convinced that youth training has offered them a better start to working life than unemployment could have done and it is from this basis, together with the importance they attach to work experience providers, that they assess the likelihood of their training leading directly into work. Far from being totally convinced about the merits of youth training for a job, however, most trainees remain keenly aware of the limitations inherent in the organization of the scheme.

What is more, the recognition of those limitations also lies at the heart of understanding the scheme's inability to retain trainees for the full dura-tion of their programmes. Since its inception, the vast majority of trainees have shown the value they attach to their schemes by voting with their feet. A review of the scheme's first three years showed that early leavers accounted for about half of all entrants and that for the 12-month pro-gramme average time spent training per entrant amounted to about 40 weeks. Overall, one-third of all trainees left before six months' training had been completed (Gray and King, 1986).

Despite the optimism that surrounded the extension of the scheme to two years, and the consequent legislative moves which later introduced its effective compulsion, working class young people have persistently refused to embrace youth training and have continued to resist its disciplines by leaving in large numbers before completing their programmes. A 1988 study into early leavers reported that the average length of stay for trainees on the two-year scheme was just a little over 16 months and for those on the one-year scheme it remained at around 10 months (Maclagan, 1988). This massive vote of no confidence has also consistently been illustrated by the figures from the *Two Year YTS 100 Per Cent Follow-Up Survey*, which reveal that between April 1988 and March 1990 around two-thirds of trainees nationally left their schemes early (Table 6.2). Again, Coventry loosely mirrored the national picture, with around 63 per cent of trainees leaving their schemes early over the same period. However, even these levels of mass defection represented a small improvement on the scheme's previous performance where, for example, the 1986 to 1988 figures show national early leaving rates of 74 per cent (Training Agency, 1989a).

As comparable data are no longer available, it is difficult to gauge more recent trends but it would not be unreasonable to suggest that the recent surge in unemployment levels, together with the scheme's effective compulsion, have left most working class school leavers with even less room for manoeuvre. The data that have emerged largely confirm this picture, and the post-TEC survey points towards a drop in the number of early leavers, despite the continuation of large-scale defections. Between April 1991 and December 1991, the latest available figures, around 48 per cent of all young people nationally were still absconding early, with Coventry and Warwickshire TEC reporting a slightly higher rate of 53 per cent (Unemployment Unit/Youthaid, 1993a). While the figures show little difference between early leaving rates for young men and women, black trainees have proved even less willing to tolerate the specific forms of discrimination they have been subjected to. In the 12 months up until January 1990, 71 per cent of Afro-Caribbean trainees in the Coventry area left their schemes early, compared with 69 per cent among trainees of Asian descent and 67 per cent among white trainees (*Hansard*, 10 January 1990, col. 672). Since then, figures from the post-TEC survey show that nationally 59 per cent of people from ethnic minorities left early compared to 48 per cent across all ethnic groups (Unemployment Unit/Youthaid, 1993a).

It is through these figures that the large-scale discontent and disruption which has persisted in and against youth training's development manifests itself, as trainees have sought to escape its new impositions by leaving early in large numbers. This is again clearly illustrated by the data from the follow-up survey, which reveal the extent to which discontent and

Table 6.3 *Youth Training Early Leavers – Reasons for Leaving Early for Great Britain and Coventry between April 1988 and March 1990, as a Percentage***

	Britain	**Coventry**
Full-time job	52	53
Another youth training scheme	6	7
Illness	4	3
Not getting training needed	14	14
Unhappy with way scheme run	14	19
Not getting advice/help	7	5
Learned enough to get job	3	2
Not enough money	20	22
Dismissed	5	5
Other reason	20	19
Not answered	3	3

*Early leavers' replies were 236 855 for Britain and 3692 for Coventry. Respondents could give more than one reason.

Source: Training Agency (1990)

dissatisfaction remain a major motivation in the decision of early leavers to depart. As Table 6.3 shows, in the two years up until March 1990 nearly half of all reasons for leaving early reflected this large-scale dissatisfaction with the scheme. For Britain as a whole, of the 236 855 leavers who left their schemes early, around 14 per cent left because they were not getting the training they felt they needed, another 16 per cent expressed discontent with the way their schemes were run, around 7 per cent felt they were not getting the help they needed and 21 per cent were dissatisfied with the amount of money they were receiving. When these figures are put against the experiences of training detailed in the previous chapter and the earlier trainee assessments of their schemes' general benefits, it should come as no surprise that substantial numbers of trainees continue to oppose this low-skills regime and the bitter forms of discipline it entails.

Completing Their Training

Table 6.3 also demonstrates that by far the largest single reason for early leaving is the movement of trainees into 'full-time jobs' outside youth training. This corresponds to the continuing significance of 'real jobs' for working class school leavers discussed throughout this book, so at one level this should not be unexpected. After all, this is what young people see as their primary objective on leaving school and, for trainees, this is the purpose of their training. However, the scheme was first and foremost supposed to be a training scheme, and research among early leavers has shown that many trainees become or remain deeply disillusioned with their schemes, seeing the possibility of a job as the most effective route of escape (Maclagan, 1988). This is in stark contrast to the scheme's stated intention of providing school leavers with a period of quality foundation training, and points towards young people's predominant use of the scheme as a period of temporary refuge. Moreover, government-commissioned research has clearly shown that to leave the scheme early for work usually means the type of 'blind alley' work that youth training was supposed to usurp, as just over half of all employed 16- and 17-year-olds in Britain receive no formal training whatsoever (*Times Educational Supplement*, 27 January 1989).

Even where trainees have only completed their first year's training, the signs of a readiness, even an eagerness, to leave are already clearly evident. Only 17 (41 per cent) expressed with any sincerity the belief that they would stay for the full two years, although this represented a higher proportion than were likely to do so (see Table 6.2 for the number of trainees staying for the full duration of their schemes in Britain and Coventry). Interestingly, their motivations for staying lay primarily in the direct instrumentality of their training schemes, as these young people were either young men who were apprentices, or looking to secure apprentice status in the near future, or those trainees who had already had some indication that they could be taken on. For the apprentices: 'an apprenticeship leads to a job . . . why should I leave when I've got a good chance of a job at the end?' (Harinder – construction trainee carpenter). Similarly: 'It would be silly to stop what I'm doing because it'd mean the waste of a year's training . . . I should have a job when I finish here' (Patrick – engineering trainee).

Others also expressed the intention to remain on their schemes because to leave would have jeopardized the hard work they had already put in, trying to carve out some opportunities for work: 'It was getting a job in the first place that got me on to the scheme . . . I should get taken on when I've finished, so why should I leave now?' (Terry – PSV trainee). A small number also felt that to leave early would undermine the wider investment they had already made through their training schemes:

> What's the point of doing something if you're not going to see it through? . . . It's a waste of time leaving your scheme before you've finished, you lose out since you never learn anything properly.
> (John – horticulture trainee)

Overall, however, references to the short-term investment, the human capital that ministers are so fond of alluding to, were remarkably absent, and wider ideas about empowering themselves through the scheme were generally absent. For these young people the decision to stay for the full length of their schemes was a simple and rational choice: 'I should get a job here [the council] so I'll stay . . . If I don't then I'll probably leave' (Bhovinder – clerical trainee).

This is not to argue that the remainder of the trainees had made up their minds to leave the scheme and were merely biding their time, although this was the case for some. To do so would drastically underestimate the complex ways in which trainees confront the opportunities and constraints endemic in the youth training form. Nonetheless, the remaining 25 young people did, in more or less spirited ways, express the view that their status as trainees consistently came into conflict with their wider objectives of securing real jobs and that if an opening appeared, whether through the scheme or outside, they would not hesitate to leave before their training's scheduled conclusion.

Seven (17 per cent), however, did feel that they would 'definitely' leave their training schemes early, a much smaller number than in Coventry as a whole (see Table 6.2). This included a group who had already made up their mind to leave and had gone some way to doing something concrete about it. One young man had already been accepted for a Nursery Nursing Education Board (NNEB) course at a local college and another was applying for the same course. The failure to get a second year's apprenticeship with the city council had totally destroyed any credibility youth training may have initially possessed for two other trainees, one of whom felt

> there's no point in staying on any more . . . you're expected to do the
> same work as the others [apprentices], you get next-to-nothing money
> . . . and next year it's all writing and I don't fancy that.

He had already started looking for work outside of the scheme but, like those of many of the others, his efforts had continually come up against the solid wall of mass unemployment: 'It's all YTS now, there ain't nothing else open to you . . . they don't tell you that in the ads because it puts kids off' (Jim – construction trainee plumber).

After these young people had been on their schemes for nearly a year, youth training had achieved little or nothing in convincing them to stick their training out to the end. Moreover, participation on the scheme had paradoxically reinforced their convictions of the need for a 'real job' and it was this knowledge that fuelled their belief and determination to leave soon. For two of these, the desire for work at times almost verged on desperation, as it became increasingly evident to them that youth training was a dead end and that time was rapidly running out: 'I've got to find a job. If I don't get one with the Post Office then I'll carry on looking somewhere else until I find something' (Tony – retail trainee). Similarly:

> No way, I won't stay here for two years. I'll leave and get a job
> anywhere if I have to, a shop or something, and maybe go to night
> school. Or I could get work in an old people's home, you don't need any
> qualifications to work in an old people's home. (Anne – community care
> trainee)

The remaining trainees (42 per cent) were considerably more unsure about whether they would complete their training programmes. For them, the decision to leave was contingent on whether any opportunities for real jobs came their way, or whether their own determination or resource-fulness could fashion an opening. They could see themselves as staying but were more likely to comment that 'hopefully I'll get a job before then' (Julia – clerical trainee). They also continued to place their faith in getting jobs with their work experience providers: 'I hope to get taken on before then' (Bhovinder – clerical trainee). With less certainty, some sought to find a job independently of their schemes: 'Jobs do come up, you just have to keep looking in the paper. I'm not saying they're easy to come by but you just have to keep searching' (Jane – catering trainee). Indeed, it was the knowledge that jobs were 'not easy to come by' that was the principal constraint in holding them on their schemes, so that 'If nothing else comes up then I'll stay' (Glenn – PSV trainee). Most would have already left could they have realistically done so: 'If I can find a job then I'll take it' (Jane – catering trainee). Youth training might not have been what they wanted, it might mean enduring new demands and disciplines, but unemployment constituted an even greater disciplining force: 'I don't want to stay unless I have too but I'd rather stay here than go on the dole' (Richard – construction trainee plumber)

Real Jobs: 'I'm Always Looking'

Despite the fact that these young people were compelled to enter youth training, most had clearly not taken the scheme's offer of quality training for jobs at face value. They were uncertain of its usefulness, challenged the claim that it would lead to jobs and directly questioned its overall efficacy through a propensity to desert in large numbers. Furthermore, this ambiguity was further underlined by the 19 trainees (46 per cent) who stipulated that they were currently looking for work. This was not a casual or a randomized activity in the hope that a job would turn up, but was often a central activity undertaken with great activity and gusto, and pursued in a systematic and considered way: 'I've been looking in the paper recently so I'm serious about it' (Neil – community care trainee). Job-hunting represented a concerted and well-thought-out activity: 'I'm always looking . . . the papers, the [Council's] internal vacancies list, keeping my ears open' (Clive – clerical trainee). This was further borne out through one young woman's successful capture of a full-time clerical post at the city council and by the fact that another had been offered a job as a nanny. However, on finding out what it would have involved, the latter trainee considered

> It was no better than YTS . . . it meant living in, you had to work weekends, got one night off a week and had to let them know in advance if you wanted to go out.

In addition, it meant moving away from the area and therefore confronting an important barrier which has traditionally restricted working class young women's job search activities (Rees, 1992): 'You'd have to pay me more than £70 [a week] to do that . . . I'm serious about finding another job but one that gives me a bit of free time' (Anne – community care trainee).

Constantly looking for a 'real job' was therefore an important part of being a youth trainee and a way to challenge and overcome youth training's low-skilled work experience regime: 'I've always been looking for something ever since I started the course' (Jane – catering trainee). However, trips to the Jobcentre, scrutinizing the situations vacant columns in local newspapers and exhausting possibilities through families and friends, all those job-search methods more commonly undertaken by adults (Employment Gazette, 1989), merely confirmed their feeling that 'young people don't get a look in these days . . . you're right up against it if you can't get a job'.

What also clearly emerged from the trainees' comments was the direct link between looking for 'real jobs' and the low level of allowance (explored in more detail in Chapter 7). However, even here, where they clearly appreciated the opportunities offered by their schemes, the constraints imposed by such a low income constantly provided a bitter reminder of its limiting force: 'I quite like what I'm doing but I wouldn't mind something else with more money' (Elaine – catering trainee). To this end, this young woman had looked for jobs in the local newspapers, followed up vacancies advertised in shop windows and had just 'applied for a job working on the check-out at [a local supermarket] . . . the extra money would come in very handy'. Similarly, the need for more money meant that another young woman had recently started to think about finding a part-time job: 'A job would be better than this, even a part-time job would be better. You can still earn quite a bit from a part-time job, enough to get by on anyway.' However, like those of many of the others her efforts to find work had merely confirmed her existing knowledge that 'there ain't much going around here' (Frances – retail trainee).

For others, the prospect of 'real jobs' was also inextricably linked to ideas of greater security. For one young man, applications to the Royal Mail for a place on their youth training scheme meant 'union [rates of] pay and a guaranteed job at the end' (Joe – MaC trainee). He had also applied for jobs with some of the big car manufacturers in the area but since they were still laying off workers, and their remaining apprenticeship schemes faced a deluge of new applications each year, this constant failure was turning into outright frustration:

> I've been on this course a long time. Too long. About a year too long.
> I'm getting more and more pissed off with it as it goes along . . . It's
> important to me to keep looking for a job. I need the money.

A measure of the low value which many continued to attach to youth training was further illustrated by the fact that many saw the prospect of any
job outside youth training as offering greater security. In the context of
their general experiences of training this was not too far from the truth and
it was therefore not surprising that for a trainee on the PSV scheme, whose
training had degenerated into sweeping up and making the tea, the sense
of insecurity was great:

> I don't feel secure at my placement. They got me for nothing so they
> probably don't really need me when I finish, so I'll carry on looking until I
> find something. (Glenn – PSV trainee)

He too had continued to apply for apprenticeships, again searching
through the situations vacant pages and enquiring directly to employers,
but he was now 17 and rapidly becoming too old to be considered. For
another,

> A real job would give me a proper wage and a bit of security . . .
> openings for motor mechanics are difficult to find . . . I want a full-time
> job with a proper wage. It's important to me. (Mick – MVM trainee)

This is not to neglect the other 20 trainees (49 per cent) who indicated that
they were not currently looking for work. Two of these were already leaving their schemes, one to start a NNEB course and another hoping to do
so, and a third was moving to a training scheme in a different area. A
fourth trainee had been successful in already landing a job with the city
council. Of the remaining 16 (38 per cent), two more admitted to
previously having looked for work only to give up because of the constant
lack of success:

> When I first started I did [look for work] but I couldn't find anything
> except temporary work, like filling in for somebody while they were
> having a baby . . . I'm waiting till I get a bit closer to finishing now.
> (Sarah – clerical trainee)

A large number of the remaining 14 trainees indicated that they were not currently looking for work, largely because they had put their faith in being taken on by their work experience providers. The importance attached to work experience placements as a source of work is well illustrated by Table 6.2, which shows that around one-third of trainees going into work, both nationally and locally, found jobs with their work experience placement providers. The Youth Cohort Study also illustrates the ways in which trainees appreciate the importance of placements as a source of work, with again around one-third of trainees indicating that they had either been offered places with their work experience providers or were expecting to be kept on (Courtenay, 1988). Indeed, in assessing the one-year scheme's contribution to finding young people jobs, one study concluded that

> the main contribution of YTS1 to trainees' later job success . . . seemed
> to be through opportunities in placements, and the value of even
> established training seemed at best ambiguous or at least not proven.
> (Lee *et al.*, 1990, p. 136)

These young people hoped to be 'taken on' (Wendy – clerical trainee), and the importance of placements as a way of leaving youth training for 'real jobs' was repeatedly advocated: 'I think I'll get taken on where I am' (Niki – clerical trainee) or 'I'll stay on until my time runs out and hope I get taken on at the end' (Luke – retail trainee). Similarly:

> I'm on 6 months' trial at my placement at the moment, that's what
> placements are for. To see if the gaffer likes you and to see if you can do
> the work. (Adam – horticulture trainee)

Whatever Happened to the New 'Golden Age'?

The ways in which youth training remains a fragile social relation were also further underlined by concerns that were generated by the prospect of a return to relatively buoyant labour market conditions for school leavers towards the end of the 1980s. Although recession quickly undermined its promise, this so-called *new golden age* resulted from a temporary upturn in the economy and changing demographic factors, leading some to comment that 'the market for youth labour has swung from slump to boom in a decade' (*Independent*, 17 May 1989). Such triumphalist claims were supported by projections from the Department of Employment which estimated that the number of young people leaving school to become available for work would decline by one-third between 1982–1983 and 1992–1993 (Employment Gazette, 1991a). By 1995, the number of young people in the 16–17 age group would be the smallest this century. Indeed, official concerns noted that the anticipated 'fall will be sharpest among families whose children have traditionally left full-time education at minimum school leaving age' (Training Agency, 1989b, para. 5), leaving analysts to predict a shortage of young labour, a rise in its price and continuing skill shortages for the future (Cassells, 1990).

The superficiality of such arguments was cruelly exposed as the British economy once more lurched into recession at the beginning of the 1990s. Yet, importantly, even such a temporary and superficial recovery quickly illustrated that the scheme's foundations were extremely weak and that youth training would be unable to endure even a modest improvement in school leavers' job prospects. Large-scale research has argued that even if increases in the availability of work for young people were limited to semi-skilled and unskilled work, trainees would most likely desert their schemes in droves (Roberts *et al.*, n.d.).

Both the enthusiasm with which the trainees here sought to find work outside the scheme and the types of job that dominated their job-search activities emphatically underline this point. Furthermore, the ease with which the trainees indicated that they could be tempted away from their schemes and the type of work that would do this further emphasize the frailty of youth training. Indeed, most of the trainees here indicated that they could be tempted away from their schemes, with only three (7 per cent) stating that they were happy with their training and that it was unlikely they could be attracted away. Another three also indicated that they were unsure about what sort of work would tempt them to leave and, when pushed, two felt they would most probably stay. This was either because 'You're more likely to get a job if you stay on the scheme' (Adam – horticulture trainee), or

> It's my best chance of a job at the moment . . . Both my dad and my brother say that the main thing to do is get your [apprenticeship] papers and once you've got your papers you can go anywhere and do anything. (Robert – engineering trainee)

The remaining trainees (85 per cent) all indicated that they would be prepared to leave their schemes either if a job opportunity came their way, or if one could be manufactured. Only one of these talked in definite terms about the specific type of work that could have tempted him to leave: 'I think about being a postman all the time . . . if it came to it I'd probably take anything' (Tony – retail trainee). Two more defined the types of work which could attract them in opposition to their training schemes: 'anything that didn't involve horticulture' (Clare – horticulture trainee) or 'if I could walk into a job with no training' (Louis – construction trainee carpenter).

The other trainees were more likely to talk about the types of work which could tempt them to leave their schemes in terms of general advantages which, more often than not, represented only a modest improvement over what they were doing already. In particular, 'a job that pays a bit more' (Colin – community care trainee) was seen as more worthwhile than a training scheme, and 'something which would give me a bit extra money at the end of the week' (Jane – catering trainee). The importance of a little extra money was plain where 'something in the same sort of work but something a bit better paid' (Niki – clerical trainee) or 'something that I would enjoy and something where the money wasn't too bad' (Carol – catering trainee) would have caused them to leave with little hesitation.

However, money was not the only consideration and others indicated that the grip of youth training could also be loosened by a modest improvement in their other terms and conditions: 'something that paid a bit more and where you didn't have to work for so long' (Keith – PSV trainee). Others felt that 'something that had better hours, better days and better pay . . . a job which you can keep for a while' (Derrick – MaC trainee) or 'something more secure really' (Glenn – PSV trainee) would tilt the balance against their schemes. Indeed, the extent to which any work outside youth training was largely associated with increased job security meant that virtually any job could have tempted them to leave, despite the fact that most of the work destined to come their way would most likely involve insecure, low-skilled and short-term jobs. This was expressly summed up by two of the trainees: 'If it [a job] was permanent then I'd take any job' (Rajesh – MVM trainee). For another: 'A proper job is much more secure. I need that sort of security . . . a job which doesn't finish unless you are made redundant' (Neil – community care trainee).

Conclusion

Despite its claims to represent a revolutionary solution to Britain's longer-term skills problems, youth training has clearly failed to provide the young working class with the opportunity for skills training. When the scheme's provision is examined in closer detail, it quickly becomes evident that the vast majority of trainees are subjected to a diet of repetitive and low-skilled work experience, undertaking tasks which are quickly and easily grasped. For their part, trainees have not remained oblivious to this and many are all too well aware that youth training has failed to deliver its promise of quality foundation training for school leavers. In doing so, it has established a new set of contradictions and struggles centred around the inability of the scheme to provide young people with training for real jobs.

The fact that trainees remain at best unconvinced about the ability of their schemes to lead to jobs is most clearly evident from the tentative and uncertain ways in which they evaluate the benefits of their schemes. Most remain convinced that their schemes are of benefit but putting a finger on what this actually means remains problematic. What they do see as beneficial, however, are the ways in which the scheme has succeeded in providing them with general work experience and training, measured by its continued ability to bring them into direct contact with employers and the world of work more generally. These uncertainties are even more pronounced in relation to trainees' assessments of how well their schemes have prepared them for work and again they remain, at best, only partially convinced of its usefulness as a period of preparation for subsequent working life and, at worst, highly sceptical. Even during a period of relative prosperity for school leavers, large numbers of trainees remained unsure of youth training's usefulness as a stepping stone into work.

The bottom line for most trainees is that youth training represents a better alternative than unemployment and to this extent most trainees remained generally optimistic about their chances of finding work. Yet most of the trainees also knew that finding a 'real job' is no easy matter and that competition for even the most basic of jobs is intense. Nonetheless, they did retain some limited faith in the ability of youth training to contribute to their employment prospects and most adhered to the belief that their prospects of a job were better than when they had started. Significant numbers of trainees also gave strong emphasis to the role of their work experience providers in finding 'real jobs', either hoping to be taken on or anticipating being taken on at some point during their training. Yet behind this cautious enthusiasm lay the acknowledgement that unemployment is never far away, and many trainees remained unconvinced that they would leave their training schemes for jobs. In this way, working class young people on training schemes have continued to resist youth training's claims to quality training for jobs and many continue to understand that the scheme remains unresponsive to their needs.

The fact that these young people had a clear and realistic appreciation of youth training's inability to lead to jobs is patently evident from a closer inspection of the scheme's successes in finding trainees work. Official pronouncements continue to portray youth training as a runaway success but even the most optimistic interpretations of these statistics cannot hide the fact that youth training's stated aim of becoming a stepping stone into jobs remains largely unaccomplished. The claims made for the scheme's extensive successes in finding trainees jobs are not sustained by any close inspection of the statistics, and unemployment levels among leavers continue at around three times higher than that for the population as a whole. Black and disabled school leavers are even more likely to find themselves unemployed on leaving, thereby questioning the ability of the scheme to perform much more than a simple holding operation in the face of sustained unemployment. The fact that the scheme continues to be unable to confront the real roots of young people's unemployment is not lost on large numbers of trainees.

It is in this context that young people have continued to resist the imposition of youth training for jobs and it is here that the significance of the scheme's chronic inability to retain trainees for the full duration of their training lies. Throughout youth training's development, trainees have resisted the low-quality training, the arduous and repetitive forms of work and the scheme's inability to act as a way into work by deserting their schemes in large numbers. Two-thirds of all trainees left their schemes early and the reasons given for doing so were dominated by criticisms of the content of the training, widespread discontent with the way schemes are run and the schemes' continuing inability to meet even the most basic needs of the trainees. The return to recession and the schemes' effective compulsion have acted to curtail these large-scale revolts but they have by no means stopped them completely. With unemployment now pushing one million among the 18 to 24 age group, around half of all trainees are still voting with their feet and leaving their schemes early.

Again this makes more sense in the context of the trainees' evaluations and assessments of their scheme's benefits and effectiveness as a route into jobs. Young people have responded to youth training's promise of training for jobs by staying on their schemes for only the shortest possible time, while they are maintaining a constant watch for a much-prized 'real job'. Large numbers of trainees are therefore permanently on the look-out for alternative sources of work and had it not been for the faith placed in the ability of work experience placements to lead into work, the numbers would undoubtedly have been higher. Nevertheless, many trainees continued to pursue their job-search activities with considerable vigour, and if an opening for work is found or engineered, few stop for more than a moment to contemplate the possibility of staying on their schemes.

This inability of the scheme to respond to the need of the young working class for work most vividly illustrates the continuing frailty of the youth training movement. The majority of trainees do not want to remain on their schemes for longer than is really necessary and continue to resist its impositions. Indeed, any improvement in the prospects for work among school leavers would undoubtedly see a wholesale defection from the scheme. This is certainly not the hallmark of a quality training programme which has found its way into the hearts and minds of the young working class, and even the temporary improvement in job prospects towards the end of the 1980s vividly illustrated the rate at which they would abscond. If the economic 'miracle' had provided anything other than another mirage, the youth training scheme, as a mass training scheme for school leavers, would have undoubtedly collapsed.

7 TRAINING WITH NO MONEY

Youth training has failed to establish itself as a credible alternative on leaving school, with its poor-quality training and low-skilled work experience unable to satisfy school leavers' demands for real jobs. In turn, these aspects of youth training have all engendered new forms of behaviour among working class young people, as new sets of tensions have been established around the more general claim that the scheme represents quality foundation training for jobs. Large numbers of young people remain unconvinced about the ability of the scheme to prepare them for working life and even more concerned about the prospects of their training leading into work. At their most obvious, these tensions have expressed themselves through the decisions of trainees to desert their schemes in large numbers before the planned duration of their training.

Another important dimension to youth training which also highlights school leavers' attempts to resist the scheme's impositions has also fuelled this decision to leave early. Second only to the promise of a 'real job', the biggest single reason given for leaving has consistently been young people's dissatisfaction with the level of the basic training allowance. As the *Two Year YTS 100 Per Cent Follow-Up Survey* showed (Table 6.3), nationally, one in five early leavers gave 'not enough money' as a reason for leaving, and 22 per cent did likewise in Coventry. Clearly, the offer of a period of structured work experience together with the opportunity for work experience-based training has failed to diminish the powerful attraction of the labour market, and youth training alone has not proved capable of resisting the lure of 'real jobs', despite their often 'dead end' nature, with the promise of a wage at their core.

In this way it is significant that many trainees continue to resist the legitimacy of the basic training allowance because youth training evolved with the explicit intention of driving down the price of young labour. Legitimized by an analysis of rising unemployment which argued that employment levels among the under-18s lessened as waged differentials between adult and young workers declined (e.g. Wells, 1983), the over-pricing of the young became the pretext for a sustained attack on young workers' wages. From the highest level downwards it was being argued: 'the wages of the young are often too high in relation to those of experienced adults. Employers cannot afford to take them on' (Margaret Thatcher, *Hansard*, July 1981). Youth training therefore evolved as a central thrust of successive government's stated intentions of bringing 'about a change in the attitudes of young people to the value of training and acceptance of relatively lower wages for trainees' (Department of Employment, 1981, p. 5.8). To this end, employers were actively encouraged to avail themselves of the

> opportunity (through YTS) to take on young men and women, train them and let them work for you entirely at our expense, and then decide whether or not you want to employ them. (Quoted in Davies, 1986, p. 59).

Despite the fact that 'there is no empirical data to sustain the Government's claim that growing rates of young workers deter kindly capitalists from taking on school leavers' (Allum and Quigley, 1983, p. 9), youth training took a central place in attempts to reconstitute young workers as a cheaper form of labour power. Institutionalized under the YOP, the level of allowance paid to YOP trainees consistently failed to keep pace with inflation. Given a more aggressive form under successive Thatcher governments, in 1982 the Young Worker Scheme, and later the New Worker Scheme, offered employers a subsidy to take on young people below a fixed wage level and, throughout the 1980s, the regulation of young people's pay was systematically removed from the limited protection of the wages councils. Indeed, in its original form, youth training proposed to pay trainees only £15 per week and it was only after vociferous opposition from trade unions, educationalists and others that a figure comparable with that for the YOP was agreed upon, giving trainees on the new Youth Training Scheme the princely sum of £25 per week (Ainley and Corney, 1990).

The centrality of youth training in the attack on young workers' pay has been plainly outlined by a Low Pay Unit survey:

Clearly, it is necessary to create a climate of belief in the 'pricing out' concept if young people are to be convinced that there is no alternative to low pay. It is, however, possible for governments to take direct action to suppress wage levels in those areas where it has ultimate control and in this respect the importance of holding YTS pay only marginally above unemployment benefit rates is obvious. After two years on such low levels of pay, almost any increase will seem luxurious even if in reality it represents working for poverty wages. (Low Pay Unit, 1988, p. 3).

The Low Pay Unit's report concluded that, historically, there has been a 'clear acceptance' among young workers that they should be paid a lower rate than adult workers and that these assumptions feed through into their anticipation of what adult workers should be paid. As such, 'the tiny minority who advocated wages in excess of £150 per week is depressing when average wages are currently in excess of £200 per week' (Low Pay Unit, 1988, p. 5).

A Growing Independence

It appears that the assault on school leavers' pay has, to some extent, been successful in lowering young workers' wages relative to those of adults. Towards the end of the 1980s, data from the New Earnings Survey showed that the proportion of wages received by 16- and 17-year-olds, in relation to adult rates, had dropped from 61.3 per cent in 1979 to 57.7 per cent in 1987 (Potter, 1989). Independent estimates suggest that increased differentials between 'youth' and 'adult' wages were even more significant than the New Earnings Survey allowed and that, in particular, women and black young people were suffering even greater wage discrimination than their white male peers. In addition, more localized studies have also highlighted that young workers remain extremely vulnerable to attempts to force down the levels of their wages. For example, the Low Pay Unit in Manchester recently found that, between April 1990 and April 1992, average pay rates for young people dropped from £1.69 to £1.45 a hour (Greater Manchester Low Pay Unit, 1992).

However, school leavers have not taken easily to these attempts to reduce their real level of income and evidence points out that, contrary to the Low Pay Unit's warnings, they remain largely unconvinced that there is no alternative to low pay. In particular, opposition to the level of the youth training allowance has remained widespread. Not only has this persuaded many trainees to leave their schemes early but, as we saw in Chapter 3, one of the main reasons young people of school leaving age have remained opposed to entering youth training in the first place is that it has consistently been seen as a 'cheap' or 'slave labour' scheme. It is precisely this appreciation of youth training as an attempt to further impose new forms of low pay on the young that has remained a central feature in young people's opposition to the scheme (Raffe and Smith, 1987; Gray and King, 1986; Horton, 1986). Rather than a gradual acclimatization, or an increasing acceptance among the young working class that they must 'price themselves back into work', the real sense of exploitation engendered by the scheme's low allowance has been consolidated throughout its development, as trainees have had to confront directly the material realities of living on a low wage.

The extent of the assault on school leavers' wages is illustrated by the fact that in real terms, the current level of youth training's first-year allowance is worth between two and four times less than it would have been if the original YOP allowance had kept pace with rises in prices and incomes. Since the beginning of the scheme, the allowance has been raised only slowly from the original £25 in 1983 to £26.30 in 1985. A two-tier system of payment was introduced when the scheme was extended to two years in 1986, with the first-year allowance rising to £29.50 by 1989, where it has since stood still, and the initial £35 second-year allowance remaining unchanged over the past seven years. The value of payments to trainees was once again frozen for the year 1993–1994 and recent comments from ministers imply that no immediate future rises are likely, owing to a concern that to do so would bring 'youth' rates too close to those received by under-25s on adult training schemes (*Times Educational Supplement*, 13 May 1989).

For successive generations of youth trainees, this has meant facing up to the erosion of their major independent source of income. Under youth training's new 'flexible' organization, non-employed trainees under 17 still have to be paid only the minimum £29.50 per week, and the minimum payment for trainees aged 17 and over remains the same as the second-year payment when it was introduced in 1986. Estimates show that if the overall training allowance had kept pace with average earnings since the training allowance was introduced with the YOP in 1978, trainees under 17 would currently be receiving a minimum of £77.63 and those 17 and

Table 7.1 *Breakdown of Pupil Reactions to the Fairness of the Allowance, as a Percentage (School Pupil Survey)*

	Stayers	Leavers	Total	Male	Female
Fair	5	8	13	8	5
Not fair	31	55	86	52	34
Other	0	1	1	0	1
Total (*n* = 147)	36	64	100	60	40

over £99.55. Even keeping up with the retail price index would have meant a current allowance of £54.99 for 16-year-olds and £70.50 for 17-year-olds (Unemployment Unit/Youthaid, 1993b).

As Table 7.1 illustrates, the level of allowance remains deeply unpopular across the range of young people approaching school leaving age, as 86 per cent of the pupils felt the current rate was unfair. This represented the single most emphatic response to any question in the survey, with over eight out of 10 pupils from both the stayers and leavers, and the girls and boys, judging the level unjust.

Table 7.2 illustrates the pupils' justifications for why they felt the allowance was or was not fair. The small number of reasons supporting the fairness of the current level of allowance tended to endorse official arguments concerning the status of trainees, whether arguing that 'It's about right if you're training', 'School leavers can't expect any more', or 'It's what school leavers should be paid.' A very small number also expressed the view that the training allowance would teach school leavers 'how to deal with money' or 'you learn to cope with money'.

In contrast, these endorsements were swamped by the pupils' argument concerning the unfairness of the allowance. Around a quarter of the responses from the pupils argued that such a level of allowance constituted 'slave' or 'cheap labour'. This was not simply a knee-jerk or rhetorical dismissal of the allowance but constituted an objection which was grounded in the knowledge that a trainee was expected to 'work next to somebody else getting paid properly so it's slave labour'. These pupils argued that the allowance was unfair precisely because it did not come close to reflecting the value of the work they were expected to put in. They argued that trainees were expected to work next to full-time workers, do

Table 7.2 *Reasons Why They Thought the Level of Allowance Was or Was Not Fair, as a Percentage* (School Pupils Survey)*

	Stayers (resp. = 78)			Leavers (resp. = 132)		
	Male	Female	Total	Male	Female	Total
Positive reasons						
Right for training	1	0	1	2	2	4
Right for school leavers	1	4	5	1	2	3
Learn about money	1	0	1	0	2	2
Negative reasons						
Cheap/slave labour	10	13	23	16	13	29
Money to live	36	28	64	38	24	62
Same as benefit	3	2	5	1	0	1
Total	**52**	**47**	**99**	**58**	**43**	**101**

*Pupils could give more than one reason

the same jobs and work the same hours but with significantly less pay: 'You work with others who get a proper rate of pay' or 'You are working with other employees so should be paid like them'. It was this understanding of the youth training allowance which allowed them to argue that 'They just exploit you', 'The employers get free or cheap labour' so 'It isn't worth working for 50p per hour'.

Importantly, around two-thirds of the pupils also saw the unfairness of the allowance in relation to their expectation or assessment of the levels of money which an increasingly independent school leaver needed to live on. For this group, the allowance was considered unfair because 'It doesn't give you enough money to live on', 'You can't live on that', or 'There's no way you could get through the week with money like that'. Recently, research has become more interested in the ways in which young people gain some form of independence from their families of origin (see Jones and Wallace, 1992) and the ways in which different factors influence their movement out of the parental home. Empirical research has led Finn to suggest that 'it is precisely around jobs and educational options that many

. . . youngsters saw their transition out of the family of origin' (Finn, 1984, p. 32), and this is supported by studies from elsewhere. Very few young people expect to leave home before they reach 18 but the vast majority do so between 18 and 24 (Leaving Home Project, 1990), with the decision to do so closely tied in with the expectation of work and an independent income. It is in the progressive desire to become independent and an evolving understanding of what this involves that many of the pupils rooted their criticisms of the current level of allowance. Approaching the end of their compulsory schooling, these young people could not accept the equity of the allowance because they knew they would need 'more money for independence if a person wants to leave home' and that the current level was only 'enough just to get through the week'. It meant 'no money to pay the rent', 'not enough to pay board money', or 'no money to pay the bills'.

'I Work as Hard as Anybody at That Place'

These school pupils had yet to be convinced of the merits of such a low allowance and the vast majority bitterly opposed its imposition. What remains a distinctive feature of pupils' antagonism to the restructuring of work and employment for school leavers is their adherence to levels of remuneration for young workers which challenge the logic of youth training's market criteria, and their continuing insistence on a fairer level of allowance rooted in moral considerations. For them, trainees are clearly used as cheap or slave labour and this is to be rejected, even in the face of the state's claims that the market could not sustain any higher levels of pay. However, the pupils also presented their objections in terms of the need for young people to be given a level of allowance commensurate with their attempts to develop new forms of autonomy and independence. What this adds up to is something akin to Thompson's (1978a) 'moral economy', whereby the young working class refuse to accept youth training's economic arguments, insisting that the level of allowance involves social and moral considerations too.

Moreover, these sentiments were shared by the young people actually training on the scheme. Among the trainees, 34 (81 per cent) argued that the level of the allowance was not fair, another seven (17 per cent) felt that it was fair and one claimed that they did not know. For four of the seven trainees who felt the allowance was satisfactory, this was clearly related to their current levels of earnings. This group of trainees were some of the select few who were either receiving, or expecting to receive, apprentice rates above the youth training minimum, or were trainees lucky enough to benefit from the ability of work experience providers to 'top up' the basic minimum. The latter included one of the young women on the chamber of commerce's clerical scheme, who clearly appreciated her relative fortune: 'I know I'm lucky to get more than the rest' (Fiona – clerical trainee). For the apprentices, the minimum rate was considered fair while they were based largely in the training centre, but once they left for their work placements these young people were inclined to argue that their wage should rise accordingly: 'After all, we're expected to work like any other worker. They don't make many concessions' (Patrick – engineering trainee). Similarly: 'At the moment it's mainly being in the workshop all day so the money's fair enough . . . but once I leave I think I should get more' (Bob – engineering trainee).

The remaining three in this group were all receiving the basic training allowance, arguing that 'as trainees you can't expect any more' (Luke – retail trainee). The people in this small group were the only ones to accept that being a youth trainee necessitated short-term sacrifice for longer-term gain. They alone were willing to endorse the argument that the state was

> giving you an allowance; this is better than those of your colleagues who are still at school or in colleges of education are receiving, and I would have hoped that everybody concerned would look at it in that light. (Norman Tebbit, then Secretary of State for Industry, *Hansard*, 2 May 1982, col. 42)

The majority of trainees, however, were distinctly unwilling to see the level of the training allowance in the light recommended by Norman Tebbit. In a situation where they were expected to work like full-time workers yet were treated as low-paid trainees, levels of discontent ran high. Indeed, it is this facet of youth training more than any other which gives the scheme's description as slave or cheap labour such a high degree of resonance among the working class young, as trainees are constantly forced to confront the material barriers imposed by such a low wage. While many go some way to accepting that as trainees some financial sacrifices may be needed, the fact is that trainees are all too well aware that youth training represents an attempt to reconstitute the wage relationship, and this constantly impinges on any desire to take advantage of the scheme's limited opportunities.

This was demonstrated in the range of arguments deployed by the trainees to support their claims that the allowance was unfair. Twenty-six (62 per cent) argued that the allowance was unfair because it patently refused to acknowledge the time and effort they were required to expend training: 'We are doing the same jobs as other people but it's slave labour . . . I have to work as hard as anybody at that place so why shouldn't I get paid the same?' (Niki – clerical trainee). A number were acutely aware that being a trainee involved taking extremely low equivalent hourly rates. 'For 60p or 70p per hour you're just being used as a dogsbody' (Helen – retail trainee). This often necessitated taking a drop in the rates they were receiving as child workers: 'They [her school-time jobs] were better than the YTS. You get less than 80p per hour on the youth training, it's ridiculous' (Anne – community care trainee).

Not only were criticisms of the allowance rooted in a real appreciation of the demands of waged labour, young people were also well aware that the imperative to get a 'real job' meant that they were required to work harder than other comparable groups of young workers merely to prove themselves to employers. These young people were insistent that trainees were caught in a double bind which, on the one hand, financially penalized them for being trainees, and on the other hand required them to work even harder to overcome the stigma that being a trainee entailed. The difference between impressing and failing to impress an employer was not measured by some abstract criterion, but was judged by the harsh reality of whether or not they got jobs at the end of their scheme:

> I want to make an impression so I end up working twice as hard as those I work with . . . Status comes into it. You obviously can't expect to start on that sort of wage [a permanent employee's wage] but I work harder than anybody and get paid a lot less for it. (Clive – clerical trainee)

For most trainees on placements with work experience providers, the distinction between training and work had very little meaning anyway. They saw themselves as workers, were judged by the same criteria as other workers, were penalized in similar ways and largely accepted that their work experience providers demanded that they perform as such:

> When you are down here [the training centre] it's not so bad, but when
> you get to the placement they make you work hard for your money . . .
> You can't expect a lot as you're training, they ain't gaining from you, but
> when you're on placement they should have to pay something towards
> your wages. (Rajesh – MVM trainee)

Similarly: 'I know we're learning at the same time but when we're on
placement we do the same work as anybody else' (Sue – catering trainee).
Again:

> I work very hard . . . It was more boring at [the garden centre] and the
> work was not so hard, but where I work now I'm expected to pull my
> weight with the gaffer. (Adam – horticulture trainee).

It has been suggested that

> in judging a fair return for their labour, few young people appeared to
> take the productivity of juvenile labour or the market value (if any) of a
> trainee's output into consideration. (Raffe and Smith, 1987, p. 257)

Yet the above comments readily indicate that the majority of trainees are
well aware of the contribution they are required to make and that this often
means putting in extra effort above and beyond that expected from other
workers. Furthermore, the trainees' comments show that most appreciate
that they are on trial and that this at least means 'pulling their weight'
while out on placement. Indeed, research found that in the service sector,
particularly in the repair of consumer goods and vehicles, retail distribution and personal service work, trainees' contribution to output clearly
exceeded the level of the allowance where trainees were directly involved.
Only in some manufacturing industry did trainee output fail to match the
allowance, reflecting 'the low productivity of trainees in their first year of
training for skilled work' (Deakin and Pratten, 1987, p. 493).

A Fair Level of Allowance

So young people in general and trainees in particular remain, at best,
unconvinced and, at worst, steadfastly opposed to arguments supporting
the low level of allowance paid on youth training. Trainees continue to be

an unwilling source of cheap labour and are quick to dispute its legitimacy. However, as already indicated, levels of pay among the young have in reality undergone a steady decline. It is therefore to be expected that this assault on young workers' wages has, to some extent, worked its way through into young people's expectations of what a fair level of training allowance should actually be.

However, even though the level of allowance was near universally condemned, Table 7.3 shows that a large majority of both the pupils and the trainees felt a fair allowance to be between £33.50 and £50 per week. This represented only a modest increase in the allowance levels these young people were then experiencing and one which considerably underestimated the actual decline in its level in relation to wider variations in average earnings or prices. It also represented a level well below the then current levels of pay 16- and 17-year-olds could expect if they were lucky enough to enter work directly. As indicated in Chapter 3, towards the end of the 1980s gross weekly earnings for 16- and 17-year-olds stood between £65.50 and £74.50 per week. Further evidence has suggested that in 1988 gross weekly earnings for young men and women in manual jobs averaged £75 to £85 per week, and for 17-year-olds were around £90 per week (Cassells, 1990). The young people here clearly had ideas of a fair training allowance which were well below both market rates and the real value of the original allowance.

What is also noticeable is the contrast between what both groups of young people who took part in the survey felt was fair. Although broadly

Table 7.3 *What Trainees and Pupils Considered a Fair Level of Allowance for Youth Training, as a Percentage (£s)*

	Trainees	Pupils
33.50–40	48	20
41–50	28	48
51–60	5	18
61–80	7	4
81 +	3	7
Don't know	4	3
Total	**100**	**100**

similar, the pupils' idea of a fair allowance tended to be higher than that of the trainees. Whereas the biggest group of trainees felt £33.50 to £40 would be fair, the biggest group of pupils felt that £41 to £50 was more realistic. Similarly, the pupils were much more likely to consider what constituted a fair level of allowance to be even higher, while the trainees were more likely to think it slightly lower. Such a pattern indicates that youth training has been, to a certain extent, effective in dampening wage expectations among trainees in ways conceived of as desirable by its proponents and this has worked its way through into subsequent levels of pay. Wider evidence from the Youth Cohort Study of England and Wales has pointed out that

> participants [in the scheme] earn approximately 5 pence per hour less than non-participants and that those in jobs with youth training employers earn 9 pence per hour less than those with non-scheme employers. (Whitfield and Bourlakis, 1989, p. 13)

In all, 40 of the 42 trainees had an idea of what they thought a fair level of allowance should be, the lowest of which was £33.50 from a trainee still receiving the first-year allowance (then £28.50). Overall their judgements about what constituted a fair rate were not significantly higher than the then current levels, with 19 trainees (48 per cent) believing an allowance of £40 or under to be fair, and 32 (76 per cent) feeling £50 or under to be fair. Again, their ideas of a fair allowance had failed to keep pace with wider changes in prices and incomes.

Ideas about the equity of the allowance also tended to reflect earnings differentials across the different schemes, and those already earning above the basic allowance tended to think in higher terms. Of those who thought an allowance of over £50 per week would be fair, two were already receiving apprentice rates of pay and a third was anticipating it in the near future. Another felt he should be paid around £115 per week, but considering he had recently filled in as a temporary clerical worker where he was earning £65 per week this was less surprising: 'It's the going rate for the job' (Clive – clerical trainee). The other three trainees in this group of seven were receiving the basic training allowance, but one's cousin was training on a scheme paying £60 a week: 'I think that would be fair pay for what I do then I could spend a bit of money on myself and possibly go out more' (Niki – clerical trainee). For another,

£70 to £80 a week seems right for the work that I'm supposed to do, especially out on placement. The others there get around £200 a week for doing almost the same sort of work. They've just been there a bit longer. (Mick – MVM trainee)

Many of the trainees tended to justify their claims of the fairness of a higher allowance in terms of the contribution to production they felt they were making. In all, 12 (29 per cent) felt that their effort alone legitimized claims for a more equitable allowance: 'We work hard and ought to get something decent in return' (Lorraine – horticulture trainee). Similarly: 'I work hard. I want a good report so I have to work hard . . . They should pay us the right amount if we work OK' (Derrick – MaC trainee). However, economic arguments were not the only weapons deployed and a further 24 (57 per cent) trainees appealed to moral reason, claiming that such an increase was justified because it would enable them to live a little better: 'It would give me a little bit extra to do what I like with' (Helen – retail trainee). Despite the time demanded by their training and the effort they were required to put in, many accepted that as trainees this should involve some financial sacrifice: 'It's not a proper job and I am being trained, but I think we should get £50 a week, then I'd have a bit left for myself' (Keith – PSV trainee).

The trainees also linked the idea of what constituted a fair allowance to growing ideas of independence and adulthood. A higher training allowance meant 'I could live on that sort of money . . . spend a bit more on myself, give a bit more to my mum' (Luke – retail trainee), or 'If they put it up a little, say by £5 a week, it would make a big difference. That's not asking too much, is it?' (Lucy – community care trainee). This big difference would allow them greater freedom and autonomy: 'I'd be able to buy clothes and things like that, and would have something to show for it' (Samantha – clerical trainee). Similarly: 'I know you're training but if they gave us that [£50 per week] we would get something out of it. We would be able to spend something on ourselves' (Carol – catering trainee). It would also 'make it possible to spread it out a bit more and possibly save some for the end of the week' (Carol – catering trainee), or 'putting the money up a bit [£45 per week] would allow us to be a bit more independent' (Joe – MaC trainee), which meant buying their own clothes and even the possibility of living independently. At present, 'there is no way I could ever move out on that sort of money' (Fiona – clerical trainee).

The Level of Allowance

The trainees gave little sign that they had accepted as legitimate the values embodied in youth training. More importantly, it has engendered new and more diffuse patterns of resistance and opposition as the young working class struggle in and against the barriers and disciplines the scheme seeks to impose. Working class young people continue to act in ways not considered desirable by the scheme's advocates and this is particularly evident in the case of struggles over the training allowance, where the young working class have continued to resist the imposition of such a low level. Large numbers have shown the lack of value they attach to the training allowance through their continuing hostility towards the financial sacrifice it entails and by the more spectacular large-scale desertions from their schemes in search of more money.

The significance of the low level of the allowance has further been compounded by more recent moves to decentralize the provision of youth training and the concomitant imperative that employers take more financial responsibility for training young workers. Such demands were originally premised on the belief that falling numbers of school leavers and an upturn in the economy would necessitate a greater investment on the part of employers in their new young recruits (Ball, 1989b; Finn, 1988). It was believed that this would feed through the youth training system in the form of more responsive and attractive training schemes, and that employers would increasingly utilize their prerogative either to give trainees employee status, whereby they would be trained on the scheme but receive a wage and a guarantee of a job, or to top up the minimum training allowance. To some extent this has taken place and although no statistics are available regarding the number of trainees benefiting from top-up, in September 1985 only 8 per cent of trainees nationally had employee status. This figure rose to 11 per cent by 1987 and again to 24 per cent by May 1989 (*Hansard*, 3 July 1989, col. 74), but between October 1991 and September 1992 it had levelled out at 29 per cent (Unemployment Unit/Youthaid, 1993b).

What this means in reality for trainees is far from clear but a local newspaper article in 1989 reported that growing anxieties over the implications of a likely shortage of young workers were already beginning to work their way through youth training and that 30 per cent of Coventry trainees had been given employee status. Quoting the Training Agency's area manager: 'It means they have been offered a job, are being paid the going rate but are still receiving training through YTS' (*Coventry Evening Telegraph*, 14 March 1989).

However, as Table 7.4 points out, the majority of trainees had yet to experience the benefits of employee status pointed out by the area manager. In fact, although the wider statistics looked impressive, the reality for trainees turn out to be considerably more complex, and only four (10 per cent) of the young people here had experienced employee status at one time or other. One of these had just left their scheme to take up a 'real job' with the city council and another had previously filled a temporary clerical vacancy before returning to his scheme with non-employee status. Another two were apprentices and were therefore receiving apprentice rates of pay and were almost certain of a job at the end.

Evidently, the benefits of employee status were not filtering through to all youth trainees but were confined to specific groups and, more importantly, were sometimes limited to exclusive periods of their training. This suggests that as well as using trainees as an internal pool from which to recruit (see Chapter 5), employers were also using trainees to fill temporary vacancies, albeit with the benefit of employee status and a much superior wage. However, for the majority of trainees, 36 (86 per cent) in this case, the direct benefits which accompany employee status had yet to be made available and the vast majority of the trainees were still receiving the basic allowance.[1] As Table 7.4 also shows, only two trainees were benefiting from the much flaunted but little utilized ability of employers to top up trainees' allowances above the basic minimum. Both were clerical trainees with the chamber of commerce and both did their work experience placement with private sector employers. One received an extra £10 per week and the other got her first-year allowance topped up to the second-year level.

Table 7.4 *Level of Weekly Training Allowance or Wage Received by the Trainees*

Level	Male	Female	Total
Basic training allowance	21	15	36
Basic training allowance plus 'top up'	0	2	2
Apprentice rate/wage	3	1	4
Total	24	18	42

It must be pointed out that even employee status does not guarantee trainees the payment of more than the national minimum paid to non-employee status trainees. Before the TEC initiative, employed trainees had to be paid a minimum wage at least equivalent to the training allowance but current regulations allow individual TECs the discretion to decide whether or not to stipulate a minimum wage for trainees. Furthermore, disabled people, black young people and young women have all been considerably less likely to benefit from employee status than other comparable groups of trainees (Ball, 1989b), and more anecdotal evidence points towards a significant drop in the number of schemes which now offer trainees top-up on their basic training allowance. In fact, now the demographic bubble has burst, some TECs and LECs are actually paying employers an additional payment to take on school leavers and train them (Unemployment Unit/Youthaid, 1993b).

Facing the Squeeze: Making Ends Meet

Despite provision for top-up and the ability to give trainees employee status, for the vast majority of young people training means only the basic allowance. Most trainees continue to resist claims that this represents a fair reward for the work they are expected to do and the effort this involves, particularly where this involves working next to full-time employees. Not only has this involved a rejection of repeated calls to the working class young to give way to the necessity of youth training's economic logic, but this rejection has also in large part been rooted in young people's increasing inability to cope on the training allowance without further relying on other forms of material support. As with the school pupils' reluctance to endorse the fairness of the allowance, trainees too evaluate remuneration for training in relation to ideas about their evolving status as increasingly independent adults.

This was highlighted by the fact that only four (10 per cent) of the trainees claimed that they could make ends meet each week on their income and even then this was only with considerable difficulty. These young people indicated that they could 'cope quite well on the money . . . but I usually get a bit of help from mum and dad' (Martin – engineering trainee), or 'at the moment I can get by on it because I get help from my mum and dad' (Carol – catering trainee). The remainder of the trainees indicated that making ends meet on the allowance was considerably more problematic. This must be seen in the context of the erosion of the youth training allowance, to the extent that it is now so low that it is actually outstripped by the level of income support that 16-year-olds may be entitled to *if* they are living independently and could suffer severe hardship if it were denied. Only non-employed trainees are allowed to claim income support, which amounts to a mere £5.30 extra a week, but this, together with any other benefits derived from receiving income support, for example entitlement to full housing benefit and other related concessions, means that it can represent a considerable addition to a young person's total weekly income.

These difficulties were well illustrated by another group of eight trainees (19 per cent), for whom getting by meant 'a tight squeeze . . . to make ends meet . . . After you've paid your board [money], got a travel pass, paid money for my [mail order] catalogue there isn't much left over' (Wendy – clerical trainee). For others too, 'It's a tight squeeze at the moment, but I manage' (Patrick – engineering trainee). Managing involved developing budgeting strategies where

> just enough money to last the week . . . [meant paying] my allowance straight into my bank account where I can't get at it. I don't get the time to go to the bank so I have to get my mum to lend me some from time to time. (Lorraine – horticulture trainee)

Another managed in a similar way by giving his parents £20 keep each week on the understanding that they would make the £8.50 weekly payments due on his mountain bike:

> After I've bought my bus pass it leaves me with about £4 in my pocket for spending money . . . My parents will help me out if I get into trouble with debts but so far I've managed to avoid it. (John – horticulture trainee)

Another 14 (33 per cent) also complained that it was a tight squeeze but gave greater emphasis to the problems entailed in coping each week. These trainees felt that the allowance represented the minimum they could live on and that it was just enough to make ends meet but nothing more: 'It's just enough to get by on, no more' (Sarah – clerical trainee). For these young people there was little alternative: 'I've got to get by. Getting by isn't difficult but there's nothing left over to spend on yourself' (Thomas –

construction trainee), or 'You can manage on the money but you have to go without and what you do buy you have to be careful with' (Helen – retail trainee). If these young people wanted to buy something that other young people might have taken for granted, such as clothes or a record, it meant saving over a number of weeks or going for the much more expensive option of buying something through a mail order catalgoue.

However, getting by was also the product of necessity and something in which they had no choice. Put plainly, getting by meant 'you have to make the money last or you don't survive' (Richard – construction trainee), or 'you have to get by, there's nothing you can do about it' (Clive – clerical trainee). This meant making their money last through rationing, going without or both: 'I just can't afford the things I'd like to be able to buy. Not just big things. Little things like soaps or perfume or a record' (Samantha – clerical trainee). Or it often meant going into debt or borrowing money from parents or relatives: 'It's hard if you get into debt, but it's even harder not to' (Chris – PSV trainee).

Sixteen of the trainees (38 per cent) stated categorically that they could not make ends meet on their weekly allowance. These young people too experienced many of the conflicts and antagonisms voiced by the other trainees, and tackled them in similar ways through rationing or planning ahead, or by having to make hard and fast choices about how they were actually going to dispose of their severly limited incomes. For them too, just getting by meant major inroads into their modest resources, like paying board or keep money, or finding money for a bus pass or for clothes: 'After you've given your mum some money for board, you haven't got much left' (Elaine – catering trainee), or 'I have to give my mum some money for my board each week, then I have to pay for my travel and my clothes and I have to spend some money on leisure' (Luke – retail trainee). Similarly, 'If I want to go out at the weekend, which I usually do, then I'm skint the rest of the week. It's a choice I have to make' (Frances – retail trainee), or 'If I go out my dad has to give me money so I can afford things like clubs, pubs and fags' (Colin – community care trainee).

Living at Home as a Trainee

Despite the differing emphasis on how easy or difficult it was to make ends meet each week, all the trainees experienced similar conflicts and demands related to the extremely low level of the allowance. Moreover, the importance of the family was also particularly evident in the way in which trainees got by. This reflects the family's long-standing importance in subsidizing the movement of young people from full-time education into full-time employment.

> Materially, young adults were dependent upon parents for their daily physical reproduction whilst at school, but moving to a position where they were partially responsible for their own costs of reproduction.
> (Wallace, 1987b, p. 19)

Historically, this took the form of a young person being required to contribute to his or her own physical upkeep through paying keep or board money into the househole. Set a nominal levels, this payment tended not to involve a strict economic relationship as it usually failed to cover fully the entire costs of a young person's daily physical needs. It also usually meant a reciprocal relationship of indirect support back to young people as, in return for their keep, not only did they enjoy protection from paying the full market value of their upkeep, they also enjoyed a number of subsidies from the household, including food, clothing and money for cigarettes and drink, that were often not fully repaid. Although the level of indirect support was itself dependent on the economic status of the family, the cushion this provided was particularly important when the young person was unemployed or on a low income.

One of the explicit aims of youth training was to restructure young workers' relationships to the family by throwing back on to the family a greater part of the burden of their daily physical upkeep. Under the YTS 'parents would be expected to provide any necessary financial support to these trainees' (Department of Employment, 1981, para 36) above and beyond the basic allowance, an intention which became more explicit in the run-up to the scheme's launch. As Norman Tebbit, then Secretary of State for Employment, commented at the time:

> it would be right for young people, whether in education, the new training scheme or unemployed, to be regarded as dependent on their parents for the first year after reaching the minimum school-leaving age.
> (Hansard, 21 June 1983, col. 22–23)

Youth training was therefore to restructure this relationship through driving down the price of young labour, thereby redistributing the burden of physical reproduction further back onto the family. For many working class young people, youth training has therefore effectively extended their period of reliance on parents and family and, in doing so, has erected new forms of obstacles to their growing aspirations for independence.

All 42 trainees were living with one or more parents during the period of the research and 38 (90 per cent) indicated that they gave their parents some money each week for board and lodgings – a total which confirms the findings of research elsewhere (Jones, 1991; Huston and Jenkins, 1989; Wallace, 1987b). These included one young woman who had given her parents money for keep but had found it impossible to manage on what was left and had persuaded them to forgo any further payments until she had found a 'real job'. For the other four, it was accepted that as trainees they were still unable to contribute to their keep but that they would be expected to do so on finding full-time work: 'She [her mother] said I could wait until I started work' (Kath – clerical trainee). Three of these young people lived with a mother and father, both of whom worked, with the fourth living solely with her working mother. They were therefore the exception rather than the rule, something which they were ready to acknowledge: 'I'm lucky. Most of my friends have to pay board but my mum says I don't have to until I get a job' (Louis – construction trainee).

Table 7.5 confirms the general pattern established by other research (see Wallace, 1987b) that £10 a week appears to be a standard rate for board or keep money. Nine trainees did contribute a lower sum each week, with a further eight paying more. Seven of this latter group were young men, and two young men claimed they were paying £20 per week for their board. For one of these this £20 figure included the £8.50 hire-purchase weekly payment for his mountain bike and the other paid money for both himself and his wife, who was currently not working: 'It's sort of rent money for us both and they don't charge us any bills for heating or cooking or using the phone' (Rajesh – MVM trainee).

However, although Wallace (1987b) has suggested that such payments are nominal or have little direct economic rationale, considering that most of these trainees were only receiving the basic training allowance the amount of keep they were paying represented around one-third of their regular weekly income. For these young people it represented a real and direct commitment to participate in the family economy, especially where board money represents an important addition to the general household coffers, and this is reflected in the greater level of contributions from young people in households where the father is unemployed (Jones, 1991). Even

Table 7.5 *Levels of Board Money That Trainees Paid to Their Families*

Amount (£)	Male	Female	Total
None	2	2	4
5–6	2	2	4
7–8	2	3	5
9–10	11	10	21
11–15	5	1	6
16 +	2	0	2
Total	24	18	42

here, however, 32 (84 per cent of those who paid board money) received some form of indirect support, either through money payments to subsidize leisure or in the purchase of clothes or other necessities: 'If I want to go out my dad has to give me money' (Colin – community care trainee) and 'There hasn't been a week gone past without me borrowing another £15 off my mum and dad' (Anne – community care trainee). There was often an implicit agreement that these subs did not have to be repaid: 'If I'm hard up my mum gives me a sub and it doesn't really matter if I can't pay her back' (Elaine – catering trainee).

Six of the young people (14 per cent) identified several ways in which these antagonisms manifested themselves. It made some feel that they were not fulfilling their responsibility as young adults:

> I give them £10 a week for my keep. I'd like to give them more but I just can't afford it. If I get a little short during the week then they have to help me out. (Terry – PSV trainee)

Others realized the burden it meant for their parents: 'They can't afford it, really' (Richard – construction trainee plumber) and 'I wouldn't ask them directly, they haven't got much money themselves, but my dad is good that way' (Carol – catering trainee). Indeed, asking for additional money conflicted with developing ideas of independence: 'My folks help me out occasionally but I don't like asking them for the money. I should be standing on my own two feet by now' (Clive – clerical trainee).

The low level of the allowance effectively prohibited any move to stand on their own two feet and only two young people spoke of their desire to leave home. Growing difficulties in their relationships with parents or other family members meant that moving out was looked on as an increasingly attractive option. However, financial obstacles meant that considerable barriers needed to be negotiated before this could become a reality: 'I'd really like to move out but I can't afford to. I argue with my mum a lot and I'd seriously like to get a place on my own but I haven't got the money' (Elaine – catering trainee). Another summed up the position for most of the young people: 'I couldn't afford to move away even if I wanted to on that sort of money' (Mick – MVM trainee).

Additional Sources of Income

For the majority of the young people, a basic training allowance was their main regular source of income but it meant that getting by each week necessitated considerable strain. It was therefore unsurprising that since they had begun their period of training, 21 (50 per cent) of the young people, nine women and 12 men, had developed alternative ways of bringing in some much needed extra income. This did not include one young man who played snooker for money in local pubs and clubs or two young women, both catering trainees, who stated they were in the process of trying to find part-time jobs on top of their training schemes but had so far been unsuccessful:

> I'd like one [a part-time job] but they are difficult to find, there's quite a demand for them. Quite a few of the girls have them but they're difficult to find. Most find them through their placements, but some had them before they came on the course. (Jane – catering trainee)

As this young woman comments, retaining jobs which had been undertaken while still at school provided an important additional source of income for a signigicant number of the trainees. In all, 11 of the young people (24 per cent), four women and seven men, indicated that they had continued working in this way after they had started on their schemes. This meant 'an extra few quid here or there' (Derrick – MaC trainee) labouring at weekends for a builder, or a more regular source of income by continuing with Saturday or evening jobs:

> I just stayed on for a while because I knew the money on YTS was pretty
> bad and the few extra pounds would come in useful, but I couldn't keep
> it up for very long. I found I needed my weekends to get over the last
> week and to prepare for the next. (Kath – clerical trainee)

Some stuck it out longer: 'Until recently I was working in [the shop] but
I had to give it up because with that and doing a full week it was getting
too much' (Fiona – clerical trainee).

A smaller number of the trainees, four (10 per cent) in all, had earned
extra money through doing jobs they had found after starting their training schemes. Much of this type of work was intermittent and represented
an unreliable source of money. It involved work like selling pictures at
shows and exhibitions for a brother-in-law and receiving payment on a
commission-only basis. It could also mean 'doing some plastering for a
builder who lives across the road from us. When there's work and he needs
me to help then I give him a hand' (Joe – MaC trainee). At £2 per hour
it brought in much needed money but meant 'sometimes taking the week
off, telling them here [the training centre] I'm ill, or doing a Saturday or
a Sunday for him'. Another young woman occasionally worked as a
cashier at an exhibition centre, taking time off sick if necessary for the
chance to bring in around £100 a week.

Work experience providers also utilized this source of keen and willing
labour, although only six trainees (14 per cent) claimed to do extra paid
work at their placements. These young people earned extra money not
through top-up but by doing what they described as 'overtime' (Sue –
catering trainee), above and beyond the maximum 40 hours they were
required to train each week. These trainees worked 'when the boss wants
me and when the work is available' (Luke – retail trainee) and were paid
'depending on how hard I work' (Elaine – catering trainee). This usually
meant working the occasional six-day week, with the extra day bringing
in an additional £12, or a Saturday morning bringing an extra £7 to £10.
One young woman did 'the odd day, like a Sunday or Bank Holiday . . .
he gives me £12 cash in hand for that' (Lorraine – horticulture trainee),
and another young man worked 'overtime whenever and wherever I can
get it . . . I might earn an extra £20 a week that way' (Adam – horticulture
trainee).

However, working in this way was not always easy. For the 10 trainees
who worked regularly, this meant an average extra $8\frac{1}{2}$ hours per week
on top of their 40 hours' training. What this meant in additional income

was also important, ranging from an extra £8.50 for five hours' work on a Saturday morning to £16 for a day's work in a fashion chain store. On average these young people were supplementing their training allowance by approximately £14 per week: 'It means the difference between going out and staying in on Saturday night' (Joe – MaC trainee).

Conclusion

Trainees have been and remain consistent in their criticisms of the level of allowance paid to trainees on youth training. Large numbers of working class school leavers continue to see youth training as a low-wage work experience scheme and it is immediately apparent from the state's own research that over one in five trainees continue to give lack of money as a reason for leaving their schemes early. The working class young are all too well aware that in becoming trainees they risk subjecting themselves to youth training's new forms of economic logic, but it is something that they have not taken to easily.

Some trainees have undoubtedly benefited from the ability of employers to give their trainees employee status and to top up the level of training allowance above its basic level. At best this has been a sporadic movement with the benefits involved being spread unevenly across the scheme as a whole. Yet with further recession, even this small concession looks vulnerable and trainees once again have been forced to face the prospect of a further erosion in their living standards. As employers have shown even greater reluctance to take on school leavers any further improvements in the level of the training allowance have been ruled out.

The idea that as trainees young people should make a short-term financial sacrifice for longer-term training gains has held little sway with most working class school leavers. Many young people both on and off training schemes continue to question the fairness of the allowance, bearing in mind the considerable contribution they know they are expected to make at work experience placements. Not only do they consider the allowance unfair in relation to the demands made of them as production workers, but this feeling of injustice is further heightened by the fact that many are working alongside full-time workers receiving substantially more money for doing essentially the same types of work. Not only are they expected to behave like full-time workers and to share their burden of production, but, in their eagerness to be taken on, many set out to impress employers by working considerably harder than others they work alongside.

However, economic arguments, as powerful as they may be, are not the only reason why young people continue to reject the economic logic behind the youth training allowance. Importantly, many continue to see leaving school as the beginning of their independence from their families of origin and continue to argue that these factors need to be taken into consideration when assessing the value of the training allowance. Working class young people do accept that trainees may have to forgo the level of wages available in the wider market-place, but they also remain firmly committed to the belief that it should also take into consideration non-market criteria related to quality of their lives. Trainees may only have modest aspirations when it comes to calculating a fair level of allowance, and ones which bear little relation even to historical trends had the original YOP allowance kept pace with changing prices and incomes. Nonetheless, their ideas of fairness involve constantly relating economic arguments to their changing social context and therefore represent an implicit rejection of the power of the market.

A further dimension needs to be taken into consideraton when evaluating working class young people's responses to the low level of the training allowance. The low training allowance also means that many school leavers do not have access to sufficient funds to enable them to get by each week without drawing on other sources of material support. Most trainees continue to pay keep or board money to their parents as a contribution towards the cost of their physical reproduction, but this represents only a nominal contribution and one well below the actual market value. Therefore, trainees are forced to rely on their parents and family for indirect forms of material support just to survive, a subsidy which is usually consolidated by parents' willingness further to extend to their offspring money to finance social and leisure activities. However, trainees have not taken lightly to this period of enforced dependency and many continue to resent the increased stress it places on their family relationships. Not only does it contradict their growing ideas of independence and autonomy, but also it comes into conflict with the fact that increasing numbers of families have themselves been thrown into poverty in recent years.

For these reasons trainees have been forced to look to other areas for their changing material needs. We have already mentioned that struggles in and against youth training has seen large numbers of trainees leave their schemes in search of more financially rewarding options, despite the fact that many of these are in dead-end jobs. Also, many trainees attempt to maintain or develop alternative sources of income to supplement the meagre allowance. Significant numbers continue in jobs they had held at school and many more seek out other opportunities for part-time or alternative forms of work. A significant number of trainees therefore hold what are for all intents and purposes two jobs and more are all too willing to undertake overtime for their work experience providers. Yet the strains of working what usually constitutes an extra working day are clearly visible and many trainees feel the considerable pressures involved in such extensive forms of working.

Note

1. The basic allowance rose form £28.50 to £29.50 during the period of research and the change affected a small number of trainees.

8 YOUTH TRAINING FOR THE FUTURE

The preceding discussion has set out to explore the ways in which working class young people confront the prospects of beginning their adult working life as youth trainees. It has taken some of the key assumptions and assertions on which youth training's many claimed achievements and successes have rested, and has examined them in relation to working class young people's everyday experiences of the scheme. Such an exercise is considered essential because youth training is seen by many as an important step in the development of post-school training provision for working class school leavers. Not only was it to challenge the anachronistic and under-developed training structure which dogged postwar Britain but, more importantly, it was to provide school leavers with a structured and enhanced first stage to their working lives proper. Its self-stated intentions were therefore not only to tackle the grotesque levels of unemployment that plagued many school leavers' searches for work but to do so through a period of quality foundation training which would, it was claimed, set up a new generation of young people for their subsequent working lives.

The claims made for the scheme since then suggest that it has gone a long way towards meeting many of these original objectives through bringing about a 'revolution' in Britain's training provision. More than this, however, its advocates have argued with some force that it has also proved successful in generating great enthusiasm among school leavers who, they assert, have responded dutifully in large numbers. Accordingly, it has been claimed that youth training has been successful in providing school leavers with the opportunity to equip themselves with the skills and attributes they are told they will require if they are to build a successful working life; that the scheme has been highly successful in bringing about

a radical change in school leavers' evaluations of the importance of structured training; that it has succeeded in instilling in young workers an
appreciation of those attitudes considered necessary for the maintenance
of a successful modern economy; that young people have embraced youth
training's opportunity for quality training leading to jobs; and that it has
gone a long way down the road towards convincing school leavers that
there is no such thing as a free lunch and that it is time they priced
themselves back into work through the acceptance of the 'going rate' for
a trainee. In short, it has been argued, with varying degrees of vehemence,
that youth training has totally transformed British working class people's
appreciation of training and their understanding of the organization of
work.

The account presented here takes these claims seriously but its conclusions tell a different story. Most immediately, its findings point away from
claims that youth training has brought about a radical change in school
leavers' attitudes to, and understanding of, work and training. In its place,
it begins to paint a picture which sees the scheme more as an extension of
pre-existing forms of discipline and control than as the beginning of a new
and welcome chapter in the lives of many working class young people.
Through youth training, many school leavers have found it necessary to
subject themselves to the disciplines and impositions of a period of training
dominated by the demands of low-skilled work experience, rather than the
promise of quality skills. They have had to endure the constraints of a
training programme which has taken them out of unemployment, often
forcibly through the withdrawal of social security benefits, only to impose
upon them the insecurity of training rather than the promise of a job. It
has meant for many others having to eke out an existence on a pitifully low
level of allowance and, to cap it all, it has merely returned large numbers
of trainees to unemployment rather than providing them with a stepping
stone into work. This is an account, therefore, which sees youth training
as adding up to little more than a concerted attempt to squeeze even tighter
the ways in which young workers' introduction to work has historically
been constituted as an alienating and negative experience.

Yet another, and more important, theme of this account has been the
ways in which working class school leavers have consistently rejected and
opposed these impositions, despite the enormous resources deployed by
the state. Certainly, large numbers of school leavers have now experienced the reality of what it means to be a trainee, but one of the most
significant characteristics of the progress of youth training has been the

steadfast refusal of working class school leavers to accept at face value the actions and pronouncements of the state. So as the new vocationalism and its institutional forms have impacted more and more on their lives, and as it has sought continually to process and control their aspirations for meaningful work and training, working class young people have acted consistently to resist and deny these measures. Far from creating a new generation of young workers embracing the spirit of the new vocationalism, internalizing and rehearsing its imperatives and values and celebrating its institutional forms, youth training has given rise to a whole new set of contradictions which themselves have established new forms of resistance and denial.

To begin with, working class young people are constituted as distinctive forms of labour power from an early age. The majority of young people grow up in communities intimately shaped by the social relations of production. Most immediately, working class young people constitute a whole population of hidden workers operating in an often subterranean world of wage labour who, more often than not, experience the realities of paid work at its most exposed. Negotiating employment relationships, arduous tasks, insecurity, low pay and employers' discriminatory recruitment practices all add up to give child workers an often bleak and uncompromising insight into what it means to be at work. Yet adolescents want to work, despite what we are usually told, and in the face of this often harsh and alienating introduction to working life most continue to see their school-time job as a valuable asset. Not only do they provide school pupils with a welcome source of income, something in these times of austerity which itself should not go underestimated, and a greater degree of control over their lives, but they also represent an important source of continuity as young people seek to leave behind the confines of compulsory education and embrace the relative freedoms of adult working life.

Such an early insight into the freedoms and constraints of waged labour is not lost on those young workers, and their school-time experience of the material realities of paid employment plays a considerable part in determining their opposition to youth training. Through their work as children, young people know what it is like to find, secure and hold down paid employment and come to recognize its freedoms and constraints. Yet through their indirect knowledge of schemes and their direct contacts in the community, with family and friends, they also increasingly come to know what it means to be a trainee and it is through this, set against their immediate knowledge of work and working, that early opposition to youth training is formed. Without doubt, it is significant that the training state, through the new vocationalism and beyond, seeks continually to deny the validity of these experiences, because to acknowledge the reality of what it means to be young and working class would be to expose fully the brutality of the workless state. So, however much the training state seeks to deny this fact and the more it seeks to tell school leavers that they are deficient in the qualities needed to find and hold down work, it can never totally obscure the ways in which the social relations of production continue to exert a determining pressure on the ways their lives are shaped.

It is therefore unsurprising that school leavers continue to view the prospect of youth training with considerable reservations. The young working class know that the prospect of unemployment, and the pressures on family and finance it brings, is to be avoided at all costs and that the portrayal of them as deficient, 'work-shy' and unprepared for the rigours of working life bears little correspondence to the realities of their adolescence. Measured against the harshness of unemployment, however, youth training for many becomes a preferable alternative and one that school leavers know can open up opportunities with employers which are otherwise denied. Consequently, working class young people have developed a deeply instrumental attitude towards youth training. This is an instrumentalism which not only sees the scheme as a way of providing a more direct possibility of leading into 'real jobs', but also captures their refusal to subject themselves totally to the training state's offer of quality foundation training for life. Certainly, the ways in which school leavers tenaciously cling to the desire for a 'real job' – that is, any job so long as it falls outside a scheme – is itself confirmation of this deep-seated opposition. Yet in their instrumentalism towards youth training, working class young people have also gone some way towards subverting its hollow promises of quality training and skills, in their place recasting the scheme as an opportunity, however frail, to gain a temporary respite from the sheer weight of unemployment but an opening from which they contrive to escape at the earliest possible chance.

That such a critique has developed should come as no surprise to anyone who begins to explore the conditions that most trainees are expected to endure. Unrewarding and alienating work dominated by the imperatives of repetitive and easily acquired tasks, and work experience which usually represents little more than an extension of domestic or manual labour and few opportunities for personal development are endemic to the experience of youth training. Again, many trainees appreciate this absence of skills training for jobs through a recognition of their schemes as training which is easily and quickly learnt and accomplished. Yet the fact that this does not necessarily evoke too much frustration or disillusionment rests in trainees' anticipations of such training regimes beforehand and through a recognition that most young people do not enter schemes expecting skills training in the more traditional sense of the term. Youth training for most school leavers represents a way to escape the emptiness of unemployment and the boring routines of further education, while providing access to employers in particular and the world of work more generally. The promise of quality skills training is not a precondition of their participation on a scheme, whereas experience, access to work and the possibility of a 'real job' remain their over-riding aims.

However, even here, most trainees remain unconvinced by the promise of youth training for jobs. Overall, trainees' assessments of the likelihood that a scheme will lead to 'real jobs' remain astute and sober, considering the schemes' indifferent track record in leading trainees into work. Most see the opportunity of any form of paid employment as the best way to escape the confines of their schemes, itself a poor reflection of the scheme, and most actively conspire to ensure that they remain a trainee for as short a period as possible. Others have also come to an appreciation of their schemes which equates the greatest possibility of a 'real job' with the willingness of their work experience placement provider to take them on. Yet this too does not mean that trainees have accepted the training state's claim that they are individually responsible for the predicament they find themselves in. Rather, many trainees continue to recognize that their wider chances of work depend upon factors beyond their control, such as the whims of their work experience providers, the sheer pressure of unemployment and the fact that employers continue to have no responsibility to trainees beyond the duration of their schemes. This too then represents an awareness among trainees that their schemes can never fully deliver their promise of quality training for jobs and, in this respect, most continue to see youth training for what it is: the best of a poor deal.

Alongside this rejection of its training opportunities, a further indication of how young people have come to recognize youth training's impositions is also evident. As if routinized work experience was not enough, school leavers have also come to appreciate that youth training means subjecting themselves to an enforced period of low pay. Certainly, the consistent opposition to the bitterly low level of allowance provides young people with one of the clearest indications of the real intentions of youth training, especially when many find themselves working alongside other better-paid workers while expected to do the same tasks. It is this, together with their own wider experiences of work, that gives trainees' assessments of their schemes as exploitation, and as cheap or slave labour, such a enduring resonance because it is an evaluation grounded in actual experience of what it means to be a trainee. Now that it has become unfashionable among certain sections of the left to acknowledge capitalism's drive to ever intensify its methods of exploitation, any cursory glance at the evidence will show that working class school leavers are only too well aware of its exploitative social relations. What is more, most young people continue to reject the cold economic logic of the market and, in its place, seek to articulate their own alternative.

In and Against the State Revisited

What is being outlined is the everyday patterns of resistance and refusal, whose individual parts constitute the sum of being a trainee in Britain today. This is an account which rejects the state's assertion that trainees have embraced the new vocationalism in its varying forms, yet it is also one which rejects the assertions of others which give a unity and power to the 'New Right' project that it does little to deserve. What both the state and these more critical accounts must face is that attempts to recompose traditional forms of working class behaviour through youth training have met with only limited success. In varying degrees of intensity, the young working class have consistently failed to internalize the ideas, values and contexts which have been used to give legitimacy to the practices of the state and, in this way, they have continually sought to reject the legitimacy of the new vocationalism and its attendant schemes. On the contrary, the young working class have not been the passive recipients of the politics and ideology of the training state but have remained active in resisting its impositions and demands and, in doing so, have gone some way towards articulating their own needs.

This is not to argue that the working class experience school, work, training and the prospect of unemployment in identical or consistent ways. Clearly this is not the case. Yet the collective basis to the trainees' social existence continually resurfaces through their own accounts, experiences and actions. What appears as a problem or an opportunity for one individual or group of trainees is, more often than not, a problem or opportunity for another group or individual. It is this that unifies what appears to be a collection of individual, disparate and seemingly unrelated actions and events, and it is out of these commonalities that a logic to their responses can be found. This is a logic which unites these seemingly differing and isolated accounts through an appreciation of them as a set of responses to the conditions of exploitation and domination into which the trainees are propelled. Whether or not the individual trainees themselves appreciate this significance (and, as we have pointed out, many actually do), their experiences and actions point towards the ways in which young labour is collectively constituted in opposition to the tendency of the social relations into which they voluntarily or involuntarily enter to increasingly reduce the organization of their social life to relationships of exploitation and domination.

It is here, in and against the exploitative relations of the training state, that the significance of their experiences and actions lies: a set of experiences and actions which is made and constantly re-made through the constitution of young people as a potential and latterly real source of labour power, yet a set of experiences and actions which is also the outcome of young people's conflict with the needs of capital to restructure its social relationships in order to accumulate. Through the social construction of labour, young people are increasingly implicated in this process of exploitation and are progressively forced to confront the ways in which capitalist social relations can never fully meet their needs. Specifically, through the new vocationalism, and youth training in particular, the social relations of production have taken on increasingly aggressive form. It is because of this that working class school leavers necessarily confront the barriers to their needs and aspirations that the organization of youth training represents. In the movement from school to work, many working class young people face the prospect of submitting themselves to training defined by unpleasant and alienating types of work. It means a protracted period of work experience which offers little financial or personal reward, and it means suffering the insecurity and threat of unemployment that being a trainee usually entails. Nevertheless, it is out of a struggle with these everyday limitations and obstacles that a sense of opposition and refusal will inevitably be forged.

Resistance and opposition, however deeply embedded in the social organization of daily life, does not by itself mean the beginning of a new alternative. This can only be the outcome of a more conscious, organized and coherent response. Yet without ever establishing an adequate understanding and analysis of the ways in which working class school leavers experience and act in relation to youth training, the beginnings of an alternative will never start to emerge. The prospect will mean that the needs of most young workers will remain unacknowledged and the process of leaving school will continue to signify an increasingly alienating and unresponsive beginning to adult working life. Moreover, if the needs of working class school leavers are not given paramount importance in debates about the organization and structure of work and training, then the struggle to establish a fully rounded and more fulfilling working life for all will not get very far. More of the same has nothing new to offer subsequent generations of working class school leavers, as the bankruptcy of low-quality training without jobs becomes increasingly apparent.

However, as we have also seen in some detail, there is a material basis for an oppositional politics to youth training, despite the jettisoning of such a strategy by many in the name of modern socialist politics. It is an oppositional form of politics which demands that the Labour Party develop policies which tackle the real issues facing working class school leavers, such as unemployment, low wages, employers' discriminatory recruitment practices, increasing poverty, pressures on young people to drop out of the labour market completely and empty promises of training without jobs. Linked to this, it needs to be an oppositional form of politics which urges the trade union movement to go beyond its preoccupation with waged workers and begin to address the specific problems of trainees, while making connections with the wider implications of the development of the training state for all groups of workers. Trade unions need to recognize that not only are trainees potential trade union members of the future, but the growth in training schemes parallels the development of insecure, low-paid, flexible and temporary forms of working more generally. Only by going beyond the limitations of traditional forms of workplace organization can wider allegiances be constructed which draw new groups, like trainees, into active forms of participation and which seek to make connections with initiatives already underway. The work of claimants' rights groups and unemployed workers' centres, and broader campaigning, organization and lobbying around issues of work, unemployment and training all offer opportunities for building collective forms of opposition.

This is not to argue that such a task is easy or that none of these approaches is without its problems. Nonetheless, the experience of the past twenty years has confirmed the hollowness of claims that the right could deliver a vibrant and dynamic capitalism which would offer social harmony and material reward for all. In place of such rhetorical claims, the reality has been the further subjection of large sections of the working class to the horrors of mass unemployment, and for those still in work it has meant increasingly bitter forms of poverty and exploitation. Although the process of renewal appears daunting, there could be no better place to begin to reverse this degradation than through collective organization around the needs of working class school leavers. Because of the ways in which large numbers of working class school leavers have consistently refused to accept the authority of the training state, trainees have attempted, albeit in partial and tentative ways, to articulate an alternative set of needs. Giving priority to the importance of 'real jobs', the creation of useful and rewarding forms of work and training, a rejection of the hopelessness of unemployment, and a more equitable and moral assessment of the rewards represents a condemnation of the politics of training and the foundation on which an alternative can be built. Without an attempt to do so, the prospects for a large section of the population remain bleak.

REFERENCES

Ainley, P. (1988) *From School to YTS: Education and Training in England and Wales 1944–87*, Milton Keynes: Open University Press.

Ainley, P. and Corney, M. (1990) *Training for the Future: The Rise and Fall of the Manpower Services Commission*, London: Cassell.

Allum, C. and Quigley, J. (1983) 'Bricks in the wall: the Youth Training Scheme', *Journal, Conference of Socialist Economists*, Winter.

Ashford, S. and Bynner, J. (1991) 'Whither the enterprise culture: an examination of young people's job values', *British Journal of Education and Work*, Vol. 4, No. 3.

Ashton, D. and Field, D. (1976) *Young Workers*, London: Hutchinson.

Audit Commission (1993) *Unfinished Business: Full-Time Education Courses for 16–19 Year Olds*, London: Office for Standards in Education and Audit Commission.

Ball, L. (1989a) 'What future YTS?', *Unemployment Bulletin*, No. 30, Summer.

Ball, L. (1989b) 'Employed status on YTS', *Unemployment Bulletin*, No. 31, Autumn.

Banks, M., Bates, I., Breakwell, G., Bynner, J., Emler, N., Jamieson, L. and Roberts, K. (1992) *Careers and Identities*, Buckingham: Open University Press.

Bates, I. (1984) 'From vocational guidance to life skills: historical perspectives on careers education', in I. Bates, J. Clarke, P. Cohen, D. Finn, R. Moore and P. Willis (eds) *Schooling for the Dole? Against the New Vocationalism*, Basingstoke: Macmillan.

Bates, I. (n.d.) *'No Bleeding Whining Minnies': The Role of YTS in Class and Gender Reproductions*, ESRC 16–19 Initiative, Paper No. 19, London: City University, Social Statistics Research Unit.

Beechey, V. and Perkins, T. (1987) *A Matter of Hours: Women, Part-Time Work and the Labour Market*, Cambridge: Polity Press.

Bell, D. (1973) *The Coming of the Post-Industrial Society*, New York: Basic Books.

Benn, C. and Fairley, J. (eds) (1986) *Challenging the MSC: On Jobs, Education and Training*, London: Pluto.

Blackburn, R. M. and Mann, M. (1979) *The Working Class in the Labour Market*, London: Macmillan.

Blissett, E. (1989) *Recent Trends in Industrial Relations in Coventry*, Coventry: Coventry City Council, Economic Development Unit.

Bonefeld, W., Gunn, R. and Psychopedis, K. (eds) (1992) *Open Marxism*, Vols 1 and 2, London: Pluto Press.

Brake, M. (1980), *The Sociology of Youth Culture and Youth Sub-cultures*, London: Routledge and Kegan Paul.

British Youth Council (1992), *The Time of Your Life? The Truth about Being Young in 90's Britain*, London: British Youth Council.

Brown, C. (1984) *Black and White in Britain*, London: Policy Studies Institute.

Brown, P. (1987) *Schooling Ordinary Kids: Inequality, Unemployment and the New Vocationalism*, London: Tavistock.

Brown, P. and Ashton, D. (eds) (1987) *Education, Unemployment and Labour Markets*, Basingstoke: Falmer Press.

Burnham, P. (1991) 'Neo-Gramscian hegemony and the international order', *Capital and Class*, No. 45.

Callinicos, A. (1989) *Against Post-Modernism*, Cambridge: Polity Press.

Carter, M. P. (1962) *Home, School and Work: A Study of the Education and Employment of Young People in Britain*, Oxford: Pergamon Press.

Cassells, J. (1990) *Britain's Real Skill Shortages and What to Do About It*, London: Policy Studies Institute.

City of Coventry (1993) *Coventry Job Market Trends*, February, Coventry: City of Coventry, Economic Development Division.

Clarke, G. (1991), 'Defending ski jumpers: a critique of theories of youth subculture', in S. Frith and A. Goodwin (eds) *On Record: Rock, Pop, and the Written Word*, London: Routledge.

Clarke, J. (1979) 'Capital and culture: the post-war working class revisited', in J. Clarke, C. Critcher and P. Johnson (eds) *Working Class Culture*, New York: St Martin's Press.

Clarke, J., Hall, S., Jefferson, T. and Roberts, B. (1976) 'Subcultures, cultures and class: a theoretical overview', in S. Hall and T. Jefferson (eds) *Resistance through Rituals: Youth Subcultures in Post-war Britain*, London: HarperCollins.

Clarke, L. (1980) *The Transition from School to Work: A Critical Review of Research in the United Kingdom*, London: HMSO.

Clarke, S. (1988) *Keynesianism, Monetarism and the Crises of the State*, London: Edward Elgar.

Clarke, S. (1991) 'Marxism, sociology and Poulantzas's theory of the state', in S. Clarke (ed.) *The State Debate*, Basingstoke: Macmillan Academic and Professional.

Cockburn, C. (1983) *Brothers: Male Dominance and Technological Change*, London: Pluto.

Cockburn, C. (1985) *Machinery of Dominance: Women, Men and Technological Know-How*, London: Pluto.

Cockburn, C. (1987) *Two Track Training: Sex Inequality and the YTS*, Basingstoke: Macmillan.

Coffield, F. (1991) 'From the decade of the enterprise culture to the decade of TECs', *British Journal of Education and Work*, Vol. 4, No 1.

Coffield, F., Borill, C. and Marshall, S. (1986) *Growing Up at the Margins*, Milton Keynes: Open University Press.

Cohen, P. (1972) *Subcultural Conflict and Working Class Community*, Working Papers in Cultural Studies, Birmingham: University of Birmingham, Centre for Contemporary Cultural Studies.

Cohen, P. (1983) 'Losing the generation game', *New Socialist*, Nov./Dec.

Cohen, P. (1985) 'Beyond youthopia?', *Marxism Today*, Vol. 10, October.

Cohen, P. (1986) *Rethinking the Youth Question*. Working Paper 3, London: University of London, Institute for Education.

Cohen, P. (1990) 'Foreword: Transitions in transition', in R. Hollands (ed.) *The Long Transition: Class, Culture and Youth Training*, Basingstoke: Macmillan.

Combes, A. (1987) 'Not such a nice little earner', *Times Educational Supplement*, 4 December.

Commission for Racial Equality (1982) *Massey Ferguson Perkins Ltd: Report of a Formal Investigation*, London: Commission for Racial Equality.

Confederation of British Industry Special Programmes Unit (1983), *Coventry: Report*, West Midlands: Confederation of British Industry.

Conservative Party (1992) *The Best Future for Britain: The Conservative Manifesto 1992*, London: Conservative Central Office.

Corrigan, P. (1979) *Schooling the Smash Street Kids*, London: Macmillan.

Corrigan, P. and Frith, S. (1976) 'The politics of youth culture', in S. Hall and T. Jefferson (eds) *Resistance through Rituals: Youth Subcultures in Post-war Britain*. London: HarperCollins.

Costello, N., Michie, J. and Milne, S. (1989) *Beyond the Casino Economy*, London: Verso.

Courtenay, G. (1988), *England and Wales Youth Cohort Study* Report on Cohort 1, Sweep 1, Sheffield: Manpower Services Commission.

Coventry Careers (1988) *Destination of School Leavers*, Coventry: Coventry Careers.

Coventry Careers (1993) *Annual Report*, Coventry: Coventry Careers.

Coventry City Council (1989) *Economic Monitor*, No. 4, December.

Coyle, A. (1982) 'Sex and skill in the organisation of the clothing industry', in J. West (ed.) *Women, Work and the Labour Marker*, London: Routledge and Kegan Paul.

Craft, M. and Craft, A. (1983) 'The participation of ethnic minority pupils in further and higher education', *Educational Research*, Vol. 25, No. 1.

Craig, R. (1986) *The Youth Training Scheme: A Study of Early Leavers and Non-Participants*, YTS Evaluation Series 2, Sheffield: Manpower Services Commission.

Cross, M. (1987) 'Black youngsters and the YTS: the policy issues', in M. Cross and D. I. Smith (eds) *Black Youth Futures*, Leicester: National Youth Bureau.

Cross, M. and Smith, D. I. (1987) *Black Youth Futures: Ethnic Minorities and the Youth Training Scheme*, Studies in Research, Leicester: National Youth Bureau.

Cross, M., Wrench, J. and Barnett, S. (1990) *Ethnic Minorities and the Careers Service: An Investigation into Processes of Assessment and Placement*, Research Paper No. 73, London: Department of Employment.

Curran, J. and Blackburn, R. A. (1990) 'Youth and enterprise culture', *British Journal of Education and Work*, Vol. 4, No. 1.

Davies, B. (1986) *Threatening Youth: Towards a National Youth Policy*, Oxford: Open University Press.

Deacon, A. (1981) 'Unemployment and politics in Britain since 1945', in B. Showler and A. Sinfield (eds) *The Workless State*, Oxford: Martin Robertson.

Deakin, B. M. and Pratten, C. F. (1987) 'Economic effects of the YTS', *Employment Gazette*, October.

Department of Employment (1981) *A New Training Initiative: A Programme for Action*, Cmnd. 8450, London: HMSO.

Department of Employment (1985), *Education and Training for Young People*, Cmnd. 8450, London: HMSO.

Department of Employment (1988a) *Employment for the 1990s*, Cmnd. 540, London: HMSO.

Department of Employment (1988b), *Training for Employment*, Cmnd. 316, London: HMSO.

Department of Employment (1990) *Preliminary Results from the Labour Force Survey for Great Britain and Revised Employment Estimates Incorporating Those Results*, London: Department of Employment.

Dex, S. (1983), 'Second chances? Further education, ethnic minorities and labour markets', in D. Gleeson (ed.) *Youth Training and the Search for Work*, London: Routledge and Kegan Paul.

Dutton, P. (1987) *The Impact of YTS on Engineering Apprenticeship: A Local Labour Market Study*, Institute for Employment Research, Coventry: University of Warwick.

Elias, P. and Owen, D. (1989) *People and Skills in Coventry: An Evaluation of the Education, Training, Qualifications and Work Experience of Coventry People*, Coventry: City of Coventry.

Employment Gazette (1985) 'A survey of youth training scheme providers', *Employment Gazette*, August.

Employment Gazette (1989) '1988 Labour Force Survey – preliminary results', *Employment Gazette*, April.

Employment Gazette (1991a) *Education and Labour Market Status of Young People in Great Britain*, London: Department of Employment.

Employment Gazette (1991b) *Young People Leaving School*, London: Department of Employment.

Fawcett Society (1985) *Class of '84: A Study of Girls on the First Year of the Youth Training Scheme*, London: Fawcett Society.

Finn, D. (1982) 'Whose needs? Schooling and the "needs" of industry', in P. Atkinson and T. L. Rees (eds) *Youth Unemployment and State Intervention*, London: Routledge and Kegan Paul.

Finn, D. (1984) 'Leaving school and growing up: work experience in the juvenile labour market', in I. Bates, J. Clarke, P. Cohen, D. Finn, R. Moore and P. Willis (eds) *Schooling for the Dole? The New Vocationalism*, London: Macmillan.

Finn, D. (1986) 'YTS: the jewel in the MSC's crown', in C. Benn and J. Fairley (eds) *Challenging the MSC: On Jobs, Education and Training*, London: Pluto.

Finn, D. (1987) *Training Without Jobs: New Deals and Broken Promises*, Basingstoke: Macmillan.

Finn, D. (1988), 'Training and employment schemes for the long term unemployed: British government policy for the 1990s', *Work, Employment and Society*, Vol. 2, No. 4.

Frith, S. (n.d.) *Coventry City Centre Project*, mimeo.

Frith, S. (1980) 'Education, training and the labour process', in M. Cole and B. Skelton (eds) *Blind Alley: Youth in a Crisis of Capital*, Ormskirk: G. W. & A. Hesketh.

Frith, S. (1983) *Sound Effects: Youth, Leisure and the Politics of Rock and Roll*, London: Constable.

Fyfe, A. (1989) *Child Labour*, Oxford: Polity Press.

GLARE (1989) *A Report on Race Equality in London's Careers Service*, London: Greater London Action for Race Equality.

Gray, D. and King, S. (1986) *The Youth Training Scheme: The First Three Years*, YTS Evaluation Series No. 1, September, Sheffield: Manpower Services Commission.

Griffen, C. (1985) *Typical Girls? Young Women from School to the Job Market*, London: Routledge and Kegan Paul.

Greater Manchester Low Pay Unit (1992) *Set Fair?*, Manchester: Greater Manchester Low Pay Unit.

Hall, S. (1983) 'The great moving right show', in S. Hall and M. Jacques (eds) *The Politics of Thatcherism*, London: Lawrence and Wishart.

Hall, S. (1988) 'Thatcher's lessons', *Marxism Today*, March.

Hall, S. and Jacques, M. (1989) *New Times: The Changing Face of Politics in the 1980s*, London: Lawrence and Wishart.

Hall, S. and Jefferson, T. (eds) (1976) *Resistance through Rituals: Youth Subcultures in Post-war Britain*, London: HarperCollins.

Head, J. (1988) 'Children's hours', *New Society*, 26 February.

Hoel, B. (1982) 'Contemporary clothing "sweatshops", Asian female labour and collective organisation', in J. West (ed.) *Women, Work and the Labour Market*, London: Routledge and Kegan Paul.

Hollands, R. (1990) *The Long Transition: Class, Culture and Youth Training*, Basingstoke: Macmillan.

Hollands, R. (1991) 'Losing the generation game', *Youth and Policy*, No. 33.

Holloway, J. (1987), 'The red rose of Nissan', *Capital and Class*, No. 32, Summer.

Holloway, J. (1991a) 'The state and everyday struggle', in S. Clarke (ed.) *The State Debate*, Basingstoke: Macmillan Academic and Professional.

Holloway, J. (1991b) 'Capital is class struggle (and bears are not cuddly)', in W. Bonefeld and J. Holloway (eds) *Post-Fordism and Social Formation: A Marxist Debate on the Post-Fordist State*, Basingstoke: Macmillan Academic and Professional.

Holloway, J. and Picciotto, S. (1977) 'Capital, crisis and the state', *Capital and Class*, No. 2.

Holloway, J. and Picciotto, S. (1978) *State and Capital: A Marxist Debate*, London: Arnold.

Horton, C. (1986) *Nothing Like a Job: A Survey of Unemployed School Leavers Who Could Have Gone on the Youth Training Scheme but Who Did Not*, London: Youthaid.

House of Lords (1990) *Vocational Training and Re-Training*, Select Committee on The European Communities, 21st Report, HL Paper 28, July, London: HMSO.

Howieson, C. (1990) 'Beyond the gate: work experience and part-time work among secondary-school pupils in Scotland', *British Journal of Education and Work*, Vol. 3, No. 3.

Hubbuck, J. and Carter, S. (1980) *Half a Chance: A Report on Discrimination against Young Blacks in Nottingham*, London: Commission for Racial Equality.

Hutson, S. and Cheung, W. (1992) 'Saturday jobs: sixth-formers in the labour market and the family', in C. Marsh and S. Arber (eds) *Families and Households: Divisions and Change*, Basingstoke: Macmillan.

Hutson, S. and Jenkins, R. (1989) *Taking the Strain*, Milton Keynes: Open University Press.

Industrial Training Research Unit (1979) *The A–Z Study*, London: Industrial Training Research Unit.

Jackson, M. P. (1985) *Youth Unemployment*, London: Croom Helm.

Jones, G. (1991) 'The cost of living in the parental home', *Youth and Policy*, No. 32, March.

Jones, G. and Wallace, C. (1992) *Youth, Family and Citizenship*, Milton Keynes: Open University Press.

Keep, E. (1986) *Designing the Stable Door: A Study of How the Youth Training Scheme Was Planned*, Industrial Relations Research Unit, Papers in Industrial Relations, No. 8, Coventry: University of Warwick.

Keil, E. T. (1976) *Becoming a Worker*, Leicester: Leicestershire Committee for Education.

Keil, E. T. and Newton, P. (1980) 'Into work: continuity and change', in R. Deem (ed.) *Schooling for Women's Work*, London: Routledge and Kegan Paul.

Keil, E. T., Riddel, D. S. and Green, B. S. (1966) 'Youth and work: problems and perspectives', *Sociological Review*, Vol. 14.

Kirby, R. and Roberts, H. (1985) 'YB on YTS?', *Youth and Policy*, No. 12, Spring.

Kumar, K. (1978) *Prophecy and Progress: A Sociology of Industrial and Post-Industrial Society*, London: Pelican.

Lamb, H. and Piercy, B. (1987) 'Big Mac is watching you', *New Society*, 9 October.

Lancaster, B. (1986) 'Who's a real Coventry kid? Migration into twentieth century Coventry', in B. Lancaster and T. Mason (eds) *Life and Labour in a 20th Century City: The Experience of Coventry*, Cryfield Press, University of Warwick.

Lash, S. and Urry, J. (1987) *The End of Organised Capitalism*, Cambridge: Polity Press.

Leaving Home Project (1990) *Leaving Home: Young People's Housing Aspirations and Expectations*, London: Leaving Home Project.

Lee, D., Marsden, D., Rickman, P. and Duncombe, J. (1990) *Scheming for Youth: A*

Study of YTS in the Enterprise Culture, Buckingham: Open University Press.

Lee, G. and Wrench, J. (1983) *Skill Seekers: Black Youth Apprenticeships and Disadvantage*, Leicester: National Youth Bureau.

Lees, S. (1986) *Losing Out: Sexuality and Adolescent Girls*, London: Hutchinson.

London Edinburgh Weekend Return Group (1980) *In and Against the State*, London: Pluto.

Low Pay Unit (1982) *Child Labour in London*, London: Low Pay Unit.

Low Pay Unit (1988) *School Leavers Survey 1988: Pay and Conditions*, Birmingham: West Midlands Low Pay Unit.

Low Pay Unit (1991) *The Hidden Hours: Children at Work in the 1990s*, London: Low Pay Unit.

McCrudden, C., Smith, J. and Brown, C. (1991) *Racial Justice at Work*, London: Policy Studies Institute.

MacDonald, R. and Coffield, F. (1991) *Risky Business? Youth and the Enterprise Culture*, London: Falmer Press.

McGuigan, J. (1992) *Cultural Populism*, London: Routledge.

Maclagan, I. (1988) *Early Leavers and YTS*, London: National Council for Voluntary Organisations, Community Schemes Unit.

Maclagan, I. (1993) *Four Years' Severe Hardship*, London: Youthaid/Barnardos.

MacLennan, E., Fitz, J. and Sullivan, J. (1985) *Working Children*, Pamphlet No. 54, London: Low Pay Unit.

McRobbie, A. (1978) 'Working class girls and the culture of femininity', *Women Take Issue*, Centre for Contemporary Cultural Studies, London: Hutchinson.

Makeham, P. (1980) *Youth Unemployment: An Examination of Youth Unemployment Using National Statistics*, Research Paper No. 10, London: Department of Employment.

Manpower Services Commission (1977) *Young People and Work: Report on the Feasibility of a New Programme of Opportunities for Unemployed Young People*, Sheffield: Manpower Services Commission.

Manpower Services Commission (1981) *A New Training Initiative: A Consultative Document*, Sheffield: Manpower Services Commission.

Manpower Services Commission (1982) *Youth Task Group Report*, Sheffield: Manpower Services Commission.

Manpower Services Commission (1985) *The Development of the Youth Training Scheme: A Report*, Sheffield: Manpower Services Commission.

Manpower Services Commission (1986) *Equal Opportunities Code*, Sheffield: Manpower Services Commission.

Marsh, S. (1986) 'Women and the MSC', in C. Benn and J. Fairley (eds) *Challenging the MSC: On Jobs, Education and Training*, London: Pluto.

Marx, K. (1977) 'Wage labour and capital', in G. McLellan (ed.) *Karl Marx Selected Writings*, Oxford: Oxford University Press.

Mason, T. (1986) 'Looking back on the Blitz', in B. Lancaster and T. Mason (eds) *Life and Labour in a 20th Century City: The Experience of Coventry*, Coventry: Cryfield Press, University of Warwick.

Meiksins Wood, E. (1990) 'Falling through the cracks: E. P. Thompson and the debate on base and superstructure', in H. J. Kaye and K. McClelland (eds) *E. P. Thompson: Critical Perspectives*, Cambridge: Polity Press.

Meiksins Wood, E. (1985) *The Retreat from Class*, London: Verso.

Mizen, P. (1990a) 'Race equality in London's Youth Training Schemes', *Unemployment Bulletin*, No. 32, Spring.

Mizen, P. (1990b) Young people's experiences of the Youth Training Scheme: a case study of recent state intervention in the youth labour market in Coventry, Unpublished PhD thesis, Coventry: University of Warwick.

Mizen, P. (1992) 'Learning the hard way: the extent and significance of child working in Britain', *British Journal of Education and Work*, Vol. 5, No. 2.

Mizen, P. (1994), 'In and against the training state', *Capital and Class*, No. 53, Summer.

Moore, R. (1984) 'Schooling and the world of work', in I. Bates, J. Clarke, P. Cohen, D. Finn, R. Moore and P. Willis (eds) *Schooling for the Dole? The New Vocationalism*, London: Macmillan.

Office of Population Censuses and Surveys (1992) *1991 Census: County Report. West Midlands. Part 1*, London: HMSO.

Peck, J. (1993) 'The trouble with TECs . . . A critique of the Training and Enterprise Councils initiative', *Policy and Politics*, Vol. 24, No. 4.

Pollert, A. (1985) *Unequal Opportunities*, Birmingham: Birmingham Trade Union Resource Centre.

Pollert, A. (1986) 'The MSC and ethnic minorities', in C. Benn and J. Fairley (eds) *Challenging the MSC*, London: Pluto.

Pollert, A. (1988) 'The "flexible firm": fixation or fact?', *Work Employment and Society*, Vol. 2, No. 3.

Pollert, A. (ed.) (1990) *Farewell to Flexibility?*, Oxford: Basil Blackwell.

Potter, T. (1989) *Young Gifted and Broke: An Investigation into Low Pay Amongst Young Workers*, Birmingham: Low Pay Unit.

Raffe, D. (1983) 'The end of the alternative route? The changing relation of part-time education to work-life mobility among young male workers', in D. Gleeson (ed.) *Youth Training and the Search for Work*, London: Routledge and Kegan Paul.

Raffe, D. (1987) 'The context of the youth training scheme: an analysis of its strategy and development', *British Journal of Education and Work*, Vol. 1, No. 1.

Raffe, D. (ed.) (1988) *Education and the Youth Labour Market*, Basingstoke: Falmer Press.

Raffe, D. (1989) 'Longitudinal and historical change in young people's attitudes to YTS', *British Educational Research Journal*, Vol. 15, No. 2.

Raffe, D. and Smith, P. (1987) 'Young people's attitudes towards the YTS: the first two years', *British Educational Research Journal*, Vol. 13, No. 3.

Rees, T. (1986) 'Education for enterprise: the state and alternative employment for young people', *Journal of Education Policy*, Vol. 3, No. 1.

Rees, T. (1992) *Women and the Labour Market*, London: Routledge and Kegan Paul.

Rees, T. L. and Atkinson, P. (eds) (1982) *Youth Unemployment and State Intervention*, London: Routledge.

REITS (1985) *Youth Training or White TS?*, Coventry: Racial Equality in Training Schemes.

REITS (1987) *Two Year Youth Training: Another Whitewash?*, Coventry: Racial Equality in Training Schemes.

Roberts, K. (1968) 'The entry into work: an approach towards a general theory', *Sociological Review*, Vol. 16, No. 2.

Roberts, K. (1980) 'Occupational choice: an historical romance', *Youth and Society*, February.

Roberts, K. (1984) *School Leavers and Their Prospects: Youth and the Labour Market in the 1980s*, Milton Keynes: Open University Press.

Roberts, K. and Parsell, G. (1989) *The Stratification of Youth Training*, ESRC 16–19 Initiative, Occasional Paper No. 11, London: University of London.

Roberts, K. and Parsell, G. (n.d.) *Opportunity Structure and Career Trajectories from Age 16–19*, ESRC 16–19 Initiative Occasional Papers, Paper 1, London: City University.

Roberts, K. and Parsell, G. (1990) *Young People's Routes into UK Labour Markets in the 1990s*, ESRC 16–19 Initiative Occasional Papers, Paper 27, London: City University.

Roberts, K., Parsell, G. and Connelly, M. (n.d.) *Britain's Economic Recovery, the New Demographic Trend and Young People's Transition into the Labour Market*, ESRC 16–19 Initiative Occasional Papers, Paper 8, London: City University.

Roberts, K., Dench, S. and Richardson, S. (1986a) *The Changing Structure of Youth Labour Markets*, Research paper No. 59, London: Department of Employment.

Roberts, K., Dench, S. and Richardson, S. (1986b) 'Firms' uses of the youth training scheme', *Policy Studies*, Vol. 6, No. 3.

Sharpe, S. (1981) *Just Like a Girl: How Girls Learn to Be Women*, Harmondsworth: Penguin.

Simon, M. (1977) *Youth into Industry*, Leicester: National Youth Bureau.

Stafford, A. (1981) 'Learning not to labour', *Capital and Class*, No. 15, Autumn.

Stafford, A. (1991) *Trying Work: Gender, Youth and Work Experience*, Edinburgh: Edinburgh University Press.

Thomas, D. W. and Donnelly, T. (1986) 'Coventry's industrial economy 1880–1980', in B. Lancaster and T. Mason (eds) *Life and Labour in a 20th Century City: The Experience of Coventry*, Coventry: Cryfield Press, University of Warwick.

Thompson, E. P. (1978a) 'The peculiarities of the English', in E. P. Thompson, *The Poverty of Theory and Other Essays*, London: Merlin Press.

Thompson, E. P. (1978b) 'The poverty of theory or an orrery of errors', in E. P. Thompson, *The Poverty of Theory and Other Essays*, London: Merlin Press.

Thompson, P. (1989) *The Nature of Work: An Introduction to Debates on the Labour Process*, Basingstoke: Macmillan Educational.

Tolliday, S. (1986) 'High tide and after: Coventry's engineering workers and shopfloor bargaining', in B. Lancaster and T. Mason (eds) *Life and Labour in a 20th Century City: The Experience of Coventry*, Coventry: Cryfield Press, University of Warwick.

Training Agency (1989a) *Two Year YTS 100 Per Cent Follow-Up Survey*, Sheffield: Training Agency.

Training Agency (1989b) *Keeping YTS under Review*, internal document, Sheffield: Training Agency.

Training Agency (1990) *Two Year YTS 100 Per Cent Follow-Up Survey*, Sheffield: Training Agency.

Training Agency Employment Department (1990) *ET Evaluation: Summary of Findings from the First 18 Months*, Sheffield: Training Agency.

TUC/UNICEF (1985) *All Work and No Play: Child Labour Today*, London: TUC/UNICEF.

Unemployment Unit/Youthaid (1992a) *Working Brief*, January, London: Unemployment Unit/Youthaid.

Unemployment Unit/Youthaid (1992b) *Working Brief*, November, London: Unemployment Unit/Youthaid.

Unemployment Unit/Youthaid (1993a) *Working Brief*, February/March, London: Unemployment Unit/Youthaid.

Unemployment Unit/Youthaid (1993b) *Working Brief*, April, London: Unemployment Unit/Youthaid.

Wallace, C. (1987a) *For Richer or for Poorer: Growing Up in and out of Work*, London: Tavistock.

Wallace, C. (1987b) 'Between the family and the state: young people in transition', in M. White (ed.) *The Social World of the Young Unemployed*, London: Policy Studies Institute.

Wallace, C. and Cross, M. (eds) (1990) *Youth in Transition*, Basingstoke: Falmer Press.

Wells, W. (1983) *The Relative Pay and Employment of Young People*, Research Paper No. 42, London: Department of Employment.

West, M. and Newton, P. (1983) *The Transition from School to Work*, London: Croom Helm.

Whitfield, K. and Bourlakis, C. (1989) *YTS, Employment and Earnings: An Analysis Using the England and Wales Youth Cohort Study*, mimeo, Institute for Employment Research, Coventry: University of Warwick.

Wilce, H. (1988) 'Working children's profit and loss', *Independent*, 28 January.

Williams, R. (1985) *Towards 2000*, Harmondsworth: Penguin.

Williamson, J. (1989) 'Even new times change', *New Society and Statesman*, 7 July.

Willis, P. (1977) *Learning to Labour*, Westmead: Saxon House.

Wrench, J., Brar, H. and Martin, P. (forthcoming) *Invisible Minorities: Racism in New Towns and New Contexts*, Centre for Research in Ethnic Relations, Monographs in Ethnic Relations, No. 6, Coventry: University of Warwick.

Wright Mills, C. (1959) *The Sociological Imagination*, Oxford: Oxford University Press.

YETRU (1988) *The Firms That Like to Say No!*, Birmingham: Youth Employment and Trade Union Rights Campaign.

INDEX